W9-BZI-973

A HISTORY OF THE GAMBIA

A HISTORY OF THE
GAMBIA

by

HARRY A. GAILEY

FREDERICK A. PRAEGER, Publishers
NEW YORK - WASHINGTON

BOOKS THAT MATTER

Published in the United States of America in 1965
by Frederick A. Praeger, Inc., Publishers
111 Fourth Avenue, New York 3, N.Y.

Library of Congress Catalogue Card Number 65-11999

Printed in Great Britain

TO ROSALIE

CONTENTS

Contents

PREFACE

THERE must be a greater justification for any history, than the subjective needs of the author to externalize. This becomes even more true when the area under consideration is small, little known, and fated to remain a non-influential curiosity piece among the new nations of Africa. The major reason for writing the history of the Gambia was the need for a more comprehensive treatment which focused upon the modern period. The most significant book concerning the Senegambia was Sir John Gray's *History of the Gambia* published in 1940. Admirable as was the scholarship displayed, the work dealt in only a cursory manner with the period after 1889. The printing was so restricted that the book has become a rare item and very difficult for even the largest libraries to obtain. Other books that focused upon the Gambia are either modified travellers' accounts or are outdated.

Thus a vacuum does exist in our knowledge of the Gambia. It is my hope that this work will partially fill this gap in our knowledge, primarily because the Gambia is an important area for an understanding of the extension of Europe into Africa. The Senegambia region was one of the first discovered by Europeans, and remained for centuries an important area for trade. European wars were reflected in Africa by the clash of the great powers over trading rights on the great river. In the nineteenth century one can trace the reluctant change in French and British colonial policy by observing their attitudes toward the Senegambia. France, which first changed from trading im-

ix

perialism to territorial expansion in West Africa, eventually forced Britain to adopt a similar pattern. The totally European oriented attitude of this expansion is best proved by viewing the deliberations prior to the establishment of perhaps the most ridiculous boundary ever drawn. In the twentieth century the results of British colonial policy in general, and the 'mystique' of indirect rule in particular, can be observed better in the Gambia than in other larger, more viable West African territories. Finally the Gambia presents in microcosm most of the problems which confront any newly emergent state.

I have attempted to accomplish certain specific objects in the present work. The most important aim was to present the political development of the area from a casual appendage of Britain, through the crucial period of the 'scramble', to the modern position of the tiny enclave on the verge of independence. Of necessity, therefore, the book can be considered as European oriented. The centrum of power throughout Gambian history for four hundred years has rested outside the territory. The Europeans, in addition, are the only ones to have left considerable records of their contacts with the people. The native Gambians have left few written records, and there have been few detailed anthropological studies undertaken in the Gambia. Thus, even if the nature of the work did not dictate a European bias, the paucity of research materials dealing specifically with the native Gambians would have necessitated a similar approach. The only other alternative would have been a semi-travelogue account. The inter-tribal history of the Senegambia must be left to the ethno-historians who have as yet done little of the necessary basic research.

The decision to bring the account into the pre-independence period also dictated a certain approach which limited the area of discussion. After the overthrow of the great war chiefs at the turn of the century, the Gambia loses much of its romantic lustre and one must deal with topics which are considered prosaic by many. Even in these most important matters of agriculture, fiscal policy, and political movements there is a restriction upon the researcher. The fifty year rule regarding use of documents means that only published material is available. Therefore the presentation of the modern period of Gambian

Preface

history is based upon published sources, interviews, and personal experience. To trace the development of policy before a final decision is made, the expedient of extensive interviewing is a helpful aid, but far less satisfactory to an historian than dealing with official and unofficial correspondence.

I owe many debts of gratitude for help and encouragement which contributed in large measure to this completed work. The Ford Foundation, through the generous award of a research grant, enabled me to work in the archives of Great Britain, Senegal, Gambia, and Sierra Leone, as well as to travel extensively throughout the Gambia. Professors James Coleman and John Galbraith of the University of California at Los Angeles encouraged me in my interest in the Senegambia long before Africa became a fashionable area of study. I wish to indicate my appreciation to former Governor Sir Andrew Wright, K.C.M.G., former Chief Commissioner Humphrey Smith, former Commissioner Neil Assheton, District Commissioner Richard Addis of the Upper River, and many other officials, both active and retired, for their assistance. My way in the Gambia was aided by the work, friendship, and interest of Mr. George Peters, M.B.E., the Information Officer, as well as Sir Edward Windley and his staff. I received tremendous help from Kebba and Marion Foon who welcomed me into their home and utilized their wide contacts to smooth my way in understanding the current political scene. I also wish to thank the leading politicians of the Gambia—Premier Jawara, P. S. N'Jie, I. M. Garba-Jahumpa, and Reverend J. C. Faye—for the many hours of their time which they freely gave during my residence in Bathurst. Although the form and the opinions expressed are mine, if the book has any merit, it is due in large part to the aid which I have received.

Chapter One

THE LAND AND PEOPLE

THE British Colony and Protectorate of Gambia is situated in the extreme western portion of the African continent. It lies almost entirely in the savannah belt of seasonal rains between the meridians 16° 48′ and 13° 47′ west longitude and between parallels 13° 3′ and 13° 49′ north latitude. It extends for a distance of over two hundred miles into the interior of Africa—a tiny enclave surrounded on three sides by Senegal. It is bounded on the north and east by Senegal proper and on the south by the narrow territory of Casamance. The boundaries of the Gambia are completely artificial, being dictated not by ethnic or geographical considerations, but by European politics of the latter part of the nineteenth century. The goal of the British at that time was to exclude the French from political control of any part of the river. The boundaries thus drawn were considered to be temporary until the area could be exchanged for a more profitable position elsewhere. For various reasons no such exchange of territory ever took place, and the people of Gambia have, therefore, been forced to live with a boundary roughly drawn ten kilometers on either side of the river which excluded the Gambia from its natural hinterland, Senegal. The Gambia is one of the few areas in the world where a major portion of the boundary between states has not been defined. The far eastern lines which were to be drawn on a radius from the

I

upper river village of Yarbutenda proved to be impossible to lay out by following the dictates of the Convention of 1889. Subsequent discussion did not resolve this boundary question, so for over sixty years that portion of the boundary has been left undefined.[1]

The total area of the Colony is only sixty-nine square miles and is composed of the Island of St. Mary on which Bathhurst, the capital, is located, the adjoining division of Kombo St. Mary, MacCarthy Island, the Ceded Mile, Brefet, and Bajona. Of these, only Bathurst and Kombo St. Mary are administered separately from the Protectorate. The Protectorate covers an area of over four thousand square miles and contains a mixed population of 237,000[2] The basis of economic life is agriculture, and the most dominant influence in the country's existence is the Gambia River.

The life of the Gambia is determined by this great river which meanders through the country. It is the most navigable waterway in West Africa. There is always sufficient water at the mouth to admit the largest ocean going vessel. Even at low tide there is a minimum depth of twenty-six feet of water on the bar. The entrance of the Gambia between Bathurst on the south and Barra Point on the north is only two miles wide, but immediately above the town the river widens to nearly seven miles. From this width the river narrows to slightly more than one mile above Elephant Island which is eighty miles above Bathurst. The course of the river to this point is relatively straight with numerous indentations in its banks where con-tributary streams join the main body of water. In this estuary section the river is wide and the banks low and subject to inunda-tion, particularly during the rainy season. The river is lined with mangrove swamps from its mouth to a distance of over one hundred and fifty miles inland. These mangrove swamps are so dense at times that both banks are hidden from sight. Some of the trees reach a height of fifty or sixty feet. There are a few breaks in these swamps, notably at Elephant Island. Landings can be effected at these points, but elsewhere the banks are of soft mud and are unsuitable for landings. The river channel narrows and deepens above MacCarthy Island, and the low lying banks of the river give way to banks ten to

2

fifty feet high, overgrown with small trees or shrubs. From Elephant Island to MacCarthy Island these high banks are interspersed with low shores and swamp land. Above Elephant Island the river begins its serpentine course which it follows all the way to the eastern edge of the Protectorate and thence to its source some seven hundred miles from Bathurst in the Futa Jallon Plateau near the village of Labe.

The river is navigable for almost its entire length in British territory. Ocean going vessels can go as far up river as Kuntaur, one hundred and fifty miles from Bathurst, and vessels drawing less than one fathom can proceed to Fatoto, a village close to the eastern end of the Protectorate. The river is tidal, and even at the eastern end one can discern a slight rise.[3]

Climatically the year is divided into two seasons—the wet and the dry. The wet months last from June to October inclusive, and it is this season which is the most unhealthy and oppressive. The average rainfall is from thirty-five to forty-five inches per year. The dry north-east wind known as the Harmattan begins in December. It blows cold in the morning, hot in the middle of the day, and continues intermittently until April. Bathurst and lower river areas are generally blessed with a sea breeze throughout the year. Beyond the reach of this the temperature rises sharply to some twenty degrees warmer than the coastal areas. In general, the climate all year round is the best in any British West African settlement.

Geographically the Gambia may be divided into three regions which parallel the axis of the river. The first is the aforementioned mangrove swamps. Lying behind these and on slightly higher ground are the *banto faros*.[4] and at the highest point is the sandstone plateau which is an extension of the type of soil to be found throughout the Senegal and Casamance.

The *banto faros* can be divided into two divisions—estuarine and upper river. The boundary between them corresponds roughly to the upstream limits of the Lower River Division. The soils of the estuarine *banto faros* are heavier than those found in the upper river and possess a very high clay content. During the rains, from July to October, these estuarine *banto faros* are flooded with salt water. This flooding makes them unsuitable for any form of agriculture. The upper river soils are lighter, loamy, and fertile. They are flooded during the wet season with fresh water and are important for the growing of rice. The soils of the plateau are light, sandy, high in iron content, and of limited fertility. It is, however, in such soils that groundnuts do best.[5]

The settlement pattern along the lower river avoids the mangrove swamps and the estuarine *banto faros*, and is concentrated on the plateaux. The reason for this grouping is obvious. Besides the ever present danger of saline flooding of crops, there is the presence of troublesome insects, particularly the mosquito and the tsetse fly. A change in the distribution of population is noticeable in the central part of the country where the river makes the great bend. There one finds more villages located on the upper river *banto faro*. Actually there are more villages located on these upper river flats than on the sandstone plateau. Here the incision of the river is greater, lessening the danger of flooding villages thus located. There are, therefore, fewer swampy areas and dangerous insects. A great number of villages in the lower river area and around MacCarthy Island are bluff line villages. That is, they are located near the boundary separating the *banto faros* and the sandstone plateau, avoiding the extremes of both.[6]

The Gambia is primarily an agricultural area with most of the available soil being acid and of low fertility yield. Fortunately the type of soil of the sandstone plateau is good for the culture of groundnuts. Tropical fruits, vegetables, and cereals do well on the lower soils of the Colony and Western Division. With proper irrigation and application of modern agricultural methods, the Gambia could become more than sufficient in a variety of basic foodstuffs. However, the problems of achieving this level are immense and depend upon large capital investments and the re-education of a large segment of the farming population. Some steps in this direction have been made in the past twenty years, but with the unstable condition of the groundnut market, improvements in other agricultural products become even more imperative. The Gambia has no appreciable mineral resources and thus must depend in the foreseeable future upon its agriculture.[7]

The peoples of the Senegambia region are the result of a

4

series of voluntary and involuntary migrations which took place over the past two thousand years. The exact dates and nature of these manifold movements are shrouded in the silence left by centuries of non-literary people. Modern research methods in language analysis, folklore, blood groupings, and archaeology are providing new insights into the interconnections between the present inhabitants and their shadowy past. However important these are for the general outlines of inter-relationships, the fact remains that little for certain is known before the incursion of peoples who could leave written accounts. Even these are only now beginning to be thoroughly explored. In the pre-European period the available documentary sources are few, and although one hopes that more significant materials will be discovered, this does not dispel the present ignorance. If one is partially to understand the present disposition of the peoples of the Senegambia, it is necessary with these inadequate sources to sketch the location and mode of life of some of the tribes before they came under alien influence.

West Africa is generally considered to be the land of the true Negroes who speak some variant of the Sudanic sub group of the Niger-Congo languages. Today they occupy the coastal forest belt as well as the savannah land of the Sudan to the north and east of the forests. According to evidence currently available, the major shift in the area of their occupation in West Africa was from the edge of the savannah lands into the forest area. This movement occurred at different times, but was obviously quite late, in some places occurring just before the arrival of Europeans. Before continuous contacts had been established with the north, the Negro peoples congregated together in small units based on descent. The leader of such a group was originally the eldest male. Later the right to rule tended to become the prerogative of one lineage of a common ancestor. These groups lived in small villages near the one where the chief lived. Later this rather loose organization became more formalized and was expanded to include neighbouring villages until a larger territorial agglomeration had been created.[8] This tendency was accelerated after the arrival in the Sudan of Berber peoples who became the ruling caste of a number of city states. From the fourth century onward the

5

usual pattern of political organization was that which has been labelled the Sudanic State. The ruler of such a state was regarded as having semi-divine powers, controlling his kingdom through a well ordered bureaucracy and an efficient army. This was the form of rule in the Kingdoms of Ghana, Tekrur, Mali and Songhai. As the state expanded it included at its periphery client kings who had either been defeated in battle or who had succumbed to pressure short of war. Although more free from direct control than those people close to the centrum of power, the kingdoms ruled by clients kings soon began to adopt the political, social, and religious forms of the dominant state. This synthesis was a rather late development, occurring in the Senegambia probably no earlier than the thirteenth century. But from that time, the older forms of organization were largely modified by ideas brought from the great city-states of the Niger bend.

Life in the early villages was a never ending struggle with the environment for the necessary food to keep the inhabitants alive. The society was primarily agricultural, based upon the cultivation of such crops as plantains, beans, and millet, although in some areas fish and wild game supplemented the diet. Not until regular contacts had been established with the north and south did the people have more diversified crops or the domestic animals now so common in West Africa.

The religion of these early Negroes was a combination of many factors. Usually there was a chief god, creator of all things, who was normally tied into the descent group by having especially created the first ancestor. Since the environment was a hostile one, natural objects were also venerated as lesser deities. There was some belief in an after-life which was viewed as an extension of life itself. Closely allied to this was the belief in the power of the spirits of the departed who had great powers of intervention in the world of the living. The religion of each descent group was supervised by an organized priesthood which could mediate between man and the deities.[9]

If such a generalized pattern of life is true of the Negroid peoples before alien influences were introduced, one can see how long lived these ideas and practices have been. Even though today politically the descent group has generally given way to more precise hierarchies of chiefs and priests, there are places where the older forms still prevail. In religion, despite the incursions of Islam and Christianity, the earlier forms remain with territorial and tribal variations throughout West Africa.

The major impulse for change in this sedentary, agricultural existence came from outside. The North Africans' possession of horses and camels easily overcame the resistance of the Negro in the northern savannah and semi-desert areas. These invaders tended to appoint rulers for specific conquered areas. The invaders were fewer in number than the original inhabitants and were gradually assimilated, but not before implanting new ideas and institutions among the conquered. Successive invasions, coupled with disturbances among the now more sophisticated Negro population, caused migrations and major population shifts. These later affected the present location and distribution of the peoples of the Gambia Valley. Our observations of these changes are far better documented than the earlier period because the invaders who sought to control the vital trade routes were Muslim and have left reasonably good accounts of the early kingdoms of the Sudan.

Utilizing these Arabic accounts, one can see how closely connected, ethnically and historically, is the Senegambia with the western Sudan. The peoples, customs and religion of the Gambia for the most part stem from an area north and east of the Gambia River. The great bend of the Niger River was the heartland of strong Muslim kingdoms long before the arrival of the first European. These Muslim kingdoms extended their power over an immense area in North and West Africa including what is today Gambia.

These early Muslim kingdoms were based upon the control of key centres for the trans-Saharan trade. Cities such as Walata, Gao, and Timbuktu occupied positions between the forest lands and the desert. They represented the terminal points for the caravans from North Africa and traders moving north from the Gulf of Guinea. The major items in this trade dealt with ivory, salt, gold, honey, corn, cotton, and cloves. In addition to such barter trade, local trade flourished between cities, sometimes based upon a currency of cowrey shells.

Prior to the establishment of such far flung empires as

7

Songhai, and Mali, there had been a series of petty kingdoms centred on the trading city states. Notable among these trading centres were Jenne, Gao and later Timbuktu. These were comparable to the city states of early Western Europe, and some had already been centres of trade for over one thousand years when the Portuguese first touched the coast of Africa. In the thirteenth century most of these Sudanese city states were incorporated in the rising Mali kingdom. The conquering people of this kingdom were Mandingo, and in the next two centuries they spread throughout the Niger regions and overflowed into the valley of the Gambia. Their greatest emperor, Mansa Musa, extended the Mali control westward to the Atlantic Ocean and northward to the Atlas Mountains. The Mali emperor ruled over this large area by appointing semi-autonomous judges to act in his name. At the peak of Mali power the threat of the emperor's arms was enough to dissuade any serious rebellion.[10]

The Mali Empire began to decline in the fourteenth century. Its place as the premier power in the western Sudan was gradually assumed by the Songhai Empire whose most prosperous city was Gao. Rising from subjection to Mali, they had within two centuries completely absorbed the older empire. In addition they extended their control over an even larger area than that dominated by Mali. This period was the most civilized that the Sudan had seen. The law was strictly enforced, a good police system was established, Muslim courts functioned even in the outlying districts, banking was encouraged, and a great boom in trade followed. A university was established in Timbuktu which attracted scholars from every part of the Songhai territory. The semi-centralized control of the Songhai Empire disappeared in the sixteenth century due only to a series of invasions from Morocco.[11]

The stability and unity of the empires, during the period of Mali and Songhai, were greatest in those areas closest to the emperor's centre of power. In the farthest extremities his control was only nominal, being exercised by a local chief who was in most cases free from interference from his overlord. This was the case of the petty kings or chiefs near the west coast in the region of Senegambia. Nevertheless there was a definite improvement over the conditions that had existed in Gambia before the incursions. The contact established with the Sudan created a more stable society and a more definite link with the trans-Saharan trade. Furthermore, through this contact the Muslim religion, which was to be such an important factor in later years, entered the area. The progress of Islam in the Gambia valley was slow. It has been estimated that at the time of the first Portuguese visits, Islam was only beginning to make headway there. The traders were the first to accept Muslim precepts. They transmitted their new found religion to the peasant classes and the lower grades in the society. The chiefs and their entourages were the last to succumb for Islam taught a code of self-discipline that was not congenial to some of the pagan chiefs. Many pre-Islamic beliefs conferred divine attributes on the chief. Even when this was not recognized, the chiefs and aristocracy were closely associated with the direction of religious practice. It can be assumed that where there was an organized priesthood, it reinforced the aristocratic political system. Thus it is not surprising that the ruling classes remained hostile toward Islam long after it had made substantial progress with other classes in the society. In the Senegambia area the Soninki-Marabout Wars of the nineteenth century were the final stages in the conversion of the ruling classes to a form of Islam.

The Gambia today is populated by a number of diverse peoples brought into the Gambia valley probably in the last six hundred years as a result of pressures exerted in their former homeland of the Sudan. There are five distinct major peoples inhabiting this small country—the Wolof, Mandingo, Fula, Jola, and Serahuli. They speak different languages and have differing cultural and historical backgrounds.

Alvise de Cadamosto, a Venetian explorer commissioned by Portugal, on his first voyage to the Senegambia in 1455 found the north bank of the Gambia occupied by a race of 'Tawney Moors', slight of stature and definitely not Negroid. However on the south side of the river he found a race of men who were exceedingly black, corpulent, and well made—probably Mandingos, who by this time had penetrated westward from their original homeland. Here was a very definite dividing line in the movement of races in Africa.[12] This dividing line, based on the

9

Gambia River, was not to remain for long because the 'Tawney Moors' seem to have been driven northward by the Songhai Empire.

There is good reason to believe that at least the westward extension of the Songhai was made up of the Wolof. One theory of the origin of these Wolof peoples is that they were of Yemeni or Libyan descent and conquered the valley of the Niger in the seventh century, gradually extending their position westward until they came to the Gambia. Other commentators see the Wolof as being a composite between Seres and such foreign elements as Fula, Serahuli, and Mandingo.[13] Whatever the ultimate origin of the Wolof, it is known that one section of the Songhai Empire established itself at Gualata or Julafa in the Rio d'Oro Valley from whence the present name of the tribe is derived. With the Moorish invasions from the north, these outposts were pushed back. By the seventeenth century the Wolof Kingdom was located between the Senegal River south to the Gambia.[14] Francis Moore noted in 1730 that all the towns in this area owed alliegance to the Kingdom of the Joloffs with its seat at Barsilly (Ba Saloum).[15] Their occupation was subject to some incursion by Mandingos, particularly in the immediate vicinity of the north bank of the Gambia River. However, the Wolof remained in power in most of this area until subdued by the French in the nineteenth century. At that time they were still ruled by the head of the Royal House of Songhai north of the Gambia who, it was reported, as late as 1896 could command over two thousand horsemen.[16]

The bulk of the Wolof population today, approximately three-quarters of a million, is still located in this segment of modern Senegal. In the Gambia they comprise the third largest tribal grouping, approximately 35,000 in the Protectorate, with the heaviest concentration being in the Saloum districts of the Central Division where there is an almost homogeneous block that corresponds to a large group across the border in Senegal. In addition the Wolof make up almost one half the population of Bathurst and Kombo.[17] The majority of the Bathurst Wolof came originally from the area near Dakar and the Island of Goree in the early years of the settlement of Bathurst. Racially and linguistically they are virtually the same as

10

those of the Protectorate, but historically they are a different community.[18]

The majority of the Gambia Wolof depend, as in the past, upon agriculture. With few variations they utilize methods and plant crops similar to all other agriculturalists of the Gambia. The main cash crop is groundnuts which is the responsibility of the men, while the strict sustenance crops are left to the women. Land tenure varies according to the degree of stability of the population. In general, land tenure follows the communal pattern that is common throughout the Gambia, with the village head and elders administering land utilization. The Bathurst Wolof, due to their close proximity to schools and other forms of money earning occupations, have emerged in the last fifty years as the native intellectual and economic leaders in the Gambia.

The Wolof of the Protectorate or Colony are far from being a homogeneous group. This is due to the long history of local wars, the slave trade, and absorption of other groups which had begun before the sixteenth century. Nevertheless, the Wolof has certain physical characteristics which distinguish him from his neighbours. The men are well built and of medium height. Their skins are very black and they normally have woolly hair. They are without the flat noses so common among other tribes. The Wolof profile in certain cases is slightly aquiline. Wolof women are among the most handsome in Africa. They are very careful of their clothing and are given to lavish displays of jewellery, particularly heavy gold earrings. Their dresses are modelled upon the French style which was fashionable during the empire period. In full dress the Wolof women are regal in bearing and far surpass their husbands in appearance.[19]

A second group of people in the Gambia are the Mandingos, and like the Wolof, their racial origin is also in doubt.[20] It has been suggested that they are an intermixture of Bantu stock and indigenous Negro. Another explanation is that they are of mixed Negro and Arab origin. Whatever the final solution of his origins may be, the Mandinka has certain physical characteristics which make him distinguishable from the other peoples of the Gambia. This is true despite the close association with other tribes that tends to modify the differences. He is tall, sometimes exceedingly so, with long arms and legs. The facial characteristics are striking: low brows, a prognathous jaw, and an extremely flat and broad nose. Eyes tend to be long and narrow, and with high cheekbones, a Mandinka sometimes appears to have Mongolian features.

Before their extension into the Gambia valley, the Mandingos occupied the northern slopes of the Futa Jallon Plateau, the saddle between the valleys of the Niger on the east and those of the Gambia and the Senegal on the west. The actual country of Manding or Mandi is in the Niger valley. From there the Mandingos have spread north and south from the Niger to the Atlantic. They were found by Cadamosto already firmly entrenched along the south bank of the Gambia. They formed the nucleus of the great Sudanese Kingdom of Mali, and they maintained a semi-independent role throughout the centuries against a series of invaders. Even Askia the Great at the height of his power took twelve years to complete the conquest of Mali. It is doubtful if even he was able to shake the Mandinka power in the Futa Jallon. The Mandingos were described by Richard Jobson, merchant trader to Gambia in 1620-21, as being 'the people who are Lords, and Commanders of this country'.[21] Both during and after the fall of the Mali Empire, the Gambia was ruled by petty client kings who owed their allegiance to a higher authority located outside the valley. By the time of Francis Moore's visit in the eighteenth century the Mandingos had crossed the Gambia River and established themselves at various points such as Barra and Baddibu, but they held this territory in all probability as tributaries of the Wolof.[22] From this time, however, the Mandingos assumed the premier position on the north bank as well as the south, and it was primarily with them that the English came into contact in the petty wars of the nineteenth century.

From the earliest times the Mandingos were traders and artisans. Some of the gold mines which played a large role in the prosperity of the great cities of the Sudan were located in the Futa Jallon. After early contacts with white traders, they turned more toward coastal rather than interior trade. The more prosperous Mandingos became the middle men in the barter of slaves, ivory, and gold for European trade goods. This preference for trade, together with the previously far flung Mali Empire, spread the Mandinka population throughout West Africa and made their language the *lingua franca* for commerce.

The Mandingos were among the first peoples of West Africa to accept Islam. Located as they were in many parts of West Africa, their acceptance of Islam was most important in spreading that religion. The most important Mandinka chiefs were wealthy and could hire armies of mercenaries and retainers of Tucolors, Turkanos, and others. They were in a fortunate position to force their rule upon less affluent and less powerful tribes. Thus by the nineteenth century these chiefs had become the arbiters of peace and war in the Gambia valley.[23]

Despite the important place of commerce, the life of the Mandingos was still based upon agriculture. After the pacification of the Gambia in the latter part of the nineteenth century, the Gambian Mandinka, shorn of his political power and with his economic status reduced by European firms and Lebanese traders, found that agriculture was the only remaining outlet for his talents. Today the majority of the Mandinka population apply themselves to traditional methods of clearing and farming the land. They tenaciously resist newer methods which would increase productivity and profit. The groundnut is their only really profitable crop. Rice culture, despite favourable conditions, remains women's work, and as a result is only a sustenance crop. The Mandingos are the largest single tribal group in the Protectorate, approximately 110,000. They are spread fairly evenly throughout the Protectorate with an especially heavy concentration in the Lower River Division. However they comprise only a small proportion of the population of the Colony area. They are poor and economically backward compared with the more favourably situated Wolof.[24]

The people who have been longest resident in the Gambia are the Jolas. At the present time they are located in the largest numbers in the Foni district of the Western Division. This is approximately the same area in which early European travellers found them. Andre Brue, in a trip across the Gambia from Senegal to the Casamance in 1700, noted that they were the chief people in the coastal areas between the Gambia River and the Casamance.[25] Both Brue and Moore observed that there was little tribal organization among them, notwithstanding the large area they occupied. There was no paramount chief, rule being based solely at the village level. The basis of life was millet, rice, and the possession of great numbers of cattle and goats. The Jolas normally rejected clothing, preferring nakedness, cicatrising their faces and bodies, and covering themselves with Gri-gris.

The Jolas and Mandingos were bitter enemies, and it appears that by the time of Moore's visit the Mandingos had overrun Foni and to a certain extent had subjugated the Jolas there. However their interaction was far from being a simple master and servant relationship. In all probability Foni merely became a buffer zone between the Jola settlements further south and the Gambian Mandingos, for Moore reported, 'They [the Jolas] are independent of each other, and under the Government of no one Chief; notwithstanding which, they unite so firmly, that all the force of the *Mundingos* (sic) (Tho' so very numerous) cannot get the better of them.'[26] At times these Jolas were content to be led by the Mandingos, but at other times they were in an open state of rebellion. Golbéry in 1785 also observed the Jolas, 'the physiognomy, character and manners of whom possess a kind of savageness and ferocity'.[27]

The social organization of the Jolas today is much the same as it was three centuries ago—a rudimentary communal system. Each patriarch with his relations, dependents, and servants occupies a separate village walled in and stockaded against real or imagined enemies. Compared with other races in West Africa, they are fairly industrious and hard working although they still despise clothes and remain to a great extent pagan.[28]

The Fula, the second largest group numerically, are in some ways the most interesting people of the Gambia. Their original home has been a matter of great conjecture. Some early ethnologists traced the Fula back to the *Hyskos* or Sheperd Kings of Egypt. According to this theory, around 1600 B.C. one contingent of this Asian people fled westward along the northern edge of the desert until they reached the valley of the Senegal.[29] Although this is an interesting theory, there is no way of confirming it. A more plausible explanation is that the ancestors of the Fula were Berber pastoralists or Jewish refugees who inter-

married with Mande speaking peoples of Ghana and were the
early rulers of Ghana. After their overthrow as the ruling caste
of Ghana in the eighth century, groups of them migrated to
Tekrur where they assumed a similar position of dominance
over the Wolof and Tucolor people there. Cultural and racial
assimilation continued there until the people known today as
Fula emerged, basically a Negro people speaking a Negro
language. In the eleventh century these rulers were expelled
from Tekrur and their wanderings date from this event. They
were influential later in the Sosso empire of Kaniaga and the
kingdom of Messina.[30]

In the early sixteenth century the Fula began to appear in the
higher, cooler Futa Jallon Plateau where they lived in close
conjunction with the Mandingos. From the beginnings they
were a pastoral people, basing their culture on the possession of
cattle. The western group of the Fula became Muslim at quite
an early date, perhaps as early as the fifteenth century.[31] During
the late sixteenth century the country around Futa had become
so crowded that it was imperative that some of the peoples seek
new lands for the pasturage of their large herds. One large
section of this pastoral, migratory people moved into the area
of what is now northern Nigeria, following earlier groups that
had settled in Hausaland as early as the thirteenth century.
Another important group travelled northward towards the
Senegal across the middle valley of the Gambia. This move was
a slow process and the Fula tended to mix with the tribes in the
the valley. Although a certain section of the Fula has never
intermarried with other tribes and remains relatively pure, the
greater proportion had probably already become hybrid before
they reached Futa Jallon. In the Gambia these Fula people
settled in the area from the Casamance River and Vintang
Creek to Fuladugu and Kantora, seemingly without much
trouble. The area involved was under the control of the Mandingos who utilized the Fula for very definite purposes—to
plant their crops and keep their cattle. This relationship was
at times little better than a state of slavery for the Fula. Jobson
noted this when he said, 'These people live in great subjection
to the Mandingo, under which they seeme to groone, for he
cannot at any time kill a beefe, but if they know it, the black

man will have the greatest share, neither can hee sell or barter with us for any commodity hee hath . . . '.[32] After a time of planting and harvesting these semi-nomadic Gambian Fula would move again in search of better pasturage and again would build their temporary towns under the overlordship of the Mandingos.

Although today there are few pure Fula left and many of the characteristics of these people have been lost in the admixture of Negro peoples, some of their traits remain dominant. The pure Fula contrast very definitely with their more Negroid neighbours in that they have oval faces, chiselled aquiline features, thin delicate lips, and long hair. These pure Fula, like the Cow Fulani of Northern Nigeria, remain pure nomads and herdsmen, scorning the semi-nomadic existence of the town Fula.

The last of the major tribes of the Gambia valley are also hybrids. The Serahuli are the inhabitants of that area which comprised the ancient kingdom of Wuli. They are the northern branch of the Mandingos with the admixture of Berbers from the north and the Fula, in their migrations through Wuli, from the south. In the course of the religious wars of the nineteenth century in West Africa, the Serahuli played an important role in providing mercenary soldiers for the warring factions. Today the Serahuli are generally to be found in the Upper River Division where they form the largest tribal grouping. They are primarily farmers and are handicapped by the poorness of their soil. It was in the upper river that the hungry season fell with greatest force.[33]

A description of the people of the Gambia would not be complete without some reference to the itinerant people known as the 'strange farmers'. In earlier days these agricultural workers might possibly have served as mercenary soldiers to some war chief during the Soninki-Marabout conflicts. After the wars had ended great numbers came seasonally into the Gambia to help with the planting and harvesting on a share crop basis. The individual 'stranger', ignoring the artificial boundaries, would make his own contract with the village headmen and be assigned to work for the farmers of the village who needed the most help. He was given a portion of land to work for himself in his free time. Normally the 'strange farmer' would be required to aid with the growing of additional grain and other products to provide the extra food for his sustenance. Nevertheless, the pressure on the food supplies by great numbers of non-resident Gambians did add to the problem of the hungry season. Since 1945 the government, by its taxing policy and direct intervention through the medium of the Chief's Conferences, has attempted to discourage the use of large numbers of these workers. Although there still exists an annual migration of people to the Gambia, the numbers involved grow less with each succeeding year.[34]

Chapter Two

EARLY EUROPEAN CONTACTS

THERE is evidence that some of the ancient peoples of Europe, particularly the Carthaginians, were in constant contact with West Africa.[1] Any such contacts were abruptly broken by the collapse of the Roman Empire and the spread of Islam across the northern reaches of Africa. The link between Europe and West Africa was re-established by Portuguese explorers in the fifteenth century. The Portuguese had gained a certain amount of information about the reputed wealth of Africa from Arab geographers and cartographers. Urged on by Prince Henry, Portuguese mariners pushed south into regions hitherto unknown to Europeans. Madeira was discovered in 1418, and Cape Bojador fifteen years later. In 1440 Cape Blanco was reached, and in 1446 Nuno Tristao reached Cape Verde, ninety miles north of the estuary of the Gambia. Treaties of commerce were soon entered into with the natives in the Cape Verde area, and from then on ships were sent from Portugal every year to trade with them.[2]

As a result of the information and trade thus gained, Prince Henry, in March 1455, commissioned Alvise de Cadamosto to continue exploration south of Cape Verde. He was given for this task a new caravel of some seventy tons. In this first voyage he was joined off Cape Verde by Antoniotto Usi di Mare, a Genoese with two ships acting under similar orders from Prince

Henry to explore south of Cape Verde. The two joined forces in exploring the Gambia. They entered the estuary, but were forced to turn back due to the unfriendly behaviour of the natives and the reluctance of the crew to press further inland.[3] In May 1456, these same two explorers returned to the Gambia and this time had no such hostile reception. They were met by a lord who was subject to the Emperor of Mali. He conducted them some sixty miles upstream to the land of one of his subject lords. Here they spent a pleasant fifteen days trading and observing the country. Leaving because of sickness in the crew, they proceeded to explore further south as far as Cape Mesurado before returning to Portugal.[4]

This first voyage up the Gambia River was followed in 1458 by an expedition of three vessels led by Diego Gomez who also sailed far up the Gambia until the thick growth of trees on either side of the river made navigation impossible. After some trading with the local chiefs he sent a party to explore and report on the Wolof territory through which he was passing.

There was a series of organized expeditions to the Gambia in the latter part of the fifteenth century. It was in this period that a number of Portuguese settled along the banks of the river and missionaries began to arrive, endeavouring to bring Christianity to the natives. They found this a difficult task, and no real achievement was made despite zealous efforts. The main reason for this failure was the hostility of the chiefs which was coupled with the growing tide of Islam. The reputed mineral wealth of Gambia proved illusory. Some hides, gold, and ivory were exported, but the main trade for the Portuguese was slaves.

The Portuguese settlers gradually intermarried with the natives and to a large extent lost their distinctive characteristics.[5] Those who had settled there found themselves isolated from the other Portuguese settlements on the west coast. This came to be increasingly so as the Portuguese empire expanded throughout the world. The resources of the small country were strained to such an extent that she could ill afford too much interest in an area that was unhealthy and unprofitable. Gradually the contacts between the now hybrid settlers and the Portuguese almost ceased. An occasional priest from Portugal, Cape Verde, or from the Portuguese settlement on the Rio Grande brought them in touch again with Europe and Christianity.[6]

By the mid-seventeenth century the links with Europe had almost disappeared. Richard Jobson noted:

> And there are, as they call themselves, *Portungales*, and some few of them seeme the same; others of them are *Molatoes*, betweene blacke and white, but the most part as blacke, as the naturall inhabitants: they are scattered some two or three dwellers in a place, and are all married, or rather keepe with them the countrey blackewomen, of whom they beget children, howbeit they have amongst them, neither Church, nor Frier, nor any other religious order.[7]

By the latter part of the eighteenth century these survivors of the Portuguese settlements of the fifteenth and sixteenth century had been completely absorbed into the indigenous population, thus removing the last traces of Portuguese occupation.

Long before these vestiges of Portuguese occupation had disappeared, other European countries had assumed the dominant position in West Africa. The English and French began to send trading ships to the area in the sixteenth century. Their prime motivation, as with the Portuguese, was trade. One of the earliest English contacts with West Africa was in 1553 when a Portuguese refugee piloted two small English ships to tap what were believed to be the riches of West Africa.[8] Portugal, however, remained strong enough to keep down the volume of trade in what was considered her territory. However after 1580, Portugal's position was radically altered with the passing of the Portuguese throne to Philip II of Spain. Portugal's already weak empire then had to bear the inroads of those European countries hostile to Spain.

Indirectly, Antonio, Prior of Crato, one of the claimants to the Portuguese throne, was responsible for launching English trading activities in West Africa. The good Prior, feeling himself the true King of Portugal, granted certain trading concessions in Portuguese territory to English merchants.[9] In 1588, to settle various disputes over these concessions, Queen Elizabeth granted exclusive trading rights for a period of ten years to certain English merchants trading in West Africa.[10] Due to a combination of chariness on the part of the investors and the hostility of the Portuguese, none of the ships sent out by these merchants reached their destinations in the Gambia.

This original company seemed to set the pattern for most of those that followed. In 1598 and 1618 the English government granted new concessions to merchants and gentlemen anxious to make their fortune in the West African trade. Lack of knowledge of the territory, opposition from other European merchants, and bad luck combined to produce in each case a deficit and made potential traders wary of the Gambia as a place for profitable investment.[11]

The English left little trace of their various adventures in Gambia in this early period. Richard Jobson, one of the traders, travelled up the river past Barrakunda Falls, made friends with the natives, and left an indelible account of life on the great river in the seventeenth century. His glowing reports of the riches to be gained in ordinary trade with the interior made little impression on the hard headed traders in London, but they kept alive the dream of easy riches to be gleaned from West Africa trade.[12]

The Commonwealth in 1651 formed a Guinea Company to trade with the Gambia. They, like their predecessors, expected a lively trade in wax, hides, gold, and ivory. Two expeditions were dispatched and in 1652 a trading station was established at Bintang. Members of the expedition even followed Jobson's route past Barrakunda Falls to prospect for gold. However, effort and money were expended for nothing: Prince Rupert entered the estuary in 1652, completely destroyed the station and departed with the goods he found there. This disaster ended the Commonwealth's attempt to glean the riches of the Gambia.[13]

Meanwhile the French had become active in West African trade. By 1560 the merchants of Dieppe had established a regular trade with Senegal and Cape Verde.[14] From that time forward French interest was mainly concerned with developing and consolidating their position in the Senegal valley. In 1612 France made an attempt to establish a colony on the Gambia River. The expedition failed miserably, primarily because of sickness, and was completely abandoned.[15] This experience con-

21

vinced French traders that their best interest lay not on the Gambia, but further north near the mouth of the Senegal River.

The Dutch entered into trade competition in the early part of the sixteenth century. In 1617 the States General established a company to trade between the Tropic of Cancer and the Cape of Good Hope. This company in 1621 established itself at Goree, an island lying off Cape Verde and only ninety miles north of the mouth of the Gambia.[16] This strategic position tended to discourage French penetration southward for the time being and made the Cape Verde area one of economic competition between the French and Dutch. Neither country seemed interested in opening up the Gambia for trade.

One other European state was soon embroiled in the search for West African wealth—the small, relatively unimportant Baltic country of Courland. James, Duke of Courland, saw in West Africa a chance to bolster the economy of his small country and at the same time to establish an overseas empire. Although the Courlander's venture in West Africa was of short duration, it had far reaching importance for Gambian trade in the seventeenth century. In 1651 two Courlander ships put into the Gambia River to further these imperial schemes. They purchased St. Andrews Island from the King of Barra, and Banjol (the Island of St. Mary) from the King of Kombo. They erected a fort, the first European fortified location, on the former island. Any chance of the colony succeeding was removed by events in Europe. Courland was involved in a war between Sweden and Poland. No funds were forthcoming for the stranded colonists, and in 1659 the Dutch West India Company entered into an agreement with the Duke's agent in Holland whereby the Courlander's possessions in West Africa passed into their hands.[17]

The restoration of Charles II brought England again to the fore in the Gambia. Charles, spurred on no doubt by the earlier records of Jobson and the glowing reports of Prince Rupert,[18] founded the Royal Adventurers of England Trading in Africa. There was one significant change in the type of trade to be undertaken. Richard Jobson in 1620 had refused the offer to buy slaves with the noble words that 'We were a people, who did not deale in any such commodities, neither did we buy or sell one another, or any that had our owne shapes.'[19] The avowed object of the Royal Adventurers was to supply Negroes for the West Indian and American plantations who were to be sold at seventeen pounds a head or for an equivalent value in sugar. Major Holmes, one of the participants in Rupert's previous raid, commanded an expedition which was successful in occupying St. Andrews Island, which he promptly renamed James Island. Holmes also made it clear to the Dutch and French in West Africa that he would not condone an invasion of the territory which the Royal Adventurers held to be their own.[20]

These Royal Adventurers, backed by the authority and money of James, Duke of York, soon found themselves involved in the second Dutch War. The fortunes of this war for the West African spheres fluctuated. The English captured the Island of Goree and then promptly lost it again to the Dutch Admiral De Ruyter. The Treaty of Breda in 1667 restored to their original owners all ports and territories conquered in the war.[21]

Despite royal support, the Royal Adventurers did not find the trade extremely profitable, and in 1668 they sublet their monopoly to another firm called the Gambia Adventurers. There seems to have been an agreement worked out between this company and the Dutch traders in the area because conflicts between the two nations over Gambia trade became fewer. A live and let live policy was followed by the Adventurers and this was not greatly affected by the outbreak of war between England and the Dutch in 1672.[22]

The Gambia Adventurers found, as their predecessors had, that trade in the Gambia, even with the inclusion of the slave trade, was not profitable. After a protracted litigation lasting from 1672 until 1684, both the Gambia Adventurers and their parent company relinquished their trading monopoly to a new company called the Royal African Company.[23] Through many vicissitudes this company lasted until 1750. The method of operation of this new company did not differ substantially from that of its predecessors. James Island was the main base of operation. The chief factor of the company was in command of a small number of soldiers and an even smaller civilian staff to handle the trade. In addition to this main trading station, other factories were established up river and along the coast. The number of these factories varied, but usually there was a factory at MacCarthy Island, one at Barrakunda Falls, one at Bintang, one at Banyon Point, and one at Juffure. Trade goods such as beads, cotton cloth, and leather products would be taken to these outlying districts by small sloops which would take on board the native products for transportation down river. The climate was unhealthy and the mortality rate among the white servants of the company was exceedingly high. This, combined with poor communications due to growing French rivalry in the latter seventeenth and early eighteenth century, reduced the profit to be gained in such trade to a minimum.

During the course of the century the French to the north had further consolidated their hold on the Senegal area. In 1638 St. Louis was founded and the Senegal was recognized as a French colony. The original company that set out to exploit the area was replaced in 1664 by the *Compagnie des Indes Occidentale* to which Colbert had given exclusive trading rights on the shores of the Atlantic from Canada to the Cape of Good Hope. This gigantic scheme collapsed in 1672 and the Senegal Company took its place, only to be replaced in turn by the Guinea Company which finally gave way in 1696 to the Royal Senegal Company.[24] Despite the changes in management France's hold on the area increased due to a policy first instituted by the Senegal Company of entering into exclusive commercial treaties with all the chiefs along the coast from Cape Verde to the Gambia.[25]

By the close of the seventeenth century Dutch competition had receded from the area. In 1677 France captured the important Dutch west coast Island of Goree and the annexation was made final by the Treaty of Nimeguen the following year. French control of the Cape Verde-Senegal area was now relatively secure. England was supreme on the Gambia. The history of Senegambia in the next two centuries is a story of the conflicts between these two powers. Although there was some jealousy between French and English merchants in this period, the impetus behind these clashes was dictated almost entirely by the European situation.

After the capture of Goree, the French established factors

along the Atlantic Coast of West Africa south of Cape Verde. This brought their area of trade control once again to the Gambia valley. Following a punitive expedition against the chief of Ba-Saloum in 1679, the Senegal Company obtained proprietary rights to the north bank of the Gambia as far up-stream as Juffure opposite James Island. Two years later the Senegal Company established a trading station at Albreda opposite James Island.[26] The first establishment was a very flimsy affair in charge of a single factor. Nevertheless it served as a base for trade. French trading vessels were allowed to proceed up river unmolested by their English rivals. The repre-sentatives of the Royal African Company on James Island lacked the money or the power to exclude the French from the Gambia at this time. The French company, feeling itself in a stronger position, continued to harass English shipping in the area, even going as far as taking one English ship within sight of James Island. The only reactions to such French depredations were a series of protests demanding the return of the captured cargoes.[27]

The outbreak of war between England and France in 1689 finally aroused the Royal African Company to greater exertions. The small garrison at James Fort received reinforcements, and led by John Booker, the chief factor, they overpowered Albreda. This feat was to be duplicated many times in the coming years of French-English rivalry. After this initial success the English pushed into the Senegal region and captured and sacked the main French factories there. Turning south they captured and razed Goree.[28] This forward policy was quickly reversed, how-ever. Booker's successors as chief factors were less energetic, sickness took its toll, and gradually the garrison at James Island was reduced to near impotence. It was thus easy prey for a French naval squadron sent to capture James Island in 1695. The garrison at James Fort surrendered without offering any resistance. Following this the African Company made no at-tempt to re-establish itself on the island until the close of the war. The French in turn did not seek to reoccupy their posts on the Gambia.[29]

The results of these tiny expeditions, while apparently equally disastrous to both protagonists in the Gambia, really worked

25

in favour of the English. The chiefs were not particularly interested with whom they traded. The French expedition that took James Island removed the only good trading station in the area. In addition they had alienated the feeling oi some of the powerful chiefs. Thus the French took on the appearance of mere destroyers while the English were remembered as good traders and shopkeepers.

James Fort was rebuilt immediately at the close of the war and the Royal African Company resumed its position in the Gambia. There was, however, one significant difference. The Royal African Company no longer could exercise a monopoly of the trade of the Gambia. Parliament, following the Revolution of 1688, was not prone to recognize the necessity of the Royal African Company's monopoly. In 1698, therefore, trade in West Africa was thrown open to all English merchants. The Royal African Company was still charged with the upkeep of the forts and defences of the area, and to this end they could level a duty on all exports by private merchants from the Gambia to England. Other than this private traders could establish factories and trade at will. For the loss of its monopoly the company was to receive ten per cent duty on all goods sent to and from West Africa.[30]

The seventeenth century closed with England and France at peace in Europe. This state of affairs was hardly applicable to the situation in Senegambia. The Senegal Company had dispatched Andre Brue as Director General in 1697. His one aim was to displace the English merchants in the Gambia and remove their pretensions to trade on the Atlantic Coast. In this interval between wars Brue seized a number of English ships and their cargoes. The English factor at James Island was adamant that the French should not trade above James Island. The only thing that prevented a direct conflict between the two companies was the difficulty Brue experienced with local chiefs in the Senegal.[31]

The story of the relations between England and France in the Senegambia for the next fifty years is a tale of normal trade competition enflamed by European conflicts. Immediately after the outbreak of the War of Spanish Succession a French naval squadron appeared before James Island. The outnumbered defenders put up little resistance and the French plundered the island. The garrison was reinforced in 1703, but to little avail for in 1704 the island was again plundered by a French privateer.[32]

The merchants of both countries trading in Senegambia were not happy with the disruption of trade caused by the extension of the war to Africa. No matter who the eventual victor might be, the trade of both nations suffered from raids and disruption of the normal channels of supply. This was especially true in the case of slave transport which made up the bulk of the English trade in the Gambia. Therefore an agreement was reached between the English and French companies in 1705 declaring the Senegambia a neutral area. The agreement stated that each company should prevail upon its own government to honour this neutral agreement.[33] Both companies tried to abide by the terms of the agreement but they had little control over the operations of privateers. Following a mutiny of the small garrison on James Island in 1708, the island was again plundered by a French privateer. These two blows were disastrous for the maintenance of the fort. In the following year the few remaining Europeans spiked the guns and withdrew to settle down on the banks of the river as private traders. Fortunately for English interests in the Gambia, the Senegal Company was in no position to take advantage of the situation. The French in Senegal, due to the almost complete severance of their contact with France, were in a state of semi-starvation. The Senegal Company was in dire financial straits and in 1709 sold its trading rights to a group of merchants from Rouen.[34] Thus the English private merchants were saved from French domination and through their efforts England remained dominant on the river at the close of the war.

Immediately after the Treaty of Utrecht the Royal African Company sent out a party of merchants, soldiers, and artisans to re-eastablish the fort on James Island. The fort was in no condition to be immediately reoccupied. The guns were useless and the walls and buildings were in almost complete disrepair. It was decided to use a ship as the trading depot while the fort was being repaired. The task of re-construction was no easy matter. The artisans were inexperienced, the private merchants

27

did everything to hinder the re-establishment of the fort, many of the soldiers and workers deserted, and finally sickness reduced the number of men available. It was not until 1717 that the fort could be partially occupied. On top of all this, after 1715 no relief or supplies were forthcoming from England. In all probability this failure to supply the fort adequately was a result of the failure of Parliament to renew the company's right to levy a ten per cent duty on all West African exports.[35] In such a situation the company's position in the Gambia was very vulnerable to attacks from any quarter. Taking advantage of this in 1719, pirates seized the island and carried away most of the company's property and slaves. Again the fort was abandoned by the Europeans. By 1721 there was only one man in the Gambia who remained faithful to the company. The French, following the home government's policy of peace, chose not to take advantage of the low fortunes of the Royal Africa Company, but satisfied themselves merely with re-establishing their post at Albreda and building a new fort at Bintang.[36]

The Royal African Company seems to have had no consistent policy with regard to trade in the Gambia. Following the collapse of their interests at James Island, a collapse due primarily to their lackadaisical manner of supplying the wants of the fort,[37] they sent a major expedition to try to re-establish their position on the coast. Perhaps this new effort was inspired by the fear that the South Sea Company or one of the innumerable companies then being formed in England would encroach on this vacant territory. This new expedition was more military in character than any of the previous settlement schemes and, in addition, many of the soldiers and artisans were permitted to take their wives and families. This proved a ghastly mistake for the territory was notoriously unhealthy and there were no suitable living quarters. Nineteen women and children died within five months and only three women and one child lived long enough to get away from the river.[38]

Nevertheless this expedition marked the beginning of a new epoch in the Royal African Company's occupation of the river. Inland penetration had lagged during the seventeenth century. The English traders even in times of peace had not been disposed to push further inland. They were content with the native trade near the mouth of the river. Plans had been formulated at various times to seek Jobson's and Prince Rupert's mountain of gold and to open a direct trading route to Timbuktu, but these schemes had never progressed far beyond the planning stage.[39] In 1722 a definite attempt was made to confirm the Gambia as the seed-bed of riches. A Captain Stibbs was placed in command of a new expedition. With fifteen Europeans he pushed up river to a point some sixty miles above Barrakunda Falls. On his return he reported that he had found no minerals of value and that in his opinion the mines were a myth.[40] This report tended to discourage further exploration up the river for some time.

Elsewhere, however, the Royal African Company was more successful. The gum trade with Portendic was established at this time and lasted until its renunciation by a convention with France in 1857.[41] In 1725, after a series of disputes with the French traders, Albreda and the French stations at Bintang were plundered. Soon, however, each protagonist realized that it would be disastrous to both sides to continue this bickering and after 1725 there was an effort on the part of the French company and the Royal African Company to avoid such incidents.[42]

The period between 1730 and 1740 was the most prosperous in the history of the English company. Peace with their great colonial rival in combination with honest and enterprising factors on the Gambia enabled them to exploit the area as they had never done before.

The primary product of the Gambia, as elsewhere in West Africa at this time, was slaves. Francis Moore who accompanied Stibbs to the area in 1721 left an indelible impression of the handling of this commodity:

> The same Merchants bring down Elephants Teeth and in some Years Slaves to the Amount of two thousand most of which they say are Prisoners taken in War: They buy them from the different Princes who take them . . . and are brought from a vast Way inland. Their Way of bringing them is tying them by the Neck with Leather-Thongs at about a Yard distant from each other, 30 or 40 in a String, having generally a bundle of Corn or an Elephant's Tooth upon each of their Heads.[43]

The demand for slaves to work the plantations in the West Indies had transformed the morality of English traders in one short century. The indignation of the English merchant, Jobson, in referring to the institution of slavery had given way to the approval of the educated Christian, Francis Moore, who reported that all acts of a criminal nature in the lower Gambia, whether petty or large, were punished by slavery. He related, an an example, a case of a man sold into slavery for the theft of a tobacco pipe.[44] The number of slaves transported from the Gambia fluctuated with conditions on the river. In good years as many as two thousand were transported. The average in the first quarter of the eighteenth century, according to Moore, seems to have been around one thousand per year.[45]

It is not surprising, therefore, that at the outset of the War of Austrian Succession both English and French merchants were anxious to revive the agreement of 1705 that had declared a neutral zone in that part of Africa. Neither government, however, was prepared to accept such proposals. In 1745 two English men of war destroyed the French factory at Albreda. The French made no attempt to reoccupy Albreda until after the treaty of Aix-la-Chapelle in 1748.[46]

This action, however, did not serve the Royal African Company. As before, the war brought unsettled trade conditions which this time proved ruinous to the fortunes of the company. The period before the outbreak of the war had been a prosperous one for the company. In addition, they had since 1730 received a subsidy from Parliament for the upkeep of forts in their possession. This grant was cancelled in 1747.[47] The company found itself in such financial straits that it could not keep its factors supplied. The outlying trading stations were closed and James Fort itself could no longer maintain competition with the French on the Senegal. Sickness and death reduced the trading population and the fort fell into disrepair.[48]

The Royal African Company thus ended its career under a cloud and Parliament instructed the Council of Trade to work out a scheme to save British trade in West Africa. The result of their deliberations was an Act of Parliament in 1750 creating a regulated 'Company of Merchants Trading to Africa'.[49] The company was prohibited from all trading in its corporate capacity. It was headed by an appointed executive committee of merchants and was empowered to make rules and regulations regarding trade in West Africa. The company was supported by an annual fee from Parliament for the upkeep of the forts and stations under its jurisdiction in Africa. The committee, however, was not completely autonomous. The Exchequer demanded an annual report on all money received, Parliament retained the right of review of all acts and regulations, and the Board of Trade could remove committee men or any servants of the company for misbehaviour.[50] The Royal 'African Company, however, was not finally dissolved until a divesting Act was passed by Parliament in 1752.[51]

In this interim of dual control the French at Goree again attempted to oust the English from the Gambia River. The station at Albreda was re-established, but fortunately for the English traders, their French counterparts did not resort to force. Their methods of operations at this time consisted of offering very high prices to the natives in exchange for native goods. Thus the French were well on their way towards monopolizing the river trade when the English fortunes suddenly improved. The chief factor at James Island appealed to the Captain of an English man-of-war to help them eliminate competition. Pressure was also brought to bear on the King of Barra to expel the French. The English man-of-war shelled the factory at Albreda for four days, but though very little damage was done, this display of might convinced the native king of the strength of the British Navy. With such a combination against them the French again reluctantly abandoned their sphere of trade in the Gambia while protesting to the English government their right to continue trading at Albreda. Their station was re-established on a less pretentious scale just before the outbreak of the Seven Years' War.[52]

The coming of the war found the English in a better military position than in previous conflicts. The act of 1750 constituting the new company had provided for regular inspection by men-of-war of the holdings of the company.[53] An attack upon James Fort in 1757 was successfully beaten off due to the presence of a British warship in the Gambia area. Following this action England, utilizing her supremacy at sea, captured Goree and the main French trading bases in the Senegal in 1758. She then garrisoned the main trading posts and forts with English troops. The Treaty of Paris concluding the war confirmed the English possession of Senegal, but returned Goree to the French. Nothing in the treaty altered the position of the two nations on the Gambia, and the French again reoccupied their oft vacated trading post at Albreda and the traders of the two countries resumed their task of annoying each other.[54]

At the conclusion of the Seven Years' War the military administration in the Senegal was replaced by that of the African Committee.[55] It became increasingly clear that this rule was not sufficiently strong to develop British prestige in the area and withstand the encroachments of French traders. This fact, combined with a series of small incidents on the Gambia, convinced the Board of Trade that a change was necessary. Thus in May 1765, Parliament passed another divesting Act and placed the administration of the two areas in the Crown which would administer them as colonies.[56]

The new constitution for the Province of Senegambia called for a Governor and Council responsible for executive and legislative functions, and a Chief Justice. Headquarters for the new colony were to be at St. Louis on the Senegal River. A superintendent, later titled Lieutenant-Governor, was placed in charge of affairs on the Gambia.[57] By the very nature of the governmental establishment the Gambia was relegated to a minor position. The Lieutenant-Governor was dependent upon St. Louis to sanction all acts necessary to uphold British trade as well as for all supplies and trade materials. Communications were slow and it appears that the Governors of Senegambia were not greatly concerned with the Gambia. To complicate matters further there was a constant personal antipathy between the Lieutenant-Governors and their superiors in the North.[58]

The French had again fortified Albreda and were attempting to extend their trade up river past James Fort when the American Revolution gave them a chance to recoup their lost possessions in West Africa. The conditions at the fort were deplorable. Governor Clarke, who reached the Province in 1777, reported that the garrison was undisciplined, that disorder reigned in every department, and that he had found there a complicated situation of public fraud and embezzlement.[59] It was at this time that many of the naval units, the best means of protection for the West African areas, were drawn to the other side of the Atlantic. This left the coast of West Africa all but unprotected.

Believing this to be the time to regain their lost position in the African trade, the French sent a combined land and naval force to the area in 1778. In January 1779, they reoccupied St. Louis and later the next month razed James Fort.[60] This final disaster to the English bastion in the Gambia removed it as the focal point of Gambia history. Once in the nineteenth century it was reoccupied, and then only temporarily by a small contingent of soldiers. After the action against James Fort the French removed their garrison from Goree and established themselves in as firm a position as possible at St. Louis. The English in May 1779 occupied the abandoned island. Except for occasional raids on shipping these actions marked the end of active warfare in the Senegambia. The administration of what remained to England in Senegambia passed under military rule and the Province of Senegambia remained one in name only.

The Treaty of Versailles in 1783 restored to France, St. Louis, as well as other fortified places in the Senegal region and also the Island of Goree. What was left of James Fort was admitted to be a possession of Great Britain. The French, however, refused to grant that the Gambia should be an area for exclusive British trade. In return for recognizing French rights to trade on the river, the French achnowledged the right of English merchants to the gum trade at Portendic.[61]

Parliament recognized in 1783 the utter failure of the attempt at Crown Colony government. The whole machinery of administration had been too unwieldy even if the officers charged with the administration had been excellent administrators and honest servants of the Crown. Thus in 1783 Parliament abandoned the whole experiment, revesting the control of the area in the Committee of the Company of Merchants who had relinquished control in 1756.[62]

The Committee of Merchants showed no great zeal in re-establishing themselves in the Gambia. The reason for this reluctance is obvious. Only eighteen years before they had been forced to surrender this same territory to the Crown. Now they were again given a free hand to establish themselves at their own expense in a territory that had proved a continuous source of trouble. They applied several times in the 1780s for a governmental grant to help rebuild James Fort. In every case their petitions were refused. Thereafter the Committee's work in the Gambia ceased entirely.[63] The only interest the government evinced in the Gambia before the outbreak of the new war with France in 1793 was to survey MacCarthy Island as a possible location for a penal colony. Even this scheme was eventually given up in 1785 and the fortunate prisoners were sent instead to Das Voltas lying between Angola and the Cape.[64]

Individual merchants with little or no official backing, however, maintained English trade on the river. They established themselves at Bintang, Juffure, Brefet, at Junkakunda opposite MacCarthy Island, and even beyond at Karantaba. This latter location was to prove the point of departure for Mungo Park in his first penetration of the Niger area.

The Association for the Discovery of the Interior Regions of Africa, which was founded in 1788, also helped to keep alive the interest in the Gambia. It was hoped that by using the Gambia the upper reaches of the Niger could be discovered. The Association were thus reviving the centuries old hope of linking the trade of Timbuktu to the known waterways of West Africa. To this end a Major Houghton was dispatched to the Gambia in 1790. He proceeded up river past Barrakunda Falls, and leaving the river, he reached a point west of Timbuktu where he was killed. The Association, feeling that the slave traders on the Gambia had some part in the death of Houghton, appealed to the government to appoint a Consul whose primary responsibility would be to promote trade with the interior regions. A Consul was appointed, but primarily due to financial problems the scheme was given up in 1796.[65] Meanwhile the Association, believing that the Consul would proceed to the Gambia and not forseeing any difficulties, planned to send out another exploring expedition. Chosen for this hazardous duty was an obscure Scots physician, Mungo Park who had come

34

to the attention of Sir Joseph Banks. Park left for the Gambia in 1795 without the hoped for support of a Consular official. He proceeded up river to Karantaba where he rested in the home of Dr. John Laidley, a merchant and physician, while learning Mandinka. In December 1795, accompanied only by a Negro boy, he began one of the most daring explorations ever undertaken in Africa. Eventually he reached the city of Segu on the Niger, and returned to Karantaba in June 1798.[66] The Association hailed this feat as proof of the commercial possibilities of the African interior and again revived the demand for a Consul to be sent to help exploit these possibilities. However, the government declined to act. The war with France was demanding more and more attention and it was felt that the Gambia had proved, even in times of peace, that it was not a profitable place for the government to assume responsibilities.

The Napoleonic Wars did not disturb the Gambia to a great extent. However, French privateers were active on the river, making it hazardous for the private merchants to carry on their trade. The English captured Goree in 1800 only to lose it in 1804, after which they quickly reoccupied the port and retained its possession until 1817.

Prompted by the Association, the government set in motion the ill-fated second expedition of Mungo Park. Initially the government contrived an elabroate plan to negate French influence, garrison the Gambia, and open up the trade routes to the Niger.[67] However, nothing came of this plan and Park eventually proceeded into the interior with one officer and thirty-five men from the garrison at Goree. The expedition proved to contain far too large a number of Europeans and only Park and four companions left Bamako and later they were drowned in the rapids of the Niger near Bussa.[68] The two expeditions of Park had little to do with the Gambia, except that they used it as a starting point, but they do herald a change in the attitude of merchants and goverment to all the West African colonies. Up till this time, with few exceptions, English merchants had been satisfied to exploit the trade of the Gambia at only a few places on the river. Until James Fort was destroyed the bulk of all trading was carried on there. Now under the impetus of private traders and those curious about the interior of Africa, these trading stations spread up and down the river.

Another factor that changed the character of the settlement of the Gambia was the abolition of the slave trade. According to the terms of the Treaty of Versailles, the Gambia was recognized as a British possession. Therefore trading in slaves after January 1, 1808 became unlawful. The British merchants, with few exceptions, seem to have accepted this decree. However, foreign traders refused to abide by any such curb on their profits. The greatest violators of the edict were Americans and it was necessary in 1810 to dispatch a vessel to seize any American ship carrying on the slave trade.[69] Successful as was the patrol, it proved to be only a temporary deterrent for the slave poaching continued. It seemed that the only sensible way of controlling the trade was to re-establish some fortified place on the river. To effect this Earl Bathurst, the Secretary of State, concurred with his advisers in the need either to re-establish James Island, or to construct another fort at a more suitable place. In March 1816, Captain Alexander Grant was sent with a body of some seventy-five men from Goree to select the site and build the new fort. He was much impressed with Banjol, both as a defensive site and as a place offering more room for expansion than James Island. The King of Kombo was only too glad to cede the island to the English in return for protection. Grant and his men immediately began to fortify the island and build houses and barracks. They renamed the island St. Mary and called their new town Bathurst in honour of the Secretary of State.

This venture was not underwritten by the Committee of Merchants and was only lightly supported by the government. Lord Bathurst had made it clear that while the government supported this attempt, it would not be bound by any undertaking that would cost a great amount of money. The founding of Bathurst was primarily the work of Grant and the members of the Royal African Corps—those convicts from the hulks and other offenders who were posted to Africa during the war with France. Nevertheless the new town prospered. In 1818 the civil population was over seven hundred excluding the garrison, and by 1826 the population had grown to eighteen hundred, exclusive of the garrison, of whom thirty were Europeans.[70] In 1818 Sir Charles MacCarthy, Governor of Sierra Leone, created a civil government for the new city composed of a Committee of Merchants, the head of which was designated the Mayor. MacCarthy created two courts to deal with cases arising in the city. All these actions were to be subject to disallowance by the Governor of Sierra Leone. This system was to be of a temporary nature only until the legality of the settlement was made clear. By an Act of Parliament the rights of governing and trading in the area were vested in the Committee of Merchants. As has been pointed out, the Committee had taken very little interest in the affairs of the area. Nevertheless there was a duality of responsibility until, in 1821, this situation was brought to an end by an Act of Parliament which divested the Committee of all its rights and restored them to the Crown.[71] In the same year all forts and settlements in West Africa were placed under the jurisdiction of the Governor of Sierra Leone.

Thus in 1821 a phase in British relations with the Gambia that had been operative for over two centuries ended. The government now assumed the responsibility for governing and protecting the area. Before this time such protection and executive authority had been carried out only on rare occasions. The primary responsibility had fallen to the merchants trading in the area. After England had assumed full control over the trading affairs in the territory she soon found it necessary to intervene more in areas which had completely been ignored by the traders. This is not to suggest that there was a sudden break with the policies of the past. The main interest in the Gambia throughout the nineteenth century was still trade. But other problems gradually called for an extension of government control. The task of eliminating the slave trade remained and to this was added the task of uprooting indigenous slavery. The education and religious training of the population by missionaries was a new problem fostered by the humanitarians. The assumption of control by the Crown implied an administrative and judicial system in the Colony area. Thus Bathurst and its environs became a peaceful, relatively well administered area surrounded by the native peoples who in the middle years of the nineteenth century were disrupted by religious wars. The

37

major question which occupied British administrators in the Gambia throughout the nineteenth century concerned the proper relationship between the stable and unstable area of the river valley. A correlate question was whether British trade in the hinterlands implied an extension of the laws and administration of the colony. The British government revised and broadened its administration reluctantly, but gradually in the nineteenth century the Gambia settlement became not merely a trading depot, but in a real sense a colony of the Crown.

Chapter Three

THE SONINKI-MARABOUT WARS

THE larger portion of Gambian internal history in the late nineteenth century was concerned with the internecine native conflicts that raged throughout the length of the river. Because of
the long span of time covered by these conflicts and their
complex, intertwined nature, it seems best to interrupt the
narrative of British occupation here and concentrate first upon
the Soninki-Marabout Wars. The reasons for these wars are
superficially easy to explain although the issue is later complicated by extraneous forces, not the least of which is the internal
dynamic of the conflict itself.

The Marabouts were theoretically teachers and holy men
who professed a form of belief considerably purer than that
of most of the other Gambian Muslims. These holy men had
been recruited, to a large extent, from the trader class and
possessed a wider world outlook than most Gambians. They
had received a modicum of education and represented religious
attitudes not dissimilar to those which had created the Almora-
vid explosion of the eleventh century. Most of these teachers
were extremely careful in their public devotions, and abstained
from most of the luxuries, especially liquor, so enjoyed by
many Gambians. Originally the Marabouts were pro-British

since they wanted official support against the chiefs who were predominantly Soninki. Later when such support was not forthcoming the majority of the Marabouts became anti-British.

The Marabouts had been influenced by a series of religious movements which had been generated in the western Sudan by the teachings of particular holy men. Chief among these had been Othman dan Fodio who was the mainspring of the Fulani Wars of conquest in Nigeria, and later El Hadj Omar whose teachings and leadership resulted in the Tucolor Empire. Many of the Marabouts of the Gambia had received their education and religious instruction in religious centres dominated by the new puritanical interpretations, and the Gambia region was receptive to religious ideas brought in by non-Gambians. In the early 1850s one of the chief Marabouts who preached a holy war against all infidels was a Moor, Hadj Ismail. Although he did not appear in the Gambia, his adherents were quite active throughout the river valley. Another of the agents responsible for the spate of violence in the Gambia was another Moor named Omar who had been concerned in Abd-el-Kader's rising against the French in Algeria in 1847. He settled in the western area of the Gambia at the village of Sabaji. It was from here that he influenced the coastal villages from the Gambia River south to the Casamance.[1]

The Soninkis were generally the traditional rulers of the Gambia together with their warrior class followers. They either had not accepted Islam or at best were occasional conformists. If they had been converted to Islam they were very lax in their religious observances. They did not follow the traditional taboos of Islam and they especially enjoyed alcoholic beverages. As such they were representative of most of the Gambians at that time who held to the older religions, while the Marabouts and their converts probably represented a minority of the population. However, the Marabouts and their followers were better organized and had in many places the initial advantage of mercenary troops and the backing of the trading and merchant classes. The Soninki-Marabout Wars were thus caused by political and economic factors in addition to the main religious motivation.

As the conflicts continued the political aspect overshadowed the religious, and the reasons for new outbreaks often had nothing to do with religious differences. The situation was made more complicated by the personal ambitions and selfishness of individual chieftains who used the broader issues as masks for their own aims of creating larger political units that would be subservient to them. The continuing disorders resulted in a ready made chaos for political adventurers such as Musa Mollah, Fodi Kabba, and Fodi Silla. Much of the fighting that occurred was between Serahulis, Sereres, and Jolas who had little concern for the religious differences between the two parties, but were primarily interested in selling their services as mercenaries to the highest bidder. In the closing stages of the wars the personal differences between petty chiefs became the primary cause of the revewal of the conflict in a given locale. The tendency was for power to fall to the more powerful and unscruplous of the military leaders. These wars were usually small scale affairs normally involving two villages, although there were many cases of the wars involving whole districts with many thousands of adherents on either side. In such cases the loss of life could be extensive, but in the case of disturbances between villages, the casualties were few. However these wars continued for over fifty years, and although large scale warfare was the exception, there was seldom peace in the Gambia and the total loss of life was considerable. In addition the normal life of the people in some districts was totally disrupted. Not only was the trade of Europeans and native merchants hampered, but life was so insecure that agriculture upon which the ordinary man depended became an extremely hazardous operation. The Gambia valley, already an impoverished area, became more so as the disturbances continued.

The Soninki-Marabout Wars were responsible for the breaking down of the rule by traditional authorities. Before the conflicts most districts chose their chiefs from a restricted number of noble families, or in some cases from only one. The chief's Council was composed of propertied men who also normally belonged to the restricted aristocracy. This manner of electing chiefs had existed for centuries and the royal families in many cases had remained the same since the days of the Mali empire.

These traditional chiefs were the main obstacle to the Marabouts and later to the military adventurers who seized power
and maintained themselves in position of authority by force.
When the wars came to an end in the Gambia valley in the
1890s most of the traditional ruling families had been killed or
were in exile. The end of the wars coincided with the assumption of British control throughout the Gambia. Thus the first
major task facing the new Protectorate administration was to
reconstruct the traditional political system which in certain
areas had all but been destroyed.[2]

The final factor to consider in this endemic violence which
plagued the Gambia is the role of the British administration in
the Colony areas. As will be subsequently noted, the fighting
disrupted British trade, threatened British lives, and at times
almost engulfed the settlements near Bathurst and at MacCarthy
Island. In such circumstances the administrators of the Colony
from the time of Governor O'Connor recommended an active
policy which would put an end to any threat to the British
holdings or to persons who depended for protection upon
Bathurst.[3] Such a policy would have necessitated the concentration of a large number of troops and ships in the Gambia and
an expenditure of a large sum of money. The Colonial Office
and the Treasury refused to countenance any such expansive
plans. The prevailing attitude of the home government in this
period was one of retrenchment in all overseas ventures.
Colonies, particularly those in West Africa, were not viewed as
assets, but as liabilities. Therefore the order to all administrators
from the beginning of the wars through the 1880s remained the
same—no expansion and no unnecessary expenditures.[4] The
governors were provided with such small military forces that
to undertake military ventures on their own initiative was out
of the question. In other areas of the British Empire, notably
India, the man on the spot could bind the home government by
actions contrary to its wishes. This was not possible for those
representatives of the Crown in the Gambia. Thus, throughout
the Soninki-Marabout Wars British action was totally defensive
and restricted in the main to the protection of the Colony areas
from the depredations of the warring factions. This often meant
campaigns against certain chiefs, the use of comparatively large

numbers of troops, and the expenditure of great sums of money. Far more often, however, the governors attempted to pacify disturbed regions by threats, by acting as conciliators, or by paying pensions to certain chiefs if they would keep the peace. Such a policy extended over fifty years cost the home government more than one concerted large scale effort which would have brought peace to the river area.

With these generalizations concerning the Soninki-Marabout Wars in mind one can turn to a brief description of the causes of the wars in the Gambia valley. The focal point of the first major disturbance was in the western region centring on the villages of Gunjur and Sabaji. The leader of the Marabouts in the former location was a young man, Fodi Kabba, who in the next fifty years played one of the most important roles in formenting the continuing troubles near Bathurst. One of the chief Marabouts, the Moor Omar, had taken up residence in the village of Sabaji, and it was his group which precipitated the first major threat to the security of the Colony.[5]

By the end of 1851 the local disturbances in the vicinity of British Kombo had become dangerous because Soninki refugees had taken refuge there and because the Marabouts were also disturbed by the presence of Wesleyan missionaries in the vicinity. In early 1852 Governor McDonald notified the Colonial Office that sooner or later it would be necessary for the British to intervene because of the anarchic state of affairs on the Colony borders. In addition the circumstances seemed favourable for acquiring territory in the immediate neighbourhood for the expanding population of the Colony. Permission to intervene in Kombo was refused by the Colonial authorities. Later the Colonial Office acceded to the governor's request to annex a portion of the disturbed district to take care of the growing Colony population. Therefore on May 24, 1853, some of the elders of the district gave the British a strip of land adjoining British Kombo which included the village of Sabaji.[6] This decision of the elders concerned was not popular with the majority of the villagers of Sabaji. The Governor, Colonel O'Connor, tried to overawe the village by a show of force. When this failed he sent three West Indian regiments, some of the Gambia militia, and a warship to take the village. This was accomplished on June 1, 1853, and the leading Marabouts of the city were taken away and temporarily jailed.

This was not the end of the incident for two years later Omar, utilizing his rudimentary knowledge of military organization, planned a concerted attack by all the Marabout adherents in the Kombo against the British. He delayed the launching of the attack until the start of the rainy season of 1855 in order to render the British artillery ineffective. He also preached that he had the power to turn the white man's bullets into water.[7]

The actual fighting began in June 1855 when the Marabouts of Gunjur attacked the town of the King of Kombo and in the ensuing battle killed the king. The situation did not become dangerous for the British until the following month when the chief of Sabaji forcibly kidnapped a resident of British Kombo. The Queen's advocate and a few soldiers attempted to arrest the chief. They were attacked and their line of retreat to Bathurst was blocked. Colonel O'Connor collected all the available men in Bathurst and relieved the survivors of the arresting party. His plan to attack Sabaji was forestalled since all the wooded areas were controlled by the Marabout forces whose numbers had been augmented by recruits from other villages. O'Connor retreated to Cape St. Mary, fighting a series of rearguard actions. His column lost one quarter of the original force —twenty-three were killed and fifty-three wounded. O'Connor's force was isolated on the Cape and the Marabout forces could have taken Bathurst if they had crossed Oyster Creek immediately. Their procrastination proved disastrous to their plans. The Colonial Secretary left in charge in Bathurst had sent an immediate call for aid to Sierre Leone and Goree. On July 30 the defenders of Bathurst were strengthened by reinforcements from the Commandant at Goree who had sent all the soldiers who could be spared from the garrison. Two days after their departure the Commandant had received reinforcements for his garrison from France. These troops, some of them veterans of the Crimea, were also immediately dispatched to the Gambia.

On August 4, the combined Anglo-French force marched on Sabaji, clearing the forest belt of the Marabouts by hand to hand fighting. When they reached Sabaji they found the village strongly stockaded with a large defensive force within. After a preliminary bombardment the village was taken by storm and destroyed. The government decided to prohibit its rebuilding and the majority of its inhabitants moved to Gunjur where they reinforced Fodi Kabba. O'Connor did not believe that he had the necessary force to take action against Gunjur although he was convinced that Fodi Kabba had been deeply implicated in the Sabaji affair.

Omar, the organizer of the rising, escaped from the Gambia shortly after. Haji Ismail, who had been responsible for preaching the *Jihad* throughout West Africa, was captured by the French and transported to Cayenne. These serious setbacks cut off the Marabouts of Gunjar from outside aid, but the war against the Soninkis continued to drag on. Because of his weak military position, O'Connor decided to allow the Soninkis and Marabouts to continue their fighting and to attempt to maintain a strict embargo on supplies of arms to either side.

The continued interruptions of normal agricultural production had created dire distress in the entire region. The Marabouts and their adherents were particularly poverty stricken. Cut off from outside aid, they decided to come to an agreement with the Soninki chiefs. In this search for a truce of exhaustion the British authorities were used as mediators. On April 17, 1856, the Marabout chiefs concerned signed a convention in Bathurst whereby they promised to observe the rights and privileges of the Soninki chiefs in the disputed area. Nine days later the Soninki chiefs accepted the same good offices of the British and signed a similar convention. There, for all practical purposes, the first phase of the wars ended. The events in this early period show very clearly the importance of the Colony authorities. The home government refused to sanction the logical step recommended by the governors of creating a frontier of safety surrounding the Colony.

The signing of the truce is not to be construed as the cessation of all fighting. It simply indicated that in one area there were no major outbreaks and that this uneasy peace was prevalent not only in the vicinity of Bathurst, but throughout the Gambia. In the up river areas, however, there was always violence of some type. Such disorders, minor though they might have been in the total context, plagued the European traders on the river. The position of the authorities was an anomaly. Unless they wished to see the traders entirely driven from the upper river area they would have to exert British authority from time to time. However, these brief, small forays were only temporary deterrents to the native chiefs.

It was in pursuance of this idea of occasional interference that the second phase of the wars began in 1859 and continued through 1866. In a few disturbances in 1859 a number of Bathurst traders had lost some goods pillaged by the natives up river. The Governor, Colonel D'Arcy, sent officers up river to demand redress for the grievances. Satisfaction was given by all concerned except one Soninki chief in the area of Baddibu. It became necessary as 1860 progressed either to give up any claim to British prestige in Baddibu or to teach the recalcitrant Soninki chief a lesson. Therefore in the beginning of February 1861, an expedition was fitted out under Colonel D'Arcy composed of contingents from the Navy, three West India regiments, and the Gambian militia. This expedition went first to Suwarrakunda. The town was taken by storm and later on February 21 the stockaded town of Saba also was taken. The chief was forced to come to an agreement with the governor whereby all disputes between his people and British subjects were to be referred to the governor at Bathurst. He paid an indemnity and gave hostages as guarantee of faithful performance of the treaty.[8]

Instead of ending the troubles in the vicinity of Baddibu, this only occasioned the beginning of serious conflict between the natives themselves. Although the chief of Baddibu was a Soninki, many of his subjects were Marabouts and they had merely supported him against a common enemy, the British. One of his supporters had been a man named Maba who had, however, been induced by the English to co-operate with them. After the conclusion of peace the chief of Baddibu looked upon Maba as a traitor and Maba fled to Bathurst for safety. There was a brief interlude of peace patched up between the two which was ended when Maba learned of the chief's plan to assassinate him. On the basis of this information Maba raised the standard of revolt against the chief and in an incredibly short time the

46

Marabout faction who now aligned themselves under Maba had overrun the whole of Baddibu. The chief was wounded in the fighting and later put to death, and every Soninki village was burned. Maba preached a real holy war against all of those who were not Marabouts and who would not submit themselves to having their heads shaved in token of changing their old beliefs. However, he conducted himself in a slightly different way from any of the contemporary Gambian leaders in that he simply directed the holy campaign and did not take part in the actual fighting himself. The fighting was ruthless. Any Soninki who was taken prisoner and who would not give his declaration to Islam, renounce drink, and have his head shaved was immediately put to death. Maba seems to have entertained for a brief time the idea that he could retire and dispense with the kingship.

Before he could abdicate one of his lieutenants invaded the area of Niumi, taking advantage of the death of the King of Barra, and quickly overran Jokadu. On learning of this Maba collected a force and followed his subordinate into Niumi. The Soninki population fled in haste to two of their towns, Berrending and Essau. The new King of Barra took refuge in Bathurst, but the head men of these two towns prepared to make a stand. They implored the governor to send aid, or at least give asylum to their women and children. D'Arcy was not able to give aid because no apparent British interests were involved. Even had he been inclined to give military aid it would not have been prudent since he had sent a large part of his garrison to take part in a campaign at Lagos. However, he moved all his available troops over to Barra Point and sent a warship to Albreda to evacuate British and French subjects from there. On May 26, 1862, Maba invested Essau. A number of the five hundred defenders had put on yellow clothing, symbolic of death.

The following week was a very tense one for the governor and the garrison. The two hundred and thirty men of the West Indian regiments and the Gambia militia maintained an extended defensive perimeter for seven days guarding the thousand refuges huddled in Fort Bullen. Less than a mile away Maba's forces were in the process of yelling threats of destruction upon the defenders of Essau. The expected clash did not occur since the King of Sine Saloum had taken advantage of Maba's absence to invade Baddibu, and Maba, after burning Berrending, left the area on June 1, 1862, to return to his own country.

After Maba's withdrawal, Colonel D'Arcy assembled the chiefs of both factions at Albreda and managed to arrange a type of peace. Both sides were unanimous in imploring him to take the area of Niumi under British protection. This was comminicated to the Duke of Newcastle on June 16, 1862. However, as was to be expected, he was informed by Newcastle on December 4, 1862, that such a proposition could not be entertained. In any event the peace was short-lived because Maba was immediately successful in his war of reconquest against the King of Sine Saloum. The king undoubtedly would have fallen had not French troops come to his aid and defeated Maba near Kaolack.[9]

The Marabouts in Niumi, therefore, had to carry on the war without the aid of Maba and this they did in only a desultory fashion. The Soninkis had been so decimated, however, that they were barely able to hold on to their possessions along the coastline. When it appeared that the situation was going to become difficult again, with the possible active intervention of Fodi Kabba and with Maba again taking the field in Niumi, Colonel D'Arcy was able to secure another peace whereby Maba promised to refrain from any further interference in the affairs of Niumi. The Soninkis were persuaded to accept terms. The stockades of both sides were set on fire and a formal treaty of peace was drawn up and signed on February 24, 1863.[10] Maba, however, proceeded immediately to re-attack Sine Saloum and devastate the entire area. This caused a mass migration of some two thousand men, women, and children, Wolof and Serres, into the vicinity of Barra in March and April, 1863, and five months later approximately seven hundred more. These people were generally relocated in the area of British and Lower Kombo and given land on which to settle.[11]

Maba's career was almost at an end, however, for the son of the previous chief of Baddibu gathered together a number of Soninkis and refugees and invaded Maba's territory. Maba was defeated in one of the few large pitched battles in this particular war. He fled the field of Quinella with a few horsemen, leaving behind some five hundred dead Marabouts, and took refuge at Sumbundu with some Fulas. His power was broken in Baddibu, but he still retained the capacity to make trouble, and in 1864 he collected a band of men and returned to Baddibu. Although the fighting was no longer on a grand scale it nevertheless disrupted the territory. He was successful enough for the French to recognize him as the ruler of Baddibu and give him the title of Almami. However, in 1866 he quarrelled with his French protectors and was forced to flee to Niumi. In the following year he was killed in a raid on Sine Saloum.[12]

Maba's successes had inspired the Marabouts throughout the river, and although his personal star was eclipsed, the Marabouts became extremely active in the period 1863-66. By the middle of 1864 MacCarthy Island was surrounded by a number of stockaded camps of Marabouts who seemed intent upon capturing the island itself. It was necessary, therefore, to send reinforcements to the island which ended this threat, and on June 14, 1864, the Soninki chief of Kataba and the leading Marabout chief of the same district entered into an agreement whereby they agreed to refer all future disputes to the arbitration of the Commandant at MacCarthy Island.[13]

The year 1864 also saw troubles in Kombo with Fodi Kabba renewing the wars in the vicinity of Yundum. D'Arcy was forced to send a relief column to Yundum to protect the chief. The chief urged the governor to attack Gunjur, but again D'Arcy refused to extend the scope of his activities beyond simply the protection of the immediate vicinity of Kombo. Some of the more moderate of his followers persuaded Fodi Kabba to enter into a treaty with the governor in February 1864.[14] Notwithstanding this treaty, in October of that same year Fodi Kabba also renewed the disturbances in Kombo, causing a brief period of anxiety.

Far more important in the years 1864-66 were the activities of one of Maba's former lieutenants, Amer Faal, who Gray calls just another 'very ordinary type of lawless bandit'.[15] The immediate cause for his activities was the resettlement in Banta Killing in the Ceded Mile of approximately two thousand refugees from Sine Saloum. The chief of these settlers was a

Wolof and a Soninki, and he found it very difficult to exercise any authority in his district. Amer Faal's people continuously raided the vicinity and only the opportune arrival of a gunboat in 1864 prevented large scale warfare from beginning. In 1866 a cattle raid by Amer Faal's people on the town re-opened the issue of supremacy. Colonel D'Arcy was unable to arrange a truce and he decided in the typical kick and caress fashion to teach Amer Faal a lesson by sending a punitive expedition against him. The subsequent operation lasted only four days. On July 26, 1866, two hundred and seventy officers and men took the Marabouts at Albreda by surprise and disarmed them without any bloodshed. The troops then proceeded to Amer Faal's stockaded village of Tubab Kolon with five hundred extra native allies from Essau. The town was strongly defended and had to be taken by storm. One of the soldiers, Samuel Hodges, a Gambian, received the Victoria Cross for bravery in this action. The fall of Tubab Kolon ended for the British the second phase of the Soninki-Marabout Wars.[16]

While all these disturbances were taking place in the lower reaches of the river there were constant raids in the upper part of the river by Fulas and Bambaras, and a continuation of sporadic Marabout-Soninki difficulties throughout the whole range of the Gambia valley. This second phase of the Soninki-Marabout Wars is most important because it was in this period that the old established chieftainships in the lower Gambia all but disappeared. These chieftainships were primarily Soninki and generally hereditary dynasties which, in some cases, had lasted for several centuries. Many of the remaining Soninki chiefs retained their positions after this period solely because they were in receipt of certain subsidies from the Colonial government for having placed lands or themselves under the protection of the British authorities, or in return for previous aid. The Marabouts were afraid that if they deposed the Soninki chiefs these subsidies would then be stopped; therefore they were content to rule as Mayors of the Palace behind the Soninki chiefs. Now that the Soninki chieftainships had been broken down by the Marabouts nothing stable was put in their place. Instead of being imbued with an idealism which would have enabled them to erect new political structures, many of the Marabouts were unfortunately motivated almost entirely by personal reasons. Therefore from 1866 until the resumption of some type of stable rule by the British under the Protectorate system, the area of the Gambia was allowed to drift into chaos.

All this could have been alleviated if the British had taken the obvious steps to pacify the whole valley of the Gambia. During the period of Colonel D'Arcy's governorship he constantly received missives in Arabic and English from both Marabouts and Soninkis imploring him to take a given area under British protection.[17] However, his instructions from home were quite clear on annexations and he was unable to accede to any of these petitions. In retrospect, this was a very short sighted policy on the part of the British for it meant that instead of pacifying the area in one series of very costly campaigns, they expended the same amount of money and lives over a long period of time without achieving the results that one concerted campaign would have given them.

The troubles of the 1860s ruined agriculture in large areas of the Gambia, seriously interfered with trade, and in combination with natural disasters, created a serious revenue problem for the Colony. When the colonial retrenchment policy of the home government became effective in 1864, colonial administrators such as Sir Arthur Kennedy could point to the Gambia as an area which had lost trade and revenue while expenses continued to increase. Because most of those responsible for policy were not cognizant of the developments in the Gambia these trade statistics were taken completely out of context without a knowledge of the total background of the Soninki-Marabout troubles.

Cononel Ord in his investigations in 1864 concerning British interests in West Africa confirmed Governor D'Arcy's contentions that Britain should either establish a Protectorate over both banks of the river or gradually sever all her political connections with the Gambia. Colonel Ord's report, which became the basis of British policy for twenty-five years, stated that British interests were not great enough to invest heavily in an extension of power. Ord pointed out, however, that the governors were correct in stating that a do-nothing policy towards native disturbances was an evasion of responsibility.[18]

At this crucial period of the late 60s and early 70s when the Colonial Office was re-evaluating the worth of their West African settlements, the Gambia was struck by a resumption of fighting between factions. Drought also had been the lot of the Gambian farmer for a number of years in the 1860s. As if these factors were not enough to totally disrupt trade, a great cholera epidemic struck the area in 1869-70. It began in the vicinity of MacCarthy Island in April 1869, and proceeded rapidly down river towards Bathurst. For a time there were over seventy deaths a day reported in Bathurst, and before the sickness had subsided, 1,162 persons out of a total population of slightly over four thousand had died in the Colony areas. It is reasonable to assume that in the more unsanitary up-river villages at least one quarter of the population died of cholera.[19] During the height of the epidemic normal life and trade were forgotten. It is thus not surprising that those investigating the economic value of the Gambia came to the conclusion that it was worthless.

The Soninki-Marabout Wars in the 70s and 80s were somewhat different from the preceding outbreaks. For one thing, the question of religion ceased to be a real issue. The previous disturbances had left the larger part of the Gambia valley controlled by Marabouts. The latter stages of the wars were dominated almost completely by personal interests and rivalries. There was also an increase in the amount of outside intervention in the wars. This is seen in the actions of the powerful Fula confederation that had come into being outside the Gambia. The confederation sent annually a force of several thousand men to raid, particularly in the upper river areas. The leaders of this confederation were three war chiefs—Bakari Sardu, the ruler of Bandu; Alfa Ibrahima, the ruler of Futa Jallon; and Alfa Molloh whose country was between the Gambia and Casamance River. It was easy for these chiefs to find a reason for raiding the Gambia since most of the Gambia area had by this time passed under the influence of the Marabouts, and many of these were exiles from the kingdoms ruled by the three rulers. Therefore under the guise of punishing their subjects, they would invade the Gambia on almost any pretext. In 1870 a Fodi, or teacher, came from Bandu and settled on the banks of the Gambia near Yarbutenda. After being driven away from there by Alfa Molloh, he then settled in Wuli at Tubakuta. The fame of his teaching spread and he gathered a large force around him. As this was a rallying point, Bakari Sardu attacked it in 1875, but was driven off. Four years later the combined forces of Bakari Sardu, Alfa Ibrahima, and Alfa Molloh's son Musa again attacked the town and again failed. The teacher died in 1885 and his mantle fell to his son Dembo who in the following year took in a refugee who had been giving the French a great deal of trouble in Senegal. Musa Molloh took this opportunity for revenge, and combining with a French force he attacked and destroyed Tubakuta.[20]

Another example of the fluctuating nature of this internecine warfare can be seen in the history of Kataba at his time. In 1862 Maba had invaded the land and through the mediation of the British he, the chief of Kataba, and the leading Marabouts came to an agreement whereby all differences were to be referred to the arbitration of the Commandant of MacCarthy Island. In 1870 the disturbances had grown so serious that both the chief of Kataba and the chief of Nianibintang begged the colonial government to place them under its protection. This offer was refused. In 1872 Bakari Sardu decided to intervene on behalf of the Soninkis and raided as far as Karantaba. This was quickly followed by a raid of another Marabout chief into the lands of the chief of Kataba which forced the chief to flee. As he could no longer fulfil his obligations under the MacCarthy Island Treaty of 1832 to protect the British subjects, the chief of Kataba's subsidy was taken from him and given to his conqueror. This did not bring peace to the area because in 1876 the ruling king of Sine Saloum again ravaged the district.[21]

Of all of the areas of the upper Gambia, only Wuli maintained its integrity throughout this period. This was because Bakari Sardu and his allies used it as a corridor for raids into the valley. The chiefs of this area simply became adherents to the Soninki cause and gave assistance to Bakari in his raids because it was good business. They could also call upon these more powerful outside chiefs to aid them in putting down any of their subjects who were dissatisfied.[22]

53

One of the most infamous and long remembered chiefs in these times of trouble was Musa Molloh. He was noted as a famous leader of troops, and respected for his cruelty long before the death of his father, Alfa Molloh, in 1881. In 1875 he and his followers swept down the south bank of the river as far as Kai-at Island and then turned south as far as Portuguese Guinea. He carried all opposition before him. The old kingdoms of Tomani, Jimara, and Eropina fell. Most of the Mandingo population fled these areas and Alfa Molloh's Fula followers occupied the land which has since been known as Fuladu.[23]

On the death of his father, the right to rule the large areas conquered by Alfa Molloh went to his brother, Bakari Dembel. Musa Molloh challenged this right and after preliminary skirmishes removed himself and his followers to that area of southern Fuladu near the Casamance River which he had conquered in 1875. In 1883 he reached an understanding with the French and placed the entire area over which he exercised control under their protection.[24]

Disturbances in the 70s and 80s in the vicinity of Niamina, Kiang, and Foni were mainly the responsibility of Fodi Kabba, the veteran troublemaker who had begun his career in the 50s.[25] He ruled over three districts which were isolated from one another—one area south of Bintang Creek, another comprising part of western Jarra and eastern Kiang, and the other in eastern Jarra. In between these districts the Soninkis managed to maintain a precarious independence. The failure of Fodi Kabba to control contigious districts meant that raids, looting, and burning were endemic. Fodi Kabba's control over those districts he ruled was maintained by force. He could hold his own by constantly raiding his opponents and could carry out these raids only by attracting to himself some of the worst elements in the Gambia.[26] The Annual Report for 1880 gave the British view of Fodi Kabba:

> He lives by slave hunting and robbery. None of his neighbours, unfortunately, are strong enough to drive him out and he naturally attracts to himself all the idle and worthless ruffians, who prefer living on the industry of others to doing any honest work for themselves.[27]

Such a description could apply equally well to any number of the war chiefs who kept the Gambia region in chaos.

Meanwhile in Gunjur the peace which had been arranged between the two factions in 1864 had not lasted long. As before the Soninki gradually began to lose ground to the Marabouts. By 1873 all the Soninki towns in the Kombo except two were in Marabout hands and many of the inhabitants had taken refuge in British Kombo. This presented a very great danger to the inhabitants of British Kombo and to the colonial government since three years before all regular troops had been removed from the Colony area. This had left the governor with only a local constabularly of approximately one hundred men. On March 24, 1873, however, the pressure on British Kombo was eased when the acting administrator concluded another treaty with the Marabouts whereby they undertook to maintain peace and to respect the British territory in Kombo.[28]

The full impact of Marabout power south of Bathurst was then turned to reducing the last Soninki strongholds, particularly Brikama. The chief of Brikama offered to cede his territory to the colonial government if they would only protect him from the Marabouts. Not surprisingly this offer was declined and Brikama fell to the Marabouts in mid-1874. Great numbers of the Soninkis fled from Brikama to Sukuta which in turn was destroyed in June 1874.[29] The survivors of the town fled to British Kombo. Although the administrator had concluded a treaty of friendship with Fodi Silla, the recognized leader of the Kombo Marabouts, the situation remained dangerous because Fodi Silla claimed that the Soninki from their British protected areas were a threat to his control in Kombo. The rainy season postponed the crisis until the following year when the Marabouts took the last Soninki town in Kombo. The Soninki chief, Tomani Bojang, then built a stockade within four hundred yards of British territory and appealed to the British for aid. Lacking an adequate defensive force the administrator was concerned primarily not with the fate of the Soninkis, but rather with keeping the conflict from spreading to British Kombo. However, he did offer Tomani Bojang territory for resettlement of his people in the Ceded Mile. This was foolishly refused and in September 1875, realizing the hopelessness of his position,

Bojang agreed to become a Muslim, shave his head, and destroy his stockade. In return Fodi Silla granted him and his followers land to cultivate in peace. Thus all foreign Kombo had become a Marabout stronghold by 1875.[30]

In Baddibu there had been almost incessant warfare since Maba's death in 1867. He had left an infant son, Said Matti, but Maba's old position went to his nephew, Mommadu N'Dare. Mommadu had been Maba's general who had conquered the chief of Kataba. He was subsequently recognized by the British as the ruler who had the power to protect British subjects in Baddibu, Jokadu, Saloum, and Niani. It was obvious to those who understood up river conditions that Mommadu's authority was not that extensive. In 1877 one of his lieutenants, Bairam Sisi, rebelled against his authority. The raids and counter-raids between these two continued for years without any major victories for either party.[31] By 1884, however, Mommadu had forced his rival to retreat to the Saloum area where Bairam Sisi built a strong stockade at Kaur. The situation was further complicated when Said Matti came of age and raised his own army to drive out both the pretenders. In the following year Bairam Sisi entered into a short term alliance with the king of Sine Saloum and swept through Baddibu, pillaging and plundering. Partially because of this disaster, large numbers of persons defected from Mommadu. Said Matti was the major beneficiary of the changed conditions and soon Mommadu's influence in Baddibu was reduced to that of only one town. Said Matti then turned his attention to Bairam Sisi and had by 1887 reduced Sisi's influence in Baddibu to the control of only a few scattered towns.

Trade and agriculture in Baddibu suffered in this ten year period and a deputation of Bathurst merchants in 1886 begged the administrator to intervene to try to end the war. The mediators sent to accomplish this objective were told that arbitration was useless. Each of the three claimants to power were content at that time to let the disturbances continue. Nevertheless, Administrator Carter continued in his attempts to bring peace to Baddibu, and by the end of 1886 had arrived at a workable solution. Mommadu received a subsidy from the government for maintaining law and order in the districts he no longer controlled. Said Matti wanted this subsidy. If the Colonial Office approved the shift of the pension then peace could be arranged, because Mommadu was too weak to continue opposition without the prestige factor of the grant, and Bairam Sisi was amenable to the new peace overtures. The delay caused by communicating with the Colonial Office allowed the disturbances to continue for almost another year. Finally in February 1887, peace was arranged between the factions on a basis of the above considerations. In addition all future disputes were to be referred to the arbitration of the colonial authorities. [32]

Peace in Babbidu was short lived since Said Matti soon raided into the kingdom of Sine Saloum. The French had been extremely active in the 80s in extending their spheres of influence in the Senegambia region and Sine Saloum was under their protection. They warned Said Matti to withdraw his force, and when he ignored them they sent a column of troops to co-operate with the king of Sine Saloum. Said Matti was defeated and fled to the Gambia and took refuge in Albreda. The French column pursued the defeated chief. The British authorities in the Gambia had been warning the Colonial Office continually in the 1880s of French activity in the interior that threatened the Gambia. In this period the British government was trying to secure a general agreement with France which would define the respective spheres of influence between the two powers in West Africa. Therefore Said Matti's movements in Sine Saloum were more important than just a raid by one petty chief into the lands of another. It gave the French the excuse to move to the banks of the Gambia. Sir Samuel Rowe acted with speed to forestall French occupation by taking Said Matti into custody in May 1887. [33]

The removal of Said Matti from Baddibu began a new struggle for power and the resultant disturbances threatened to spread to Sine Saloum. In such circumstances the French decided to pacify the area. French troops occupied a number of Said Matti's towns including some that were on the banks of the Gambia. They deposed two chiefs who were loyal to Bairam Sisi and authorized various chiefs in French territory to collect tribute and customs duties in Baddibu. [34] This precipitated the Colonial Office, through diplomatic channels, to protest against the actions of the French[35] and reluctantly authorize Sir Samuel Rowe to enter into treaties of protection with as many Gambia chiefs as possible. He was also warned against antagonizing the French and causing a crisis. Therefore Rowe's major treaty making efforts of 1887 were on the south side of the river. This late flurry of treaty making and occupation was designed to offset French claims to the Gambia and strengthen the hands of the British negotiators who would conclude the Gambia boundary agreement in Paris.[36]

Partly because of the declaration of British primacy in the Gambia and French hegemony in Senegal, and also due to the exhaustion of both Soninki and Marabout factions, relative peace settled over the Senegambia. With a stronger central authority pledged to law and order and a rudimentary administrative system, anarchic actions, that had originally been considered the natural order of life became breaches of the peace, which would be followed by punishment of the offenders. This is not to imply that order was immediately restored. The old habits were too deeply imbedded in the minds of Fodi Kabba and Fodi Silla for them to accept peace as the rule. The International Boundary Commission which was sent to the Gambia in 1891 met with considerable obstruction from the adherents of both Fodi Kabba and Fodi Silla. Three gunboats were therefore stationed in the river near where the commission was to begin work. Fodi Kabba retired to the Casamance, but one of his lieutenants caused the commissioners a great amount of trouble. It was necessary to bombard his stronghold, Kansalu, before the survey work could continue. By contrast the commission found the utmost friendliness and co-operation in the upper river areas.[37]

As soon as the commission and their armed protection had left the lower river, Fodi Kabba returned to raid the Jola in Foni. The administration refused to recognize his right to rule in that area and warned him to return to the French side of the boundary. On his refusal a joint naval and military venture in January 1892 attacked and destroyed one of his main stockaded towns. Fodi Kabba escaped to French territory. As a follow up to this action the administrator summoned all the chiefs of western Jarra and eastern Kiang to a meeting at

Tendcba. Those present acknowledged British sovereignty, agreed to demand only such customs and duties as the administrator might fix, and to deliver up criminals and aid the British in repelling any invasion of the territory. The one chief who did not attend, a follower of Fodi Kabba named Suleman Santa, was punished for his recalcitrance by the destruction of his town in May 1892.[38]

The next disturber of the peace was Fodi Silla who had remained relatively quiescent for two years. In 1894 he reverted to his old habits of robbing and pillaging. This activity finally brought the long delayed punitive expedition against his principal towns of Brikama, Gunjur, Sukuta, and Busumballa. After a few initial set backs the government forces took his towns and forced him into exile in French territory. He was immediately arrested by the French for some of his past activities and deported to St. Louis. The Kombo was then formally annexed by the British government.[39]

The last real troublemaker was the old war chief, Fodi Kabba, who from his base in French territory kept fomenting Gambian malcontents. He also engaged in surreptitious trade in slaves which he obtained by kidnapping. His adherents would enter British territory to raid and pillage, and then recross the border into French territory before any organized pursuit could be mounted. These raids continued for almost ten years. The murder in 1900 of one of the travelling commissioners, Sitwell, at Sankandi, a town allied to Fodi Kabba, decided the colonial authorities to take final action against Fodi Kabba and his adherents. Shortages of troops due to the Ashanti campaign and the South African War, and delays in planning a joint action with the French postponed the punitive operations against Fodi Kabba until 1901. On the British side Sankandi was taken and the whole vicinity pacified. The second phase of the campaign was that of the French against Fodi Kabba, himself, in March. His career of almost fifty years as a robber baron was closed by his death at Medina.[40] With this event peace finally came to the Gambia area.

The focus of the Soninki-Marabout Wars had changed in the long period of the disturbances. From being genuine religious and political wars they developed into opportunistic conflicts between selfish parties, motivated almost solely by desires of personal gain. For fifty years the entire length of the Gambia had been given over to these dynastic wars. Agriculture, trade, and normal life became impossible for long periods of time. The structure of hereditary and aristocratic rule was profoundly altered by these disturbances and a reconstruction of traditional political rule in the early years of British administration in the Protectorate was essential. The Soninki-Marabout Wars created a power vacuum in the Gambia which the war chiefs could not, and the British authorities consistently refused to fill. The resultant chaotic conditions gave the French in the 1880s every excuse to expand their control in the Senegambia for they were prepared to pacify the hinterlands of the Gambia. If the British after 1887 had not reluctantly moved against the disturbers and announced their decision to hold the Gambia River, the French would have occupied both banks. Thus, in retrospect, the Soninki-Marabout Wars not only disrupted the area, but laid the groundwork for the totally artificial boundaries established by the British and French in 1889.

Chapter Four

THE GAMBIA COLONY IN THE EARLY NINETEENTH CENTURY

JAMES ISLAND had been rendered useless in 1779 and not been reoccupied during the course of the Napoleonic Wars. Elsewhere on the west coast the British had successfully ousted their French rivals and had occupied the main French entre-pôts of St. Louis and Goree. In this period of over thirty years the only sign of British governmental activity on the Gambia River had been the appearance of British warships. The major reason for the reoccupation of any portion of the Gambia was to oust the slave trade in the riverine areas. Although the slave trade had been abolished in 1808, there was considerable evidence that the Gambia River would still be utilized by British as well as foreign slavers, and since there was no resident British force nearer than Goree, they could do this with im-punity. Colonel Charles MacCarthy, Governor-in-Chief of the West African territories, in 1815, therefore, recommended that James Island should be reoccupied by the British. This sugges-tion was approved by the Colonial Office and Captain Alexan-der Grant was sent from Goree with a detachment from the African Corps to survey the situation. He found the king of Barra amenable to a leasehold arrangement for James Island. However Grant rejected James Island for a number of salient reasons. Chief among these were the small size of the island, and the fact that it was located at such a distance from the mouth of the Gambia, that it would be extremely difficult to maintain close surveillance upon ships leaving and entering the river. Grant, therefore, obtained from the king of Kombo the right to occupy the Island of Banjul in return for the promise of an annual payment of 103 bars of iron (approximately twenty-five pounds).[1] The island was formally occupied on April 23, 1816 and renamed St. Mary's Island. If the Captain had tried he could not have found a more unfavourable spot to locate the new colony. The island was simply a high sandy beach thrown up by the Atlantic with a mangrove swamp behind it. Thirty years later a visitor to the Gambia noted this unpropitious location thus:

> But why a settlement has been founded amidst swamps, when higher up, and with plenty of water for ships of large size, there are dry and healthy spots, I cannot comprehend. However, Bathurst in this respect resembles our settlements elsewhere: we fix ourselves on the first spot that presents itself eligible for commerce, seemingly regardless if we perish in pursuit of wealth.[2]

It is doubtful whether Captain Grant selected St. Mary's Island as the seat of a permanent colony. It is more likely that he was thinking primarily of military considerations. His first objective had been to build a suitable military establishment from which he could control the mouth of the river. On a basis of these considerations, St. Mary's Island and Barra Point across the river were the most obvious strategic locations for any military establishments.

The task facing Grant was immense. The site which he had chosen was unhealthy and there were no permanent building materials available in the locality. All stone for the building had to be quarried at Dog Island and then floated down the river to the site of the new colony.[3] The troops under his command were not the most desirable in the British armed forces. Most of them were drawn either from the convict hulks in England or were offenders from other regiments of the army who had been transferred to the African Corps because of their bad records.[4] Despite the handicaps inherent in the environment and the appalling death rate among the troops due to the unhealthy conditions, rapid strides were made to convert the area to a settled comunity. The new townsite, named Bathurst after the Colonial Secretary at the time, was laid out by Buckle, the Colonial Engineer of Sierra Leone. The plan for Bathurst was quite advanced for its time, calling for two parallel main streets named respectively Wellington Street and Buckle Street. Wellington Street was located next to the river, and at the upper end plans were made for a large square named after Governor MacCarthy. Government House was located beyond the square, facing the river. Six other streets linked the two main streets, and these were named after six of Wellington's aides in the recent wars—Blucher, Picton, Anglesley, Hill, Orange and Cotton. By 1821 the completed public buildings of Bathurst included Government House, barracks, officers' quarters, judicial buildings, and a hospital. A three gun battery trained at the mouth of the harbour was located in the vicinity of Government House.[5] This was all accomplished in the face of the physical difficulties and a lack of revenue. Grant had been told that except for military costs, he could expect no financial assistance from Britain. All improvements had to be based on the income of the new colony. This income was derived solely from a tax on imports which amounted to only £500 in 1817, and had risen to only £3,500 by 1823.[6] The establishment of Bathurst is a monument to the strength and inventiveness of Captain Grant, and not to any far sighted policy of the home government.

The government of the new colony from the time of its establishment until 1821 was decidedly military and temporary. However MacCarthy had made arrangements for the participation of the merchants of the area in government and had seen to it that courts were established, modelled on others then in force in West Africa. This governmental organization had been based upon the idea that the new area would eventually be a separate colony. However, in 1821, the charter of the Africa Company was finally revoked by Parliament and the new colony was placed directly under the control of the Governor-General located in Sierra Leone.[7] In theory the area was to be administered by a Lieutenant-Governor resident in Government House. However, the first Lieutenant-Governor did not arrive in the Gambia until 1829, thus making it necessary for Captain Grant and the merchants on the spot to deal with the pressing matters of law and order. Even after his arrival, Lieutenant-Colonel Finley, the first Lieutenant-Governor, found that in most cases he did not have even a reasonable area of freedom of action. All legislative enactments for the Gambia had to be forwarded to Sierra Leone for final sanction. This, of course, led to considerable delay and in many cases to complete misunderstanding between the Lieutenant-Governors and their superiors in Freetown. The government in Sierra Leone was largely ignorant of the conditions then prevailing in the Gambia, yet in many cases it took upon itself to legislate for the Colony against the advice of the Lieutenant-Governors. As time progressed this anomalous situation was recognized even by the Governors-in-Chief resident in Freetown as being an awkward, cumbersome arrangement. In 1825 the Governor of Sierra Leone pointed out to Earl Bathurst that 'it would be easier for the general officer at Cork to take charge of the Barbados than for me to take charge of the three colonies of the Gambia, Sierra Leone, and the Gold Coast'.[8] But it was not until 1843 that the Gambia was severed from the debilitating control of Sierra Leone. In that year the central government of the Gambia was reconstructed and the chief executive was constituted a governor with full powers over his area of control, subject only to the Colonial Office.[9] Appointive Executive and Legislative Councils were also created for the Gambia for the first time in 1843.

Despite all these difficulties the colony area was expanded because of the necessity to control the sea-borne slave trade and to provide more adequate arrangements for housing the freed slaves that were sent from Sierra Leone to the Gambia. On April 14, 1823, the Island of Lemain near Kayee was ceded to Captain Grant by the native chief of that area. Grant guaranteed the payment annually of 110 Spanish dollars per year and in return the chief relinquished all his pretentions to control of the island and to its customs duties.[10] Part of the reason for this purchase was to gain a military post in the upper river areas in order to lend some kind of protection to merchants trading in those districts. The island was renamed MacCarthy after the distinguished Governor-in-Chief. In 1823 the Wesleyans founded a mission establishment complete with a school on the island. Eventually a number of the repatriated slaves from Sierra Leone were sent to MacCarthy Island and there some success was obtained in teaching them the rudiments of more advanced agriculture. However, the building of a fort with barracks and Government House was the signal for native disturbances directed at the island.[11] These threats to trade and the existence of the small garrison which occupied the island continued throughout most of the nineteenth century, primarily because British policy kept the number of troops on MacCarthy Island at a bare minimum.

On June 4, 1827, Grant re-negotiated the agreement of 1816 with the king of Kombo, whereby St. Mary's Island was annexed directly to the Crown.[12] In June of the previous year the Acting Governor of Sierre Leone, Kenneth Macaulay, had entered into an agreement with Brune, king of Barra, by which in very grandiose terms the chief ceded to Great Britain the right to 'full free and unlimited right, title, sovereignty and possession of the River Gambia with all its branches, creeks, inlets and water of the same as they have been held from time immemorial . . .' By article three of this agreement the first portion of land across the river from Bathurst beginning at Jinnak Creek on the west to Jakadoo Creek on the east was ceded to the British Crown.[13] In January 1832, this agreement was extended with the new king of Barra to include all of that portion of land which came to be known as the Ceded Mile.[14] In May 1827, a further agreement was reached between Grant and the king of Brikama in which the latter placed all his territories under British protection and guaranteed non-interference in the area directly controlled by Britain. Grant also received by this treaty the right to confirm the elections of the chiefs in the territory ruled by the king of Brikama.[15] The last major agreement made in this spate of treaty making was with the king of Wuli for the cession of the Port of Fattatenda to Great Britain in return for a payment of 200 Spanish dollars in kind.[16] This latter acquisition was primarily for purposes of trade in the upper river and had little or no strategic significance.

With the exception of the treaty with the king of Wuli, all these direct and indirect acquisitions were made because of two considerations. The first the control of the slave trade, was the major early consideration of the British administration in the Gambia. The second consideration was an outgrowth of the first—a growing need for the necessary land to provide a defensive perimeter around the main Colony of Bathurst.

In 1827 Commodore Charles Bullen, a veteran of Trafalgar, arrived in the Gambia and began the construction of a fort at Barra Point. This activity frightened the new king of Barra to such a point that he decided to abrogate the terms of the treaty of 1826 and force the British out of Barra. This decision began the so-called Barra War which did not end until 1831. Although small in scope, the disturbance not only threatened for a time to drive the British from their positions at Barra and the Ceded Mile, but also threatened the colony area of Bathurst itself. The situation was stabilized with the help of the French at Goree who dispatched a French man-of-war to aid the British in the Gambia. Part of the French aid consisted in the construction of a fort within the town of Bathurst itself, later named after the French Commandant, Louvel.[17] The fort stood until very recent years as a reminder of the early days of the colony. The four large calibre guns sited by Commander Bullen remained in the open until the Barra War was ended, and construction of the fort was not recommenced until 1831.[18] Fort Bullen and its three gun battery together with the guns placed in Bathurst near Government House gave the British a fairly good command of the entrance of the Gambia River.

The action of the West African squadron in combination with the armed settlements on the Gambia all but ended sea-borne slave trading from the Gambia by 1840. However, even this success caused the infant colony much trouble because little planning was done concerning the future of liberated slaves who were trans-shipped from Sierra Leone to the Gambia. They presented health problems because most of them landed in varying states of ill health from the cruisers that had brought them from further down the coast or direct from the slave ships.

66

They belonged to different tribes, coming from all sections of West Africa. Lieutenant-Governor Rendall attempted a number of projects for resettlement of these salvaged persons. A farming colony in Bathurst was first attempted which proved a failure. Later a brickwork was begun, and this in turn proved unsuccessful. The best that could be done for most of the freed slaves was to try to resettle them on portions of land in the colony areas and hope that all would be well. By 1840 the numbers of freed slaves transferred to the Gambia had decreased, and with the acquisition of a portion of Kombo many of these liberated Africans were transferred to that area where their conditions steadily improved.[19]

Little could be done about domestic slavery and the internal slave trade. The small military force available to the administrators was barely sufficient to maintain the colony areas intact during the crises of the Soninki-Marabout Wars. This weak power position, combined with chronic lack of funds, meant that however sincere individual administrators might have been in trying to rid the river of these twin problems, nothing really constructive could be accomplished. Although the home government throughout the nineteenth century pressed administrators to take active steps in the elimination of these activities, they refused to provide even the minimum support necessary for the carrying out of these wishes. In 1876 Administrator Cooper, after having completed a journey as far up river as Yarbutenda, reported to the Governor-in-Chief that the slave trade was being carried on by British trading firms:

> Your Excellency will by this perceive that my despatches written on former occasions on the subject [29 Jan. 1873 and 21 July 1873] are being now in a great measure proved and that slavery (not domestic) is being carried on to a great extent in our waters by British subjects, the slaves in many instances being brought down by Caravans to the up-river from the interior of Africa and distributed about whilst others are transported from the river Gambia to the river Jeba and Cassmanze.[20]

As late as 1893 one of the first Travelling Commissioners in the Protectorate, Ozanne, found that domestic slavery was an integral part of the culture and economics of the up-river

67

villages. In reply to requests that he should do something to eliminate these practices he stated that although the areas under his visitation were quite friendly and prepared to accept British rule, this would change if there was any serious attempt on his part to act against indigenous slavery. Even at this late date he advised a long range policy of removing slavery from the Gambia.[21] Throughout the nineteenth century all that the administrators could do was to attempt verbally to coerce the native chiefs in the interior. All treaties of cession and friendship contained provisions whereby the chiefs concerned promised to give up both slavery and the slave trade. The disturbed conditions of the Soninki-Marabout Wars brought a resurgence in the slave trade by providing the individual chiefs with more captives, and also a necessity to convert these human assets into monetary gains. The practice of wholesale slave trading was one of the major charges made by the administrators against such war chiefs as Fodi Kabba and Fodi Silla.[22]

In 1823 the first contingent of missionaries arrived in the Colony. They belonged to the Society of Friends and were headed by a most remarkable person, Hanna Kilham. The first mission establishment was at Cape St. Mary near the village of Bakau where the missionaries received a grant of land. On this land they began a school to instruct the villagers in ploughing and farm work. Mrs. Kilham herself established two schools in Bathurst, one for boys and one for girls. Two months after the arrival of the Friends the first Wesleyan missionaries arrived. At this juncture Mrs. Kilham abandoned Bathurst to the Wesleyan missionaries and went to Bakau where she and her helpers opened a girls' school. However, the usual enemies of the white settlers—death and disease—took such a toll that it was necessary to close the mission establishment.[23] The Wesleyans were more successful in maintaining their mission stations in Bathurst and later up-river, not, however, without an appalling loss of life on the part of these devoted people. The Wesleyans in the schools which they opened generally followed the plan first instituted by the Society of Friends to teach in large measure vocational and agricultural subjects. They established a mission station and school in MacCarthy Island which was maintained intermittently throughout the nineteenth century.[24] The Catholic Church first sent missionaries in the form of two French Sisters to the colony area in 1823. However, this beginning was cut short in the following year by disease. The first permanent mission establishment of the Catholic Church did not come until 1849 with the dispatch of three Fathers from France and three Sisters from the Convent of St. Joseph of Cluny. The Sisters took over the nursing at the civil hospital when it was opened in 1854.[25]

Most of the mission activities until the very late years of the nineteenth century were centred in Bathurst, because of the unsettled conditions in the native areas and the lack of protection which could be given by the governing officials of the Colony. Apart from their primary mission of building churches and bringing Christianity to the area, the foremost work of the missionaries was in the field of education. The government felt that it had neither the qualified personnel nor the necessary revenues to institute a system of education for even those inhabitants of the colony areas. The officials thus conveniently shifted their responsibility for education on to the mission establishments. Although the church groups were most willing and served in a devoted fashion in the nineteenth century, they neither had the facilities nor the money to extend education to any but a fortunate few persons in the Gambia. Once the government had decided to leave education in the hands of the mission establishments it did not even provide adequate financial grants so that these educators could contemplate any great expansion in their facilities. That this attitude continued until very recent times is shown by the fact that the sum proposed in 1900 for grants for education was only £650, whereas the cost of maintaining the police was £4,701.[26] Even as late as 1940, out of a total appropriation of £217,925, education received only the meagre sum of £5,528.[27] Although the policy of the government towards education in the period before 1890 was an inevitable one because of the small revenue, it is nevertheless true that the government pursued a hands-off policy that utilized the private agencies long after such a policy was either justified by finances or by the environmental events of the Gambia.

69

Despite the preoccupation of the government with the endemic native wars on the river and lack of funds, some progress was made, although slowly, in Bathurst. Under Governor O'Connor a new stone hospital was completed in 1851. In 1857 a large new permanent market area was constructed for the use of native traders. Colonel O'Connor was also responsible for the first real attempts at providing sanitation for the town of Bathurst by building an improved drainage system. However, the large swampy area behind the town called Half Die still presented a continual threat to the health of the inhabitants. Practically all governors of the nineteenth century reported the situation and made varying plans for the drainage and improvement of that area. The most significant of these proposals was that of Colonel Ord, whose report was so influential in many other ways. He believed that if the Gambia was retained, one of the first improvements should be in drainage, and he estimated that it would cost £7,000.[28] Invariably the reply of the home government to all such proposals was that funds were not available for such an extensive project. Even in the 1880s when a large amount of the revenue of the Gambia was diverted to Sierra Leone the colonial authorities could not find the necessary funds to carry out the sanitation project.[29] Therefore this continual threat to health remained, despite some efforts in the late 1920s, until Colonial Development funds were made available in the early 1940s.

The Select Committee of Parliament appointed to investigate conditions of British holdings on the West Coast of Africa reported in 1842 that the Gambia River possessed advantages for trade 'far beyond those of any other British settlement on the coast of Africa'.[30] This report, although it did not change the Colonial Office's attitude towards the long range importance of such settlements, did stimulate some further exploration of the up-river districts by government officials. In 1843 the first governmental steamer to be used on the river arrived. Governor Seagram encouraged and actually took part in a continuation of the survey of the river above MacCarthy Island, which had been begun in 1826 by Lieutenant Owen. In 1848 Governor McDonald travelled up the river as far as Barrakunda and then proceeded on foot along the north bank as far as Tenda and the Noreco River. Colonel O'Connor, who succeeded McDonald, also travelled sporadically in the upper river areas and is remembered for his policy of taking sons of chiefs of the lower river areas with him on his visitations. Despite these occasional governmental forays into the riverine areas, the interest of the administration was still concentrated in the area around Bathurst and little or no detailed knowledge of the conditions in the upper river area in the period of the Soninki-Marabout Wars was available to them. It was left to traders to explore and continue contacts with the native peoples in the upper river areas throughout the nineteenth century.

The only real large scale government sponsored expedition into the upper reaches of the Gambia occurred in 1881 under Governor Gouldsbury. The main reason for his expedition was to obtain a first hand view of the commercial potential of the upper Gambia. As such his report lent strength to the colonial officials who maintained that the Gambia was worthless. Although Gouldsbury entered into a number of treaties with chiefs in the upper Gambia, he did not observe any prosperous and thriving villages. On the contrary, he discovered that for miles there were no signs of clearing or cultivation of the land or of human occupancy. The reasons for this were obvious to Gouldsbury, but less so to the Colonial Office who was not interested in the effects of inter-tribal wars and slave trading in an area where there was no strong central government.[31] The treaties that Gouldsbury made with the chiefs on his visit were never acted upon by Britain.

From the very first Bathurst had become a centre of trade on the West Coast of Africa whose potential importance before 1890 equalled, if not exceeded, most. Many of the merchants who had settled at Goree when it was still in British hands moved to Bathurst after the Treaty of Paris. Until the 1850s the trade was confined to such articles as beeswax, ivory, gum, and hides in return for British trade goods. It is impossible to ascertain with any degree of certainty the volume of this trade since it was divided among a great number of British, French, and native merchants. It is safe to assume, however, from the customs duties collected by the government that the trade itself from point of volume was very small.

A major change in the activities of the merchants occurred in the 1840s and '50s when the cultivation of the groundnut began to be pursued seriously by the farmers in the Gambia valley. Groundnuts had been grown as food for many years in the Senegambia. Francis Moore who visited the Gambia in the 1730s described groundnuts growing there. Although he did not give them a name, he said that the plant produced two kernels in each shell and looked rather like a dried acorn.[32] The first recorded exportation of groundnuts from the Gambia was in 1830 and realized only £10 16s. 8d.[33] In 1860 the Gambia exported 10,000 tons, and in 1889, the year of the boundary discussions, 19,636 tons to the value of £140,086 were exported.[34] The export product second in value to groundnuts was rubber; in 1889 it brought in only a total of £3,470. Thus the Senegambia area was practically a monoculture before the transfer of political sovereignty had been completed.

With the increasing importance of groundnuts, larger trading establishments with better overseas connections were established in Bathurst. It is primarily for this reason that French traders began to assume a larger role in the export trade of the Gambia. The large part of the groundnut crop in the 1850s and '60s was exported to France rather than to Britain. Because of the twenty per cent duty which was levied on foreign ships at French ports, most of the groundnuts shipped either by French or English exporters were carried in French ships. This fact assumed major importance when the negotiations between France and Britain for the exchange of the Gambia began in the mid '60s. It appeared superficially that most of the trading activities in the Gambia had been taken over by the French companies. This was far from true and an analysis of the imports and exports of the Gambia in this period shows that as regards value British companies such as Thomas Brown, Thomas Chown, and Quinn and Company were still more important than their French competitors.

The period from 1850-1857 witnessed the British signing of a number of important treaties with native chiefs and with France. These where the last important agreements which Britain concluded with the chiefs of the hinterland until the late 1880s. In 1850 two agreements between the king of Barra and the

Governor gave Britain rights in the vicinity of Albreda which previously had been reserved for France.[35] In May 1853, an agreement between the king of Kombo and the administration ceded to Britain that portion of Kombo that directly adjoins Cape St. Mary.[36] Finally in March 1857, in an agreement between Britain and France, Britain gave up her trading rights at Portendic. In return the French abandoned their factory at Albreda and gave Britain the right to charge tolls and customs on French ships which previously had been protected from this.[37] This agreement ended an historic relationship which was as old as European settlement of the Gambia area. In the latter years of the life of Albreda, this station had been a continual economic nuisance to the British colony at Bathurst. Later observers could point out that the gum trade at Portendic was quite important and that perhaps Britain did not get the best of this particular agreement. However, for the British merchants both large and small who traded in the Gambia, the removal of Albreda as an economic threat was some small evidence that Britain had not completely forgotten its responsibility to them. With the exception of the abortive discussions with France in the '70s concerning the exchange of territory in the Senegambia region, and a number of minor defensive treaties concluded with hinterland chiefs, this was the last treaty making of any substance which affected territory in the Gambia until the French incursions of the late 1880s forced Britain to take action to protect her minimum rights.

Official British policy relating to the Gambia in the second half of the nineteenth century will be treated subsequently. However, no history of the early years of the Colony would be complete without a passing reference to the conditions of life in the Colony as recorded by numerous travellers in West Africa. The routine of living, both civilian and military, in the Gambia was a hard one made up of a composite of danger, sickness, and boredom. During the course of the Soninki-Marabout Wars the garrison was undermanned, continually threatened, and in danger of being overrun by the numerically superior native armies. There must have been a sense of futility in the minds of both common soldiers and administrators. Officials at home in Britain paid little attention to the urgent

73

requests and recommendations of the administrators. They were either not aware, or if they were they did not care much, about the problems which the government of the Gambia found to be so pressing. Thus a sense of futility and a sense of the ultimate worthlessness of what they were accomplishing was an everyday companion of these government servants. There were few entertainments for the Europeans. The unhealthy climate prevented most of the administrators and officers from bringing their families to West Africa. There were, therefore, years of separation which must be counted in assessing the contributions of the early British servants in West Africa.

A visitor to Bathurst in the 1850s was Captain J. F. Napier Hewett who recorded his first negative impressions of the city thus:

> As the greater portion of the town of Bathurst is below the level of the water, it presents a bird's-eye view to the spectator on board ship, and this view I will endeavour to describe:—The foreground is occupied by a row of buildings, which, peeping through a terrace of trees, and being detached and apparently built in the Italian style of architecture, and no shops visible, reminded me of some parts of the park at Cheltenham. In the background are seen the feathery tropical willows, and lofty drooping palms, which raise their heads between the tenements, while the town view is bounded by a light and pretty tower, apparently the tower of a church. The surrounding expanse is a vast unbroken, monotonous, swampy level, overrun with the poisonous mangrove, and studded here and there by the funereal palm, which, like the plumes of a hearse, seem emblematic of the proverbial deadliness of the climate.[38]

Hewitt continued his description of the unhealthy nature of the Gambia, and in this his account did not differ markedly from the earlier observations of Jobson or Moore. Whatever Hewitt's bias in other areas, there is objective proof of his statements regarding the debilitating effect of the climate. As an example, between May 1825 and July 1827, out of the 399 European soldiers that landed at Bathurst, 276 died.[39] After this the home authorities did not send white troops to garrison the Gambia, but recruited Africans. However, the commissioned and non-commissioned officers remained European. One must also remember that in addition to the usual dangers of malaria and dysentery, there were recurrent epidemics that periodically swept through the river valley such as the yellow fever epidemics of the late '50s and the cholera plague of 1869 that killed thousands. Hewitt dwelt a long time on a visit he paid to the barracks and the appearance of the officers, grotesquely bearded, some with their heads shaved because of previous fevers they had suffered.[40]

Another visitor to Bathurst was Sir Richard Burton who in 1863 gave a good description of the dangers to health inherent in the location of the city. His account of the medical facilities available to the sick was also extremely critical:

> The place is murderous. There is a sick ward upon the ground floor!—One night on the ground floor is certain fever in most parts of tropical Africa—and that ground floor is, like the latrene and other offices, frequently under water. In the first story the beds are crowded together, each patient having 800, whereas 2,000 feet of air should be the minimum . . . On the second floor are the quarters of the medical officers, within pleasant distance of an atmosphere wraught with smallpox and dysentery, typhus and yellowjack. This caution of a hospital is built to 'accomodate' 23, at times it has had 32 . . . I was not astonished after going the rounds to hear of 92 deaths out of 96 admissions and that at times *El Vomito* improves off everybody . . .[41]

It is, therefore, not just poetic imagination that led certain modern African nationalists to suggest the mosquito as the national emblem of any United West Africa. This small insect took a deadly toll of Europeans that dared the West African coast.

All visitors to the Colony noted the boredom and the sense of futility which permeated the European community. Some observed that one accepted panacea for the environment was drink, and that this as much as the unhealthy atmosphere was responsible for the high death rate. Even the detached, non-critical Mrs. Kilham wished that more of the white community would give themselves to work and religion rather than to liquor.[42] Hewitt seemed surprised that the garrison officers should complain that there was no society, no amusements, books, or food available, and that there was nothing to eat except poultry, and no real pleasures to be pursued except cards, quarrelling, and drinking. He later described the results of a party given for the garrison which was the beginning of a week long revel of picnics, champagne breakfasts, dinners, and dances.[43] Comparing this with earlier statements made by Mrs. Kilham, Mrs. Bowdich, Governor Huntley, and Dr. Poole, one is struck not so much by the dissimilarity of their accounts, but by the picture drawn of a backwater where so far as it was possible, the Europeans tried to recreate the life which they had left in England. Periodically it seemed necessary for them to relieve the strain of the boredom which accompanied their life by revels such as those described by Mr. Hewitt.

The sacrifices of innumerable Civil Servants, missionaries, and soldiers in such a backwater appeared to most visitors as a terrible waste of money and human talent in relation to the meagre profits that were gained from the area. In the mid '60s these private opinions concerning the value of the settlement were reinforced by the active anti-imperial moves of the government. The home government, dominated by the idea that colonies were by and large unprofitable, had been disturbed for years, not only by the turbulent state of affairs in the Gambia valley, but also by the increasing cost of maintaining their holdings in the vicinity of Freetown, the Gold Coast, and Lagos. In all these locations the cost of administering the stations seemed to outweigh the potential economic and strategic advantages gained by the maintenance of such administration. In the Gambia the continuance of the internecine warfare in the hinterland had made it necessary from time to time to dispatch relatively large numbers of West Indian troops simply to maintain the British position in Bathurst and MacCarthy Island. This meant continued expenditures in the Gambia for apparently little return on their investment.

In 1864 the home government sent Colonel H. St. George Ord as a Commissioner to West Africa to report on the conditions which he found there and to investigate possible ways of economizing. Included in his terms of reference was the question whether Britain should abandon all her responsibilities on the West Coast. Concerning the Gambia, Ord's report went far in vindicating the judgement of the administrators. He found that the charge of governing the area had been heavy, but not disproportionately so, due to the unhealthiness of the Gambia River and the need to have replacements always available. He found that although the trade of the area was small by comparison to other areas of the world, it was by and large good, and that the main reason it was not better was due to continued disturbances along the river. The hinterland disturbances affected trade greatly and therefore he hoped, that for the good of commerce and the well-being of the natives, the local government would find some way of extending protection to the natives, particularly those on the north bank. In connection with this he stated that MacCarthy Island, far from being unimportant, was most necessary for the maintenance and protection of trade in the upper river areas. To Ord there was very little choice left to the British government because a policy of abandonment was unthinkable. Britain had assumed certain responsibilities towards the area, particularly in the realm of such humanitarian activities as the destruction of the slave trade and indigenous slavery. Abandonment would have meant that in a short time all the work of fifty years would have been negated and there would not even be islands of peace and security in the troubled valley. However, for the sake of economy, he did find that it was wasteful to duplicate efforts at the four British West African enclaves and he suggested a re-imposition of the office of Governor-in-Chief to be located in Freetown. This Governor-in-Chief would be primarily responsible for law and order and for the maintenance of trade and commerce in all the British West African territories.[44]

Ord's report was followed by the appointment of a Select Committee of Parliament to investigate further and to make definite recommendations upon which the government could act. The Select Committee agreed with Ord that complete withdrawal would be impossible because of the many moral commitments assumed by Britain. However, they did reiterate the doctrine that there should be no extension of territory. By thus minimizing responsibility, Britain could plan for an eventual withdrawal from all the areas. This dictum of no expansion, first enunciated publicly in 1866 by Parliament, was closely followed by the Colonial Office in the next twenty years, notwithstanding the changes in environmental conditions which took place in that period. Contrary to the suggestions of previous administrators and of Ord himself, the Select Committee suggested that MacCarthy Island should be abandoned and that all Britain's interests in the Gambia should be concentrated in the area around Bathurst. Finally the Parliamentary report recommended the establishment of a unified form of government for all the West African areas under a Governor-in-Chief resident in Sierra Leone.[45] This latter recommendation was put into effect by Royal Commission in 1866 and later modified in 1874 by the removal of the areas of the Gold Coast and Lagos from the control of the Governor-in-Chief, leaving only the Gambia under the direct control of a chief executive located almost a thousand miles away.[46] It is doubtful whether this new policy effected any major savings in funds. The Colony of the Gambia had always been maintained on a minimum cost and with a minimal utilization of personnel. What was accomplished was the reiteration of a policy which had been found to be inefficient in 1843 whereby the administrators of the Gambia were handicapped in taking direct action on their own cognizance. Rather they were required to refer most of the major problems to the Governor-in-Chief. Because Sierra Leone was the most favoured colony, the Gambia, particularly in the later years of this arrangement, was required to provide funds to the Governor-in-Chief which were utilized in Sierra Leone and not in the Gambia. Many necessary improvements in the Colony were thus postponed even though the Gambia throughout this period of its relationship with Sierra Leone was always solvent and Sierra Leone was often in financial difficulties.[47]

The recommendation for the abandonment of MacCarthy Island was never fully put into effect, partly because of the resistance of private traders and partly because of the critical native situation in the vicinity. However, troops were withdrawn from MacCarthy Island and traders in the upper river were warned that they were there at their own risk since they were beyond the limits of British jurisdiction. MacCarthy Island was left to be administered by a factor who was also a trader in the upper river areas. This anomalous situation was not changed until after the abortive discussions with France for the exchange of territory had finished.[48]

With the administrative changes instituted as a result of the Select Committee's report, a period in Gambian history came to an end and the stage was set for the attempts on the part of the home government to find a suitable solution for the delineation of trading spheres of influence between Britain and France in West Africa. This latter stage envisaged the wholesale exchange of British territory for French territory, to give each of the powers contiguous possessions and thus minimize the continuing conflicts between French and British traders in West Africa. In these discussions which continued until the 1880s the Gambia had a major role to play since it was obvious that the French were most interested in acquiring the waterway whereas the British were more concerned with their territories further to the south.

In the fifty year period which has been discussed certain definite improvements had been made in the British position in the Gambia River. The city of Bathurst had been surveyed and permanent buildings constructed, and it had become a peaceful entrepôt of over 3,000 persons in an area otherwise plagued by disturbances. Additional territories such as British Kombo, the Ceded Mile, and Albreda had been added to the original cession obtained by Charles Grant. The discovery of the profits that could be made from growing and exporting groundnuts had benefited not only the groundnut merchants to the extent of over £100,000 a year, but also extended to the agricultural community of the hinterland areas.

But in many other ways this had not been a half century of progress. The governors were powerless to contain the disastrous civil wars in the non-colony areas. At the end of the period they were once again tied not only administratively to the Colonial Office, but to a Governor-in-Chief located in Sierra Leone. The Colony of the Gambia was almost as much of a backwater in 1886 as it had been in 1816. It was still 'the white man's grave' with boredom, danger, and disease the constant companion of any Europeans stationed there. It remained for the Colonial Office a questionable luxury which Britain could no longer afford. Thus the representations made by France for an exchange of territory was welcomed in many quarters as a logical way of regularizing spheres of influence and minimizing the costs of such places as the Gambia. The next twenty years saw the home government attempting to make a reality of the proposals first broached by France in 1866.

Chapter Five

THE LURE OF EXCHANGE

THE period after the Napoleonic Wars was one of relative quiescence for the French as well as for the British in West Africa. After regaining control of St. Louis, Goree, and Albreda in 1817, they found their interior trade almost nonexistent. For a decade the French concentrated on poorly planned plantation schemes in Senegal. After these had failed they continued a desultory interior trade, and although some new factories were founded in the upper Senegal, their activities were not impressive. In the 1830s French trading interests shifted from the Senegal to the Guinea coast where various stations such as Grand Bassam, Assinie, and Whydah were established. Not until 1854, when the government of Senegal was separated from Goree, did the French under Governor Faidherbe take an active interest in the Senegambia once again. Even under Faidherbe's direction French interest was concentrated in lower Senegal and did not impinge upon the Gambia. French lack of interest in the Gambia River is shown by the agreement whereby the French evacuated their stations at Albreda in return for British withdrawal from Portendic in 1857.

After Faidherbe's time governmental participation in trading activities on the coast almost ceased, primarily because of internal pressures upon the Second Empire. In the late '60s and early '70s the French generally neglected the trading stations which had been established earlier. As an example the garrisons were withdrawn from all their forts on the Ivory Coast in 1871 and the other trading stations were similarly neglected. One seeming exception to this lack of French interest in the late '60s was the Gambia River. This does not imply that French traders or governmental agents were extraordinarily active in the vicinity, but that the French saw an opportunity to gain the premier position in the Senegambia by surrendering spheres which they had already largely abandoned in the coastal areas further south.[1] French designs on the Gambia River throughout this period were largely at the diplomatic level because they believed there would be little opposition in Britain to their proposed solution to the problems of spheres of influence in West Africa.

The British retrenchment policy affecting their West African territories had hardly gone into effect when on March 22, 1866, the French Ambassador, M. Auverge, communicated his government's willingness to consider an exchange of territory.[2] This first proposal was for an exchange of the British possessions on the Gambia in return for the French posts at Grand Bassam, Dabon, and Assinie. M. Auverge's note indicated that the reason for this proposal was the increased volume of French trade in the area between the French possessions in Senegal and the Gambia River. The Ambassador pointed out that there had been a similar increase in British activity in the coastal area northward from Sierra Leone. Thus presumably it would be mutually advantageous for both countries to consolidate their spheres of influence. Before the Colonial Office could reply to this proposal a new note arrived from the French which suggested that perhaps the British government would prefer the French settlements on the Gabon for the Gambia.[3] This latter proposal was declined in May 1868, not because of any lack of interest in the French proposals, but because the proposal did not go far enough in delineating French and English spheres in West Africa.[4] Despite the general quiescence on the part of the French government in West Africa in the '60s, a number of French traders had established themselves in force in the area immediately north of Sierra Leone adjacent to the Mellacourie and Foracariah Rivers. The Colonial Office, desirous, as always, to protect the settlements of Sierra Leone, was afraid that the French would establish customs houses in these areas and thus bring economic pressure to bear on Freetown. The general consensus of the Colonial Office was that any exchange of territory in West Africa would have to guarantee continued British control of the areas to the north.[5]

As the Colonial Office wanted more detailed information about the conditions in West Africa, it instructed the Governor-in-Chief, Sir Arthur Kennedy, to investigate and report in detail on the situation in the Gambia. Kennedy had been appointed Administrator of the Gambia in 1852 but had never effectively held that post. Thus his visit to Bathurst in 1869 was his first personal acquaintance with the area. It should be noted that Sir Arthur Kennedy stayed only ten days in Bathurst; therefore the subsequent detailed reports which he filed for the Colonial Office over a period of some five years must be assumed to have been made up not of personal observations, but of details supplied to him by subordinates and merchants who had personal experience with the river valley. From the very beginning Kennedy adopted a totally negative attitude towards the Gambia. Even before his visit to Bathurst he had indicated the direction of his thinking in a letter to the Colonial Office in April where he stated,

> Our trade with the Moriah and Samo country, will always prove a source of profit without any outlay, while the settlements at the Gambia and Bulama will be a source of expense, with very little profit to British commerce as well as a source of anxiety, expecially the former.[6]

He favoured in general the proposal for an exchange of territory because as he said, 'This arrangement would tend to consolidate the territory belonging to, or under the protection of, both nations'.[7]

Kennedy was informed on September 20, 1869 that Lord Granville had transmitted the British proposal for an exchange of the Gambia to the Foreign Office and Lord Clarendon and his staff were preparing a proposition to be transmitted to Paris as a counter proposal to the original offers made by

France. In reply Kennedy gave perhaps the most cogent statement of the reasons for wanting to be rid of the Gambia. His dispatch included the following:

1. The cost of maintaining troops in the colony which amounted to approximately £20,000 in 1869.

2. The hopelessness of extending civilization to 'the peculiar population which surrounds and composes the bulk of the settlement'.

3. The precarious nature of the revenues based almost entirely upon the groundnut trade.

4. The utter uselessness of the place as a military post.

5. The fact that the bulk of the trade was in the hands of the French and will become predominately more so yearly.

6. The certainty of frequent clashes with the native peoples which makes it mandatory to keep a large expensive military force in the area.[8]

Kennedy was convinced, however, that the exchange of territory proposed by France in 1866 offered no real advantage. While he was opposed to Britain keeping the Gambia for sentimental reasons, he felt that it should be exchanged for something worth while. He believed that the possession of the Gaboon would be of no advantage for Britain. The Gambia should be utilized to gain from the French sufficient guarantees for a real delimitation of territory.

Rear Admiral Patey, the Administrator of the Gambia, communicated his views on the proposed exchange on October 1, 1869. Basically these were the same as those of Governor General Kennedy. Patey reported that there were five English trading firms in the Gambia which dealt primarly in barter, and of these, three were not doing well, In contrast there were four French establishments which traded in cash and all seemed to be prospering. This was primarily due to the contacts with the Casamance and the Senegal areas, as well as to a more direct entry into the main French market via Marseilles. The Administrator estimated the governmental income for 1869 to be £21,593 with an expenditure of £20,577. There was a surplus in the treasury of approximately £10,000. However, he pointed out that one part of a West Indian regiment was always quartered in the Gambia at what he claimed was an expense of £30,000 per year. Patey believed there was little reason for the British to stay in the Gambia since the slave trade was virtually at an end and there seemed to be little hope of improving the natives in the area. He concluded, 'Undoubtedly the settlements of the Gambia are maintained at a heavy sacrifice—morally, physically and pecuniarily—to the Imperial Government.'[9]

Lord Clarendon, the Foreign Secretary, bolstered up by these reports furnished him by the Colonial Office, proposed to France a sweeping exchange of territory with suitable guarantees which would presumably secure British interests and avoid the conflicts with the French. His proposal was that Britain should cede absolutely all the possessions on the Gambia and guarantee in the future not to acquire any influence on native tribes adjacent to any river in West Africa north of the River Dembia. In return France should guarantee not to acquire or to attain sovereignty over any of the natives on the Dembia River, or in the area between the Dembia south to the Sherebro River. The Foreign Secretary was at pains to point out, however, that any exchange of territory was to be subject to the final approval of Parliament.[10] The reply from the French Foreign Office in the form of a 'verbal note' by Count Daru in March 1870, was favourable.[11] At this juncture the only points which needed clarification before the exchange could be completed concerned the rights and privileges of English and French subjects who chose to remain in the territory ceded.

For almost a year after Kennedy's visit to Bathurst no official statement was given out by the government, nor was Parliament fully informed of the discussion underway with France. Nevertheless it was an open secret that negotiations were underway and the rumours spread rapidly even to the colony itself. The first discussion in Parliament relating to the negotiations took place almost two months after the acquiescence of the French government on the major proposal, on June 10, 1870, and only then did Prime Minister Gladstone assure Parliament that the government had no intention of completing the negotiations *sub-rosa* without submitting the whole matter to Parliamentary scrutiny.[12] Lord Granville in the House of Lords on

85

July 15, 1870, in reply to a question concerning a proposed transfer, said that he saw no reason to keep the place since it was of little use. He stated, 'While the colony would be of great advantage to the French in connection with their flourishing colony on Senegal, I think it no exaggeration to say that Gambia is to our country an absolute burden without any redeeming characteristics.'[13] Notwithstanding the opportunities given to the government on these occasions to discuss the details of the proposed negotiations, they did not do so, leaving those members of Parliament who were interested in the question to conjecture as to the real nature of the discussions.

The rumours of impending transfer were also rife in the Gambia. In April and May two petitions from inhabitants of Bathurst to the Colonial Office protested any ideas of a transfer. The first of these, signed by 517 people, was dismissed by the Colonial Office for the reason that most of those who signed were not property owners and therefore could have no interest in the exchange. The second petition was similarly dismissed by the authorities.[14] The uncertain state of affairs was complicated by the visit to Bathurst in June 1870, of the Governor of Senegal and the French Admiral commanding the West Coast fleet.[15] On July 5, Lord Lyons informed the Foreign Office that the Duke of Graumont had been informed that the English authorities were planning to leave the Gambia and that he had stated, 'Such being the case, the country could not . . . be left without a government to lapse into barbarism. What was it the British authorities meant? Should the French be asked to enter at once into the territory and take possession of it?'[16] The implication that the authorities in Bathurst were planning an immediate evacuation of the Gambia before negotiations had been completed was denied. Little evidence indicates that the Colonial Office communicated their plans in any detail to the Administrator and the inhabitants. The French may have been reassured on this point, but the persons most directly implicated were only allowed to speculate as to their future.

It was patent by the number of signatures on the two petitions sent to the Colonial Office that a fairly substantial number of the Gambians in the colony area did not wish to see the cession completed. One of the most powerful Gambian chiefs who had

86

been led to believe that the negotiations had been completed wrote the Queen:

> I Tomani Bojang, thank the Queen of England for all past favours; and as Your Majesty is aware that it was war that compelled me to give up a part of my territory to your people, I now beg, that should you desire to transfer your settlements to another person, I would rather you return my territory back to me as an act of friendship.[17]

The Colonial Office instructed the Administrator to inform the King of Kombo that they could not comply with such an unusual request.

The British merchants in the Gambia were concerned primarily with the possible pecuniary loss ensuing if the area changed hands. Even if one minimizes their statements concerning their investments in the Gambia, it was true that any cession would mean considerable loss of revenue. The firm of Forster and Smith outlined their situation very clearly in a letter to the Colonial Office in June 1870.[18] They claimed that they had over £100,000 invested in trade in West Africa. They wanted to be informed of the government's plans for the Gambia so that they could take steps to protect their investments. They stressed the point that they had never been able to carry on any amount of trade in areas controlled by the French. Their attitude was echoed by Thomas Brown, who apart from being the unofficial spokesman of the anti-cessionists in the Gambia, was also a member of the Legislative Council. In addition to other reasons which he put forward for keeping the Gambia, he noted that he had personally invested in the Gambia £28,500 in houses, warehouses, factories, and boats on which he expected to sustain a twenty-five per cent loss if the area was ceded. He calculated that if the cession took place he would sustain a two-thirds loss on the £35,000 that he had extended in credit to factories, traders, and natives in the upper river areas. An additional £16,000 had been invested in various goods, property, and machinery which would depreciate by fifteen per cent once the transfer had taken place.[19]

Commercial groups in England who had an interest in the Gambia, particularly the Manchester Chamber of Commerce, were also very active in trying to get a definite statement from the Colonial Office as to the policy that was going to be taken in regard to the Gambia. At the meetings of the commercial groups and in memorials they sent to the Colonial Office, the primary objections to the proposed exchange were stated. A great amount of such correspondence accumulated over a six year period, but the merchants never waivered in presenting a point by point refutation of the allegations made by Governor Kennedy.[20] In summary, their criticisms were:

1. The Gambia was the best waterway in West Africa. Sea-going ships could proceed 200 miles into the interior. Far from being, as alleged, a treacherous harbour the port of Bathurst was singularly free of fog and could moor the whole of the British fleet.

2. Trade in the Gambia was not in French hands. The statements by Kennedy and other government officials were based upon a superficial analysis of the trading situation. The merchants maintained that the bulk of the trade was in British or native hands even though most of the groundnut crop was carried in French ships. This was necessary, they claimed, because the bulk of the groundnut crop went to France. French ships were utilized because France charged a twenty per cent tax on all foreign carriers which docked at Marseilles. Despite this, the returns from trade went primarily into British hands.

3. Trade was not decreasing, but increasing. Sir Arthur Kennedy, by utilizing 1869 as the base year for his economic conclusions, used the one year when there had been a definite fall in revenue. This was because of droughts, the Soninki-Marabout Wars, and a series of plagues which struck the Gambia in the late '60s.

4. The native peoples in the Colony did not want to be French; they were happy and content under British protection, and until this opinion changed radically, British owed them continuing support.

5. The area to be exchanged for the Gambia was not comparable in value. French influence and interest in the areas proposed for exchange had failed considerably in the '50s and '60s. The Gambian colonies were as large and as affluent as any French colony on the West Coast, and controlled the waterway of the Gambia River. The potential for the future was immense.

6. British possessions on the Gambia were potentially valuable because from these the whole hinterland of the Senegambia could easily be absorbed. Thomas Brown warned, 'If you give up the Gambia to France, you virtually give up the Niger; for the French can easily get from Bathurst to Segoo on the Niger and will thus withdraw trade from the mouth of the river.'

Despite all these protests the government proceeded with its negotiations with France. After the 'verbal note' of 1870 all communications between the two governments were about technical problems such as compensation, slavery, and rights of free trade in the areas concerned. The matter of exchange had, in principle, been settled and the government assumed that when the time was appropriate Parliamentary approval would be granted. However important the settlement of spheres of influence in West Africa might be to those who had interests on the West Coast, the whole question was still minor as compared with other problems which the Cabinet had to face in 1870. Therefore Lord Granville informed France that due to pressure of other business, no transfer bill could be introduced into Parliament for that session.[21] Under normal circumstances this pause would have given the two governments time to work out the technical and specific details of the exchange. The outbreak of the Franco-Prussian War, however, presented new factors that brought the negotiations to a complete standstill. On July 23, 1870, Governor Kennedy was notified of the government's decision to postpone the whole matter until the issue between France and Prussia had been decided.[22] On August 4, the Foreign Office instructed its representatives in Paris to let the French know confidentially that nothing further could be done while the war continued.[23]

The four year period that followed before the reopening of negotiations involving the Gambia did not see any change in the official attitude towards the enclaves. In March 1871, Kennedy communicated to Kimberley further his ideas concerning the French in the vicinity of Sierra Leone and the desirability of making overtures to the new French government concerning an exchange of territory.[24] He felt that the French were prepared to agree to almost any exchange that would guarantee them the possession of the Gambia River. Kennedy reported that they were withdrawing their settlements from the leeward of Sierra Leone, which indicated to him that the time was ripe for a beginning of a *rapprochement*. Kimberley replied that while he thought Kennedy was correct in his over-all analysis, negotiations would have to be postponed for some future time when the outstanding domestic troubles and constitutional problems in France had been partly solved.

In the Gambia itself the government's declared policy to abandon MacCarthy Island had never really been put into total effect. The small garrison on MacCarthy Island had, however, been withdrawn, making it necessary for the inhabitants, under the leadership of Dr. James Horton, a Sierra Leonean who was then an assistant surgeon, to organize a militia defence of the island. Eventually the Administrator recognized the responsibility for defending the freed slaves and the defenceless population and did send a manager and some police constables to MacCarthy Island. This was, in effect, a negation of the order sent by the Colonial Secretary in 1866 concerning the disposition of the upper river areas, although the Colonial Office did not retreat from its theoretical position.[25] As has already been pointed out, the period of the early '70s saw new outbreaks of violence between the Soninki and the Marabouts. Administrator Kortright, caught up in the totally anomalous situation of trying to obey orders as well as giving protection to traders and to persons who claimed British protection in the upper river, was favourably inclined towards any kind of a shift in policy which would relieve him of this impossible task.

In April 1874, the French Ambassador, M. Gavard, called personally on Lord Derby to ascertain whether England was prepared to continue discussions. Soon afterwards the French Ambassador forwarded to the Foreign Office a memorandum stating the terms on which France would negotiate.[26] In return for the British cession of her Gambian possessions, France would give up the Mellacourie, Grand Bassam, and Assine and all claims to adjacent territory. Although convinced that proposals offered the best long range solution to any of the problems that might arise between the two powers, the Colonial Office requested their officials in the area to report their views once

again. Kortright, who at that time was faced with a new outbreak of native wars, reported his favourable attitude towards
the proposed exchange. Since he was still operating under the
no expansion dictum of 1866, the continued native disturbances
in the riverine areas adjacent to the colony presented insoluble
problems for his limited forces. Continually on the defensive
and separated from the agent on MacCarthy Island by hun-
dreds of miles of potentially hostile territory, he reported,

> These native wars in our immediate vicinity not only injure
> our trade, but are calculated at any moment to force us into a
> collision with one of the belligerents and I feel sure that the
> settlements can be safe only under the rule of a military Power.[27]

British defensive policy in the area could never provide the
kind of rule necessary to pacify the Soninki or Marabouts.
Failing this, continued occupation of Bathurst was expensive
and useless. Lord Carnarvon also communicated with Strahan,
the Governor of the Gold Coast settlements, and elicited the
opinion that possession of Assine and Grand Bassam was valuable. Strahan believed that control of this area was not only
desirable because it would exclude French traders, but also to
stop the smuggling of guns and ammunition to the Ashanti in
the north.[28] The Colonial Secretary again asked Sir Arthur
Kennedy for his opinions on the possible uses of the Gambia as
a military and naval base. Kennedy replied that the harbour
was difficult of access at all seasons and dangerous for several
months due to fog. In addition the climate was unhealthy and
there was no good water readily available. In his opinion
Goree and Dakar would always provide better harbour areas
than Bathurst.[29]

Thus armed with expert opinion, Lord Carnarvon was fully
prepared to endorse the plan to divide French and British
spheres according to the proposal that had been submitted to
him by Lord Derby. This plan was but a reiteration of the
British proposal of 1870 to divide West Africa between the two
powers on the line of the Dembia River.[30] Parliamentary
approval of any transfer, however, was necessary. It was here
that all the plans of the Colonial Office foundered. The pressure
groups acting upon Parliament were the same as those in 1870.

However, they were better organized, and from the Gambia itself there emerged Thomas Brown, a very articulate spokesman for the Gambian merchants. Brown and his colleagues in the latter part of 1875 bombarded the Colonial Office with communication after communication.[31] Since the points made were by men familiar with the whole territory of West Africa, their rebuttals had considerable effect on Parliamentary opinion.

It is impossible to ascertain ultimately how important were the petitions, letters, and pressure from the commercial representatives. Even though there was not much Parliamentary discussion on the matter in 1875-76, the government obviously believed the Parliamentary atmosphere to be far from receptive to the plan of exchange. If one understands that West Africa was considered a backwater to both the Foreign and Colonial Offices, the quick collapse of Carnarvon's plans is more understandable. There was no reason to give the impression to Parliament that the government was callously giving away British subjects and perhaps to precipitate more far reaching discussions. Lord Carnarvon explained in detail his negotiations to the House of Lords on February 17, 1876, with the assurance that nothing would be done without Parliamentary approval.[32] Two days later the matter was discussed in the Cabinet, and it was decided not to press the issue at that time. It was arranged that Disraeli should announce in the Commons the appointment of a Parliamentary Committee.[33] Thus Parliament would be made a party to any final disposition. This plan was never put into effect because of what appeared to be a sudden withdrawal by the French of their previous proposals. Acting on the French communication, the government announced on March 20, 1876, that all negotiations concerning the Gambia had been brought to an end.[34]

This sudden move by the French is inexplicable unless one believes their Ambassador's statement that France never intended to break off discussions. He claimed later that they had only intended to inquire,

what was the meaning of an expression which Her Majesty's Government had made use of with regard to influence on the

Coast, and that far from desiring to break off the negotiation, they would have been prepared to continue it on the terms of Her Majesty's Government or to agree to all that Her Majesty's Government desired.[35]

Although this may have been their intention, in the years following it became the policy of the French to procrastinate. The withdrawal of their proposal could have been an early example of these delaying tactics. Throughout the negotiations after 1876, the French believed it would be only a matter of time before the Gambian settlements became French. Their technical questions which were raised so hazily, however, coincided with what appeared to the British government to be Parliamentary opposition. The French reluctance was thus used as an excuse to postpone the question of exchange till a more favourable time.

In retrospect there are a number of reasons why the British tried so hard in this period to reach a *rapprochement* with France about the Gambia. West Africa in general and the Gambia in particular were little known to the government officials at home. Even though much had been written about the potential economic advantage of possessing a waterway such as the Gambia River, these writings were either not known by the Colonial Office officials or they were considered to be of dubious value. As has already been shown, no real thorough exploration of the hinterlands had occurred in the period from 1830 to 1880. Therefore the Colonial Office depended primarily upon their expert in the field, Sir Arthur Kennedy, to supply them with the necessary information. Kennedy saw the area as a totally backward one which was constantly draining money and equipment from what he considered to be more important areas in West Africa. Due to his lack of knowledge, therefore, he recommended that the Gambia should be traded for anything which could be conceived to be better. Part of the reason for Kennedy's point of view, of course, was the continuing Soninki-Marabout Wars. The problems caused by these wars were almost insoluble, considering the orders which the Colonial Office had given to the Administrators of the Gambia. The estimates of cost which Kennedy utilized were provided for him by the Administrator's Office. In many cases these were not very accurate statistics, and throughout the time of the negotiations, from 1866 to 1888, the Gambian estimates and expenses were calculated as a part of those of Sierra Leone. Therefore it was very difficult to arrive, at any given time, at the true cost of administering the Gambia. One fact does stand out very clearly and that is that the Gambia settlements were, despite their poverty, self sufficient entities with usually a healthy surplus in the budget, whereas Sierra Leone cost much more to administer, and its finances were in a worse state than those of the Gambia. However, no serious consideration was ever given to the abandonment of Sierra Leone primarily because of the historical connection with Britain. Sierra Leone was an experimental colony. The humanitarians would never agree to the evacuation of that colony.

In all these early negotiations the British displayed a degree of perhaps accidental statemanship not usually found in colonial diplomacy. This was particularly noteworthy considering their ignorance of the West African area and their almost overpowering desire to rid themselves of colonial responsibility. Perhaps the greatest reason for their pursuance of the negotiations was the desire, however theoretical, to get a solid block of territory which was recognized as a sphere of influence of Great Britain. This recognition would have given Britain a large territory, recognized by all European powers as the equivalent of a British protectorate, but one that would not have necessitated the expense of a regular protectorate. In order to accomplish this aim Britain had to arrive at a *quid pro quo* with France. France in the period of negotiations from 1870-76 did not value its possessions in the south any more than did Britain in the north. Therefore if the exchange could have been brought about, it would have minimized to a very large degree the clashes and diplomatic wrangling that occurred between France and England throughout West Africa in the '80s and '90s.

The collapse of the negotiations in 1876 did not mean an end of the Gambian question. However, the nature of the negotiations did change in the twenty year period after 1876. Throughout the previous negotiations the French and English had been on a relatively equal footing concerning possessions in West

Africa. The French desired the Gambia because it stood in the way of their already established bases to the north and south of that river. This did not imply a re-evaluation on the part of the French of the worth of colonies in general and the West African colonies in particular. Although the French continued to want the Gambia River after 1876, the problem of the French and British spheres assumed a real, rather than a theoretical, delineation. The proposals by the English in the previous negotiations that the line of the Dembia River should be established as a point of demarkation had been essentially theoretical. However, the French in the latter part of the '70s and throughout the decade of the '80s began to advance from their established bases in the coastal region into the deep hinterland, making treaties with native chieftains, occupying territory, and eventually conquering the stronger of the hinterland kingdoms. The negotiations concerning the Gambia in this latter period are not parochial or concerned only with the exchange of a few bases. These negotiations merge with the larger problem of a suitable settlement which would define French areas and British spheres of occupation throughout West Africa. It is in this larger context that the fate of the Gambia at the conference table must be viewed.

Chapter Six

DRAWING THE BOUNDARY

THE settlement of the question of possession of the Gambia was an integral part of the diplomacy of European expansion in Africa which has been called the 'scramble for Africa'. In this period Africa was seized territorially by the great powers and abitrarily parcelled out by a series of agreements which betrayed little knowledge of the African environment. The nation primarily responsible for precipitating this division in West and Central Africa was France. As has already been noted, France had been as little concerned with territorial acquisitions prior to 1875 as had Britain. However, new forces within France changed the older policy of trading imperialism to that of territorial imperialism. Before one can understand the lengthy negotiations which resulted in the ludicrous boundaries of the Gambia it is necessary to look more closely at these French attitudes and their consequences for the whole of West Africa.

In the first years of the Third Republic one can note three major causes for the revival of interest in an overseas empire. These were scientific curiosity, wounded pride, and the economic factor. The many expeditions that had penetrated into all sections of Africa by 1875 had uncovered secrets which previously had been hidden from Europe. The subsequent reports of the first of the explorers resulted in the formation of scientific societies throughout Europe; these then sponsored

96

more investigations. Stories of real and potential wealth mingled with exotic tales of strange people and descriptions of the horrors of the slave trade. These reports stirred the imagination of a whole generation of Civil Servants and military men.

France had been defeated in the Franco-Prussian War, and although French statesmen could dream of a war of revenge, they could not afford a resumption of hostilities in Europe. Bismarck had successfully isolated France diplomatically, and blocked in their desire to be the dominant power in Europe, many French statesmen looked beyond Europe for the fulfilment of their ideals of a greater France. In the twenty year period after 1875 this romantic notion seized a sufficient number of men who were powerful enough to implement expansion in Africa even in the teeth of Parliamentary opposition.

The economic factor, however, was the most important. This economic interest was not concerned with romantic tales of the great wealth of the interior, but with the hard headed drive for markets. France had become an industrial power, and in competition with Britain turned away from theories of free trade. French economists and politicians of the period were interested in a reimposition of a new type of mercantilism. Colonies, as guaranteed markets and as sources of raw materials were a necessity to them. One of the best statements of the economic reasons for the new expansion was given by M. Jules Ferry twice Premier of France, who said,

> Is it not clear that for all great powers of modern Europe, since their industrial power commenced, there is posed an immense and difficult problem, which is the basis of industrial life, the very condition of existence—the question of 'markets'? Have you not seen the great industrial nations one by one arrive at a colonial policy? And can we say that this colonial policy is a lunacy for modern nations? Not at all, messieurs, this policy is, for all of us, a necessity, like the 'market' itself.[1]

The vast, newly discovered hinterlands of Africa were open for the taking. Such ventures would satisfy all three needs. Further exploration would be necessary, wounded pride would be salved by the military conquests, and France would have her economic outlets in the new overseas empire.

Such ideas were not original to France. Leopold of Belgium could be said to be the first to have recognized the worth of hitherto unclaimed Africa. It was in response to his pseudo-humanitarian undertaking that in 1884 the Conference of Berlin was called, which not only recognized the Congo Free State, but defined 'effective occupation' as the final proof of ownership of African territory.[2]

The French found unexpected allies in their new expansion. Prince Bismarck, himself uninterested in colonies, welcomed the new French moves because they would upset Britain and because the French overseas victories night help them forget Alsace and Lorraine.[3] In the face of this revived French colonialism the British maintained their no expansion dictum first enunciated in the '60s. Britain finally became deeply involved in Egypt after 1882, and the French utilized these commitments as a lever to demand that Britain should recognize their new expansion elsewhere in Africa.[4] Effectively aided diplomatically by Bismarck and the new German empire at the conference table, the French, in the late '70s and throughout the '80s, expanded their control in West and Central Africa. This was accomplished in two interconnected ways. They established themselves strongly in their old coastal bases, and using these trading posts, French traders and officials moved laterally up the coast encroaching on areas that had previously been British spheres. From these same bases and from Algeria France also sent quasi-military expeditions deep into the hitherto unexplored hinterlands. Wherever the French went they signed treaties of protection or cession with the local rulers, and in some cases set up administrative posts and began to regulate trade and access customs duties.

On the Slave Coast, Cotonou was reoccupied, and in 1882, a Protectorate was proclaimed over the Porto Novo area. By 1885 France claimed control of the coast as far west as Anecho in Togoland. In 1886 the forts on the Ivory Coast were reoccupied and government officials quickly made treaties with the coastal chiefs which gave France control of the coastline from Liberia to the Gold Coast.[5] Between 1879 and 1882, France consolidated her position in the Mellacourie immediately adjacent to Sierra Leone.[6] Conakry was occupied in 1887, and in the years immediately following the French gained treaties which completed their coastal claims from Sierra Leone to Portuguese Guinea.

Concurrently French explorers and military columns were probing deep into the interior. Colonel Galleni occupied Bamako on the Niger in 1883.[7] From this strategic position the French made treaties by which Samory, titular overlord of the Mande, an adventurer who had made himself master of one of the greatest domains in the western Sudan, accepted French protection. Ahmadu, ruler of the Tucolor empire, was also linked by treaty to France, and from Bamako new quasi-military explorations were launched. Binger reached the great bend of the Niger River in 1887, and an exploring column under Lieutenant Caron arrived at Timbuctu early in 1888.[8] In the same year there were three French steamers operating on the Niger, and by 1890 a regular trade and communications link had been established between Bamako and the Ivory Coast. How serious a threat to British West African spheres these combined explorations and new Protectorates were is shown by Colonel Galleni's statement in 1889 when he wrote, 'Our Protectorate extends thus along the right Niger bank from Segou as far as Sierra Leone and the Republic of Liberia encircling thus the whole Fouta D'Jallon.'[9]

Thus by the time negotiations between France and England about the Gambia had been resumed, the colonial climate had changed. French officers and traders on the spot, encouraged directly and indirectly by their government, were systematically occupying the hinterland during the 1880s. French diplomats, fully aware of the changed conditions, followed a course of procrastination, either waiting until certain disputed areas had been occupied or until treaties had been signed between the chief, and the French representatives. France would then adopt an adamant diplomatic stand, forcing Britain to recognize that which she had at first protested against. The most astute Colonial Office official, Arthur Hemming, was almost alone in realizing this and even to him the revelation came late. In a minute written in 1887, he said of the French,

They are fully alive to the truth of possession being nine points of the law. We on the other hand are so scrupulous and squeamish that even before the discussion is opened, we instruct our Governor to refrain from taking the only steps which will check the advance of the French.[10]

Official British attitude towards the exchange of the Gambia had not altered since the collapse of negotiations in 1876. The long, drawn out correspondence involving French and English spheres in the Mellacourie area adjacent to Sierra Leone revived briefly the Gambia discussions that had been broken off three years previously. Lord Lyons, the British Ambassador in Paris, early in this phase of negotiations reported that M. Waddington had told him that one of the conditions for a satisfactory settlement of the differences between the two nations was the cession of the Gambia. Waddington was informed that since Parliament was opposed, Britain could not consider the Gambia as negotiable for the settlement of the Mellacourie difficulties.[11] The Foreign and Colonial Offices still viewed the exchange favourably, but they did not want a reiteration of the furor 1875-76. They expected to use the Gambia only as a last resort to gain French concessions. Sir Julian Pauncefote expressed this when he wrote in a memo,

> Exchange of the Gambia shows how desirable an arrange- ment it really was, and it may become a matter of Imperial necessity to carry it out even now in order to avoid the inevit- able consequences of the present complications which are rapidly increasing.[12]

Nevertheless the Foreign Office stand was maintained and the Mellacourie settlement was reached without bringing the Gambia seriously into the negotiations.

The Convention of 1882 which granted France possession of most of her claims in the vicinity of Sierra Leone also called for the *status quo* to be maintained in West Africa.[13] This conven- tion which could have become the basis of an equitable settle- ment was never ratified by France. Notwithstanding this and continued evidence that France had no intention of honouring the *status quo*, the Colonial Office viewed the agreement as binding on her officials. Despite the overwhelming evidence of French activity throughout West Africa, Britain hesitated to follow the same course of action.

Administrator Gouldsbury in his upper river explorations in 1881, entered into a number of treaties with the king of Futa Jallon and other upper Gambian chiefs. These were not followed up by token occupation nor did Britain press any prior claims to this area.[14] It was patent throughout the '80s that the depredations of native chiefs such as Fodi Silla, Fodi Kabba, and Said Matti could only be ended by intervention. This was particularly true of the north shore where in the years 1885-87, Said Matti disrupted the whole of Baddibu and eventually invaded Sine-Saloum. The British Administrator, Carter, merely tried to mediate between the protagonists. The French, however, sent a column to aid the king of Sine-Saloum and defeated Said Matti. The ensuing disturbances in Baddibu gave the French the opportunity to move into the area in force and occupy a number of towns on the very banks of the Gambia River.[15] Nor was this the only part of the Gambia where French activity threatened to gain what had been denied them at the conference table. In foreign Kombo the French were negotiating with Fodi Silla for the transfer of that area immediately adjacent to Bathurst and they were also extremely active in Kiang and Jarra.[16]

Thus, faced with losing the Gambia by occupation and still without suitable guarantees relating to respective spheres elsewhere, Britain began in 1887 to press for a new conference to settle these difficult questions finally. The French government procrastinated throughout 1888 and the meeting between British and French delegates did not begin until April 1889. Despite the presence of French forces on the banks of the Gambia, the Colonial Office would not give instructions to its officers to counter-move by entering into treaties or even by visiting disputed areas while the negotiations were pending.[17] Arthur Hemming alone of Colonial Office officials protested against this defensive position. He recommended the removal of the prohibitions against mixing in the affairs of the Gambia hinterland and believed that the Colonial Office should authorize the Administrator to 'hoist flags at all landing places which he can reach where the natives will accept the British flag'.[18] He stated this position again in August 1888, when he wrote,

101

I think we are too scrupulous on these points and that we frequently lose much by being so—e.g., we instructed Sir S. Rowe when he was at the Gambia to refrain from hoisting the British flag at any point on the north bank of the river because we were in correspondence with the French on the subject, and the consequence was that the French, being undeterred by such scruples extended their operations and established themselves at places from which we should otherwise have excluded them.[19]

Meade, the permanent Under Secretary, reflecting the dominant view, replied to the former note that Britain 'cannot begin a flag waving crusade'[20] and footnoted the latter statement with 'we cannot be too scrupulous'.[21]

On the eve of the opening of the conference the British position was theoretically the same as that stated in 1876. Sierra Leone was the most important British possession in West Africa, and therefore the major attempt of the British delegates would be to assure adequate provisions for the security of that area. Complementary to this was their desire to secure stable areas of influence between the British and French in all West Africa. The Gambia was again viewed as worthless except for bargaining purposes. Confirming this conception was the comprehensive intelligence report prepared for the Foreign Office by the Chief of Military Intelligence, General Brackenbury, and the working memo written by Hemming in November 1888.[22] Thus Britain entered the conference with her basic ideas concerning West Africa unchanged, but with the recognition that the reality of occupation had placed them at a disadvantage.

After numerous delays the Conference opened in Paris in April 1889. The British delegation was headed by E. H. Egerton of the Foreign Office and Arthur Hemming, the Colonial Office expert on West African affairs. The French delegates were M. Nisard, Director of Department of Protectorates of the Ministry of Foreign Affairs, and M. Bayol, Governor of Senegal. In a series of informal meetings which lasted until mid-June, the whole range of conflicting claims was reviewed.[23] It became apparent to the British delegates early in the discussions that it would be impossible to get the neat, clear division between spheres of influence drawn along the line of the Dembia River as had previously been sought. The French, negotiating from a position of strength, showed no intention of retreating from the coastal and hinterland areas occupied since 1882.[24] This forced a change in the direction of British policy concerning West Africa. The change of attitude was in line with General Brackenbury's advice that he would not 'recommend the surrender of the Gambia . . . unless it were accompanied by the surrender by the French of their Gold and Slave Coast possessions'.[25] He advised that if no suitable general division could be obtained, the Commissioners should try to secure the best boundaries possible, particularly in the vicinity of Sierra Leone.

The changed attitude of the British negotiators was particularly noticeable in their views of the Gambia. Where the Colonial Office had previously been more than willing to give up the whole area, the Commissioners now began to work towards getting the French to recognize British claims to both banks of the river itself. At the third general session this limited objective was gained. The French delegates admitted in principle that the Gambia was a British river and that a certain control of the riverine territory was necessary to maintain this. M. Bayol drew two lines upon a map from the mouth of the river to Yarbutenda and stated that within these lines was the territory that could reasonably be assigned to Britain. Instead of pressing for more of the hinterland, Hemming was overjoyed as he reported that 'we have obtained from the French an admission that they ought not to occupy any portion of the actual banks of the river within its navigable limits and we are justified in claiming the exclusive control of the riverine territories'.[26]

Hemming wrote to Meade on July 2 that the delegates had come to an agreement upon the British area of control on the Gambia.[27] The description of the agreed boundaries was almost the same as that of the final convention which constrained British occupation rights to ten kilometers north and south as far up river as Yarbutenda.[28] Hemming noted, 'We tried to get the French to let the line begin from a point further north than Jinnack Creek—but they were very firm on this point and it did not seem necessary to stand fast.'[29] Annexe No. 2 of the final convention further clarified the terminology which was considered important for the survey teams that would draw the boundary on a ten kilometer radius from the centre of the town of Yarbutenda.[30]

Once the French had recognized the changed picture of the Gambia in the negotiations, rough boundary agreements were established between the two nations in the coastal regions of West Africa. At Porto Novo the Ager River as far into the interior as the ninth parallel[31] was agreed upon. The boundary at Assine was tentatively agreed and in Sierra Leone the line laid down by the 1882 convention was accepted as far inland as 13° longitude.[32] Although the Convention, signed on August 10, 1889 and ratified in November was not a final, completely definitive statement of West African boundaries, it did much to regularize coastal occupation and laid the groundwork for the series of agreements of the '90s which would finish the boundary demarcation in West Africa. Hemming's comment might sum up the attitude of the Colonial Office towards the Convention. He stated,

> We have not got by any means all we wanted or perhaps all we ought to have—but looking to the position and activity of the French in West Africa and on the other hand our *passivity*, I think it is a great thing to come to some distinct and definite agreement as to boundaries so that we may know exactly where we are.[33]

The practical applications of the Convention were important for the Gambia. By excluding the French from the river Britain assumed responsibility for assuring peace, order, and government in the restricted area alloted to her. In anticipation of such an agreement, the administration of the Colony had been separated from Sierra Leone in 1888.[34] Treaties were signed with most of the riverine chiefs and a Protectorate system of government based upon these chiefs and supervised by Travelling Commissioners was declared in 1894.[35] Within a short period the chaotic conditions engendered by the Soninki-Marabout Wars were arrested and British authority recognized throughout the small enclave.

The problems of giving real effect to the agreement of 1889

proved extremely difficult due in part to the serpentine course
of the river. No really accurate survey had been made of the
river, and therefore the maps available to the home government
and to the surveying teams were far from accurate. This inadequate information led to a minor crisis in 1893 when the French
temporarily occupied Niambantang and Panchang. Governor
Llewellyn, working from an official map, reported to the
Colonial Office that both villages were on British territory and
requested vigorous protests.[36] Llewellyn was reprimanded for
what was considered his bellicose stand and the difficulty was
eventually settled by more accurate surveys which placed one
village in French territory. Surveying teams composed of both
British and French were sent to define the boundary in 1891,
1895, 1898, and 1904.[37] The first surveying parties met with a
hostile reception from adherents of Fodi Kabba and it was
necessary to send gunboats to protect them while they worked
in the lower river.[38] With the exception of the extreme upper
river area, the original convention line was only slightly modified by the surveyors. The most important modificat'ons were
those contained in a 'verbal process' signed by the Commissioners in 1891.[39] The British government was most scrupulous
in trying to see that the spirit of the agreement was in effect
carried out. This was apparent when Chamberlain refused to
consider broaching the subject of a modification suggested by
Llewellyn which would have given the British sole possession
of a creek which had been found to be navigable[40] after the
Convention.

The worst portion of the boundary to define on the ground
was the upper end at Yarbutenda. The difficulty arose because
the site of Yarbutenda as shown on the maps used in Paris was
erroneously located. The old village located on the south bank
had been abandoned. The survey Commission of 1891 discovered that traders' huts had been built on both sides of the
river, but that more had been located on the north than the
south. The surveyors in 1898 agreed to accept the northern
location as the town.[41] However, the Governor of Senegal and
the French home government refused to accept this decision
immediately. Only in December 1901 did the French accept
the proposal.[42] This decision, however, did not settle the prob-

lem and due to later complications that area of the Gambia has still not been satisfactorily determined on the ground.

Governor Llewellyn was convinced that the French government would procrastinate in every way possible in the hope that the British would reconsider an exchange of the Gambia. The Colonial Office was also not immediately reconciled to the necessity of keeping the area. Hemming had believed that British control of the river would soon bring the French to consider a more favourable exchange. In regard to British interests he had said, 'If under the circumstances our traders cannot draw the bulk of the trade to the river, they ought to be able to do so and deserve no further assistance and encouragement.'[43] This attitude was echoed by the Administrator, G. T. Carter, who felt that there had been no need to press for a more northerly boundary 'since trade will take its own course and the best way for this to go is to the river'.[44] However, Governor Llewellyn was of a different mind. When it seemed that the largest portion of troops available to him would be withdrawn from the Gambia in 1893 he wrote to Hemming,

> Don't withdraw troops. Everything I do here causes the French anxiety. We should place a high value on the Gambia. Let me proceed with my policy of extending English control. I hope that is to be the policy—it is the one I recommend and can best carry out—don't keep me here idle.[45]

Although by 1900 the boundary, with the exception of Yarbutenda, had been demarcated by three survey teams, there had been no ratification of the whole work by the French. Llewellyn continually pressed for ratification so that the temporary boundary markers could be replaced with permanent ones. This approval was not forthcoming until Sir Edmund Monson, the British Ambassador, protested directly to M. Delcasse late in 1901. Monson on the same day wrote a dispatch in which he said,

> . . . I think it right to remark . . . that the suspicion at once occurred to me that in a subordinate there may be reluctance to agree to any step which may have the appearance of acquiescence on the part of the French government in the impossibility of obtaining the cession of the Gambia as compensation for the

abandonment of their rights on the Treaty Shore of Newfoundland.[46]

M. Delcasse assured Monson that he had repeatedly given instructions to M. Cambon, their Ambassador in London, to assure the British of French acceptance of the boundary. As a result of this conversation Cambon on December 4, 1901, accepted the arrangement.[47] This acceptance led in 1904 to the replacement of the temporary markers by permanent ones.[48] Ostensibly then the major boundary difficulties were over.

The conjecture of Monson's concerning French procrastination seems reasonable, and it was probably M. Cambon in conjunction with lesser French officials in the Senegal who was responsible. A telling remark which supports this thesis was made by M. Cambon in 1912 when he was introduced to the new Governor of the Gambia, Sir Henry Galway. Cambon stated, 'Aye, for fourteen years I tried to get Gambia for France.'[49] In any event French authorities in the period before World War I continued to be extremely active in trying to gain the Gambia River. One way to accomplish this goal was to encroach legally upon the river so as to make the port of Bathurst less valuable. In 1893 Lord Roseberry had written to the British Ambassador that under no circumstances would England entertain any proposals that would extend French territory to either bank of the Gambia River.[50] Yet ten years later this was conceded by the Convention of 1904 between Britain and France respecting Newfoundland and West and Central Africa.[51] Article 5 of that agreement ceded Yarbutenda to France with the stipulation that if the river was not navigable for maritime vessels, then 'access shall be assured to the French Government at a point lower down on the River Gambia which shall be recognized by mutual agreement as being accessible to merchant ships engaged in maritime navigation'.

As a result of this agreement Governor Denton who was on leave in England was directed to meet M. Roume, the Governor of Senegal, in Paris to work out the practical details. The discussions settled nothing, but they did bring out clearly the desires of the French. M. Roume felt that the terms of the Convention granted Yarbutenda directly to France, and when informed that ships with a draft of over ten feet could not use the port, he then wanted Yarbutenda and an enclave on the lower river with four routes of access. This enclave was to be ceded and not rented. In the enclave French law, money, and customs would prevail. Denton commented upon these claims and stated that 'an acceptance of M. Roume's claim means actual ruin to the Gambia. It is not a rich Colony and even under the strictest conditions the establishment of an enclave on the lower river will most seriously injure its import and export trade'.[52]

The Foreign Office concurred in the view that French demands were exorbitant and would be resisted.[53] In 1906 the Foreign Office prepared a lengthy minute which detailed the legal position of the agreement of 1904. The salient points were:

1. Yarbutenda was ceded outright but the French cannot claim its possession and a point down river.

2. An enclave would be necessary down river if Yarbutenda was not navigable to maritime vessels. A question of what constitutes navigability therefore arose. The position to maintain was that ten feet of water was enough.

3. If enclave is given, no lease was possible. The Convention gave only rights of access for an indefinite period. The French cannot be prevented from having access to both north and south banks.

The minute paper suggested that a Commission should go out to investigate possible ways of avoiding the grant of an enclave.[54]

Support for Governor Denton's position that the situation had been created by the French to gain the whole river came from the British Consul in Dakar. He wrote,

> I have come to the conclusion that, having failed to obtain the whole Colony of the Gambia as they had hoped, an effort is now to be made to obtain such a footing in the Colony as will practically ruin it, and thereby pave the way for obtaining its complete cession at some future date.[55]

In March 1910, a French Commission under M. Hardel spent considerable time in the Gambia surveying the most likely sites for the enclave. His recommendations are contained in a ninety page report.[56] His observations were that Yarbutenda was not adequate for ocean going vessels. To be adequate a port facility should have eight meters of water. In view of the conditions of Yarbutenda, the French should demand an enclave at either Sitololo or Carrol's Wharf on the north bank. These places were approximately one hundred and fifty kilometers from Bathurst, had the required depth of water, and were conveniently located for projected rail lines to connect with Dakar. The place Hardel chose on the south bank was Oualicounda which provided seven and one half meters of draft. He suggested that the government demand on the north an enclave of 1,500 meters along the river, 500 meters deep. On the south the size should be 1,000 meters long and 200 meters deep.

Concurrent with these developments were various proposals for a direct exchange of the Gambia for other territories or the abandonment by France of treaty rights in other areas. Governor Roume suggested that certain areas of the French empire which were not very valuable to France should be exchanged. The twin islands of St. Pierre and Miquelon were briefly considered, but were rejected because Roume was certain that Britain would never agree to such an exchange.[57] A more fruitful prospect for trade concerned the liquidation of French claims to the New Hebrides for the Gambia. This seemed a logical proposal because of pressure by Australia and New Zealand upon the home government for complete British control of the New Hebrides. In a most lucid critique of the whole problem M. Roume outlined the traditional French approach to the Gambia River and strongly suggested such a trade.[58] Feeler proposals in this direction were coolly received by the British Foreign Office and the scheme was never seriously followed up.

The concessions granted by the Convention of 1904 were never claimed by the French, and after 1910 they stopped pressing Britain for enclaves or exchanges of territory. There are many reasons for this seeming *volte face*. The most important fact was that Britain was no longer a colonial rival or potential enemy. Larger political considerations dictated that no unnecessary strains should be placed upon the newly built *entente*.[59] The First World War and the building of the Dakar-Kayes-Bamako Railway and the concentration of new capital in secondary ports such as Kaolack and Ziganchour made the possession of the Gambia less important to France. After 1918, virtually all diplomatic activity concerning the Gambia ceased. Thus what was viewed by the delegates who signed the Convention of 1889 as a temporary expedient became a permanent political reality. The Gambia remained a tiny, poor, non-viable area, a charge upon the British government who could do little because of the imposition of unrealistic boundaries.

Viewed not from its present position, but in reference to its role in the 'scramble for Africa', the Gambia becomes a key factor for understanding West Africa at that time. Its present boundaries attest to the passivity of the British and the activity of the French, not only in the field, but also at the conference table. The Gambia in this type of analysis becomes a classic case of the unreality of European diplomacy in the last quarter of the nineteenth century.

The settlement of the boundary and the imposition of British rule brought almost immediate peace to the riverine territory. The Colonial Office, however, did not become reconciled to keeping the Colony and Protectorate until after World War I. Therefore the political institutions and economic policies were framed as temporary measures. The nineteenth century standard that colonies should not cost money was held to be even more applicable for an area which had been considered worthless. Any proposed political system for keeping law and order in the Protectorate would be constrained to meet this qualification of thrift first. Thus the establishment of British authority saw the imposition of indirect rule in the Protectorate. Circumstances conspired to keep this system alive long after its usefulness was at an end, and tended to nullify any bold economic or political plans for the Gambia.

Chapter Seven

GOVERNING THE PROTECTORATE

THE nature of the relationship between Britain and the peoples of the hinterland of the Gambia was changed with the sign- ing of the Convention of 1889. Whereas prior to this time Britain had followed a declared policy of minimum interference in the affairs of the interior, she now faced the problem of establishing a governmental system for the territories assigned to her by the agreement. This was necessary even though the responsible officials still viewed the small riverine enclave as only a tem- porary possession. However, little could be done to establish a thorough going system of government for the Protectorate until the actual boundary line had been settled. For the four years after 1889, therefore, the actual relationship between the Colony government and the Protectorate changed very little. Governor Llewellyn and the Colonial Office, nevertheless, were busy in this transition period trying to create a system of government to deal with the many problems presented by the new Protectorate.

Those responsible for the institution of the new rule were generally ignorant of the details of the tribal societies over which they were to rule. Equally they had little knowledge of Islamic and customary law. The Soninki-Marabout Wars which had devastated the Gambia for well over fifty years had not been successfully ended in certain portions of the territory and the deep scars that had been left by this internecine warfare were still present. Another major unanswered question was how the traditional rulers would accept their new status. It was known that some of the more prominent chiefs harboured grudges against individual European traders and the colonial administration in Bathurst. Areas of jurisdiction between rival chiefs were not known in detail by the Governor. The government was aware that in many areas the old traditional chieftainships had been totally destroyed by the wars and that in some areas there was almost a total vacuum of authority. In certain other places a new dynasty had forced itself upon a reluctant population. Slavery was another disturbing institution which had to be contended with. As long as Britain did not exercise direct authority the practice of slavery, or for that matter the internal slave trade, could be ignored, but with the assumption of responsibility it followed logically that any British agent in the Protectorate area should be morally committed to wiping out this practice. Restricting the effectiveness of a general governmental system for the Protectorate was the known fact that the colonial authorities in the home government did not wish to expend large sums of money upon ruling an area which might be transferred to France at any time. Therefore Llewellyn had to devise some system which would give the maximum latitude to native government and practices, but which would nevertheless impose the reality of British authority throughout the Gambia. This would have to be done at a minimum expense and the system devised would of necessity be based upon a restricted knowledge of the peoples and their customs in the area to be governed. Under such circumstances the only practical way of approaching the control of the hinterland areas was through some system of indirect rule.

British application of indirect rule, which later became associated with the practices of Lord Lugard in Nigeria and Sir Donald Cameron in Tanganyika, was not a new theory. Almost every imperial power from the time of Alexander the Great until modern times had resorted to some form of rule through duly constituted authorities when faced with the problem of ruling a numerically superior people. The British had been most successful in this type of administration in the conquest and continued British rule in India. Although the system devised by Llewellyn and the Colonial Office for control of the Protectorate of the Gambia was new to the African continent, there had been previous examples to follow elsewhere in the Empire.

The correspondence of Governor Llewellyn in 1893 shows some of the problems which he faced in trying to create a new administration out of little or nothing. He related from his own experience that 'I have found in most of the towns that the *Alcaides* are old and effete men quite unable to control the people and often very bigoted and prejudiced against the introduction of any changes, whilst the younger generation are far more ameanable to reason.'[1] Thus he was fully aware of the implications of officially establishing such men in control of large areas. Later that year in a letter to the Colonial Secretary, he asked to be informed about Mohammedan law as it was used elsewhere in the Empire so that he could perhaps better understand its interrelationship with English civil and criminal practices.[2] However, long before the finalization of the first Protectorate Ordinance gave a sense of unity to the government of the Protectorate, indirect rule had been established by the appointment, in January 1893, of a Travelling Commissioner for the north bank and a Travelling Commissioner for the south bank.[3] The function of these officials, Mr. Ozanne and Mr. Sitwell, was to move from village to village in the areas assigned to them and inform the chiefs of the impending changes which were to take place. They were also to gradually assert their positions, wherever practicable, to allow the chiefs and the people to know that the Commissioners represented the final authority of the Governor resident in Bathurst.

Commissioner Ozanne in his first report of July 1893 gave a glimpse of his method of operation and also of the difficulties which faced him in his position.[4] His district began at Suara Creek, thirty-two miles from Bathurst, and extended past Niambantang, approximately one hundred and twenty-six miles up river. Except for a few native servants, he travelled alone throughout most of the district on foot. His practice was to begin at the near end of his district, visit each major village until he had traversed the length of the district, and then double back and repeat the procedure in the down river direction. Ozanne would generally stay about three days at each place; he would talk leisurely to the chiefs and their advisors explaining their new position and the desires of the crown, and listen to the complaints and the problems of the people. If he discovered that there had been any fighting or any civil disobedience he would hold a trial with the *Alcaide* and, 'give a fine according to the native laws, generally reducing the penalties if I found them too severe'. Ozanne found that the natives in Baddibu who were primarily Mandingos and those in Saloum who were primarily Wolofs were very strict Mohammedans. They were almost without exception very grave and very polite individually, and he was particularly impressed with the good order which he found throughout his district. This was the more surprising because of the disorder which had been endemic throughout the area for such a long period of time and which had played such an important role in the European occupation of the hinterlands. Ozanne was struck not only with their good order, but also with their lack of ambition measured by European standards. And he noted that the one factor that made possible a control over such a large area by the Europeans was that the natives from the chief down to the lowest classes stood in awe of a white man. Ozanne reported that the chiefs and other important members in the village were afraid of only one thing—that they would not be able to keep their slaves under the new regime. However much they disliked the French, and they referred to French rule as 'the French yoke', they pointed out to Ozanne that if the French had become the major power in the river they would not have had to worry about the legality of slave owning. Ozanne's feelings toward immediate practical abolition of slavery were seconded by Governor Llewellyn who argued that to attempt mass abolition at that time would be a most dangerous policy. Nevertheless in 1894 the government abolished the slave trade by Ordinance,[5] and it was reported that in the following year the Travelling Commissioners on their own discretion had freed ninety-seven slaves.[6] The government reasoned that this much safer go-slow policy which made slave trading illegal, and the adoption by the Commissioners of a strong moral attitude against slavery, would eventually cause the practice to wither away.[7] However, little could be done to make the government policy totally effective as long as Musa Mollah and Fodi Silla were still operative. The destruction of their power in 1901 brought an end to most of the surreptitious slave trade. The punitive expedition that defeated them enhanced the position of the Commissioners and the central government, and enabled the authorities to take a hard line concerning slavery. By the time of the First World War slavery in the Gambia was represented only by the caste system which relegated ex-slaves and their children to a low position in village life.

Meanwhile the government was attempting to give a legal substance to the position of the Commissioners in the interior. In November 1893, an Order in Council gave the Legislative Council of the Colony power to make rules by Ordinances for the administration of the Protectorate.[8] This opened the way for the Administrator to quickly establish, by a series of Ordinances, the basic laws of the Protectorate without having to refer all these matters to the United Kingdom for approval. Previously in March of that year Llewellyn had submitted to the Colonial Office for their approval a draft Ordinance which was concerned with the establishment of courts of summary jurisdiction in the territories.[9] The trend of the Governor's thinking can be seen in Enclosure 5 to this long communication. He had rejected by this time the idea of creating a head *almami* to control all the other chiefs in the Gambia area and he had decided rather to confirm the present chiefs and village heads in the posts which they occupied. He wished to retain, however, the right of the government to dismiss any of these men on the presentation of proper proof of their unfitness, and also the right to appoint successors to chiefs after due consultation with the Travelling Commissioners.

The first major piece of legislation for the Protectorate was the Protectorate Ordinance of 1894 which established that, 'all native laws and customs in force in the Protected Territories which are not repugnant to natural justice nor incompatable with any ordinance of the Colony which applies to the Protected Territories, shall have the same effect as regulations made under this ordinance'.[10] The Protectorate area was divided into a number of districts which were territorial, not tribal units, and placed under the charge of chiefs. A few of these chiefs were of the royal or *mansa* traditional ruling houses, but most were those appointed by the central government to fill the vacuum of power in a territory. The Ordinance was in essence an enabling act which recognized the claims of customary law and customary procedure throughout the Protectorate. The Ordinance established native courts, such courts being appointed by the Administrator. The head chief of a district was to be the President of the native court of that particular district. These district courts were to have civil jurisdiction in areas of petty conflict. The courts had the right to determine the outcome to suits relating to ownership and possession of lands held in native tenure within a given district, personal suits not exceeding £25 between persons resident in the district, and matters relating to inheritance of goods up to a £50 evaluation. In criminal jurisdiction these courts would have control over matters which would not exceed fines of £5 or imprisonment of over three weeks. Some of the areas under the jurisdiction of the district court were to be arson, theft, extortion, cheating, slander, seduction, and disobeying the orders of a head man or a duly constituted chief. The Ordinance gave the Administrator the right to restrict or to revoke any of the district courts which were not functioning properly. It also established a form of appeal and very clearly retained for the Commissioner or the Administrator the right to stop proceedings of a given case at any time at their discretion. Defendants in either criminal or civil cases could petition the Commissioner for the removal of actions against them. Persons convicted by such district courts could appeal against the decisions through the Commissioner, who upon his own judgement could refer the cases to the Supreme Court of the Colony area, with the restriction that there was to be no appeal on cases where the fine was less than £5 or where the detention was less than seven days. British ¦subjects or other subjects of 'civilized powers' were to come under the direct durisdiction of the Commissioner who was given the same judicial powers as those already conferred upon the Justices of the Peace of the Colony or the manager at MacCarthy Island. The laws and ordinances of the Colony, with minor modifications, were to apply to all activities of such Europeans in the Protectorate.

Section 3 of the Ordinance dealt with the administrative powers of the chiefs. They were to act as conservators of the peace and executors of any laws of Parliament, Orders in Council, decrees of the Supreme Court, or orders of the Commissioners. They were to be responsible for apprehending, detaining, and sending to the Commissioners or the courts of Bathurst any persons accused of major crimes 'such as murder, robbery, or slave dealing'. This same section reserved to the Administrator the right to withdraw powers from any head man or head chief and to appoint successors to those who were deceased or temporarily incapacitated. The Administrator also retained, with the approval of the Legislative Council, the right to regulate fees to be received by head men and native courts, and the right of recording, pronouncing or executing judgements, and the form of application for relief from decisions by the Protectorate chiefs. In an ambiguous clause the Ordinance gave the Administrator the right to set aside at his own discretion any of the previous clauses by stating that he was responsible for 'all rules necessary for the better functioning of the Ordinance'.

Much of the Ordinance of 1894 was totally theoretical since the districts had not been delimited and since there were only two Travelling Commissioners to handle the details of its establishment throughout the Gambia area. The Ordinance of 1894 did act, however, as the model for all subsequent pieces of legislation for the Protectorate. It is obvious that the Governor did not expect a large portion of the Ordinance to be put into effect immediately. It was rather a system which could be established gradually over a long period of time and which would serve as the ideal for a theoretical system of indirect rule. The actual function of the Travelling Commissioners in the '90s was to be primarily that of maintaining law and order, reporting the wishes of the Governor to the chiefs, and making certain that gross violations of humanity did not occur in the up river territories.

In 1895 the role of the Travelling Commissioners and the head men and chiefs of the Protectorate was further extended

117

by an Ordinance which established a standardized Yard Tax for the Protectorate.[11] Although the total expenditure for Protectorate services in 1895 was estimated to be only £1,455 out of a total expenditure of £29,875,[12] it was known that the cost of administration would mount, and therefore the natives in various districts were to be made to share in the cost of government. For the purposes of this tax, a yard was defined as 'every parcel lot or enclosure of land (other than farm land) containing one or more huts or houses'.[13] This definition did not include granaries or cattle sheds as huts or houses. The schedule of payments under this Yard Tax Ordinance was that every owner or occupier of any yard that contained more than four huts would pay four shillings per year, and for each additional hut occupied by members of the family, one extra shilling per year. For those itinerate workers, later known as 'Strange Farmers', who did not make up a permanent part of a household, but nevertheless occupied a hut, the tax would be two shillings per year. This Ordinance also must be taken as largely theoretical since there was not the necessary means to enforce payment throughout the riverine area, and it depended largely for its operation upon the Travelling Commissioners and the honesty of the individual farmers and chiefs within a given area. The success of this Yard Tax Ordinance can be seen by the fact that in 1904 only £3,168 was collected.[14]

In 1895, Governor Llewellyn also attempted by Proclamation to create a more logical division of the Protectorate.[15] The Proclamation envisaged three divisions in the Protectorate— the North Bank with seven sub-divisions or districts, the South Bank Division with six districts, and the Kombo Division with four districts. By 1906 the government had created further divisions in the Protectorate, each under the direction of a Travelling Commissioner. This had become necessary primarily because of the settlement of differences in the extreme up river area and the inclusion in 1897, and later in 1902, of those areas that had previously been controlled by Musa Mola, as a part of the protected districts of the Gambia. Thus by 1906 there were five divisions—North Bank, MacCarthy Island, South Bank, Upper River, and the Kombo-Foni Division. Each of these was under the direction of a Travelling Commissioner.

Another far reaching piece of legislation concerned the disposition of land in the Protectorate. The key Ordinance which regulated land policy until 1945 was issued in September 1896.[16] The Ordinance declared that all lands not defined as 'Public Lands' were to be held by the native authorities and administered by their representatives according to the customs of the people of an area. Public lands were defined as all lands not in actual occupation by people, lands conquered from a deposed ruler, or lands which prior to annexation were the personal property of the chiefs. This basic Ordinance was further amplified by an Ordinance in 1897,[17] an Executive Order in 1905,[18] and a Regulation in 1915.[19] These vested the administration of the 'Public Lands' in the chiefs and head men and made them responsible for issuing permits for cutting trees, collecting gum and palm products, etc. The Regulation of 1915 provided for the issue of land certificates to enable persons to occupy the 'Public Lands'. Thus in reality all lands in the Protectorate were controlled indirectly by the Commissioners through the chiefs. The idea of private possession of lands was excluded from consideration and native tenure was supported.

Notwithstanding the Protectorate Ordinance of 1894 and later Ordinances, the early years of indirect rule in the Gambia were largely experimental and depended to a large extent upon the personalities of the Travelling Commissioners. That grandiose philosophy of indirect rule, largely attributed to Lord Lugard and Sir Donald Cameron, which served as the guide for the establishment of similar forms of rule throughout Africa had not yet been worked out. The Gambian government had little money to expend and the Travelling Commissioners in the first ten years of the Protectorate system depended largely upon their wits and their abilities to impress those who were theoretically the servants of the government. Despite the fact that a Protectorate had been proclaimed, the conditions in certain areas of the territory were still highly unsettled. Slavery was still practiced, the slave trade was endemic, and there were certain areas where the Commissioners would not venture unless accompanied by an escort. This was particularly true of the Foni area which had been brought under the Protectorate system in 1894. Reports of kidnapping, robbery, and murder reached the Travelling Commissioners and the central government. In the very early stages of Protectorate government little could be done to check these reports or to punish many offenders. The best that could be hoped for was to influence the chiefs and head men in the proper direction and to overawe them with threats of what might possibly occur if the instructions of the Commissioners were ignored.

Despite all these difficulties the Travelling Commissioners did a heroic job with the material available to them. Twelve Commissioners were appointed in the years between 1893 and 1903. Of these, three died of illness, two were killed, and one was invalided home.[20] Despite these statistics and the many dangers constant in their jobs, the only serious revolt against the Travelling Commissioners occurred in the village of Sankandi in 1900. This incident was an outgrowth of a long standing dispute between two villages over the control of rice fields. One of the original Commissioners, Sitwell, felt it necessary to adjudicate in the disagreement and decided in favour of the village which was composed primarily of Soninkis. The Marabouts of the competing village refused to abide by the judgement and a minor situation developed which Sitwell and a new Commissioner, F. E. Silva, who was to be Sitwell's replacement, felt necessary to put down. The two Commissioners accompanied by an escort of eleven native constables proceeded to the village of Sankandi with a very influential Soninki chief, Mansa Koto, to seek final settlement of the question with the Marabout chief, Dari Rana Dabo. The small group was ambushed by the Marabouts, and Sitwell, Silva, Mansa Koto, and six of the constables were killed in the engagement.[21]

This event convinced the Governor, Sir George Denton, and the Colonial Office that a joint operation with the French should be undertaken to pacify the interior once and for all. The successful campaign resulted in the death of Fodi Kabba and the negation of Musa Mollah as a power. Musa Mollah later agreed to place all Fuladu under the Protectorate system and live in peace with the British authorities.[22] The killing of Sitwell and Silva marked the real turning point in the government of the Protectorate. The relatively quick action on the part of British and French military forces in punishing those respon-

sible for continued disturbances convinced chiefs of lesser
stature that to disobey the Travelling Commissioner, let alone
take upon themselves the responsibility of harming a Commissioner, would lead only to their destruction.

The new status of Protectorate rule was indicated by a
comprehensive Protectorate Ordinance in 1902.[23] This Ordinance had been partly brought about by the incorporation of
Fuladu into the Protectorate, but it also reflected the increased
stature of the Travelling Commissioners. It attempted to put
into practice some of the lessons learned in the eight years of
Protectorate administration. Section 13 of this Ordinance
stated that 'the Commissioner shall have the superintendence
of districts within his province; and it shall be the duty of the
Head chief and Headman to be guided by any advice and to
obey all orders given by the Commissioner for the order and
general management of the district'. This was simply a more
specific statement of the powers conferred upon the Commissioners by the Ordinance of 1894. It is important to note
that by this section the Travelling Commissioners were specifically made the chief executive powers of the districts under their
surveillance. This illustrates clearly that at no time was indirect
rule what it later was advertised to be—a form of rule where
the native authorities are the chief executive power in a given
area.

The most important section of the Ordinance of 1902 dealt
with native tribunals. The Ordinance of 1894 had given the
chiefs, head men, and their advisors the right to conduct trials
of persons accused of violating the customary laws. This
Ordinance of 1902 regularized in theory the establishment of
native tribunals and the area of cognizance of such courts. A
native tribunal was to consist of three or more duly appointed
native members or the Commissioner sitting alone or with one
or more members. It was the responsibility of the Governor to
appoint, on the Commissioner's recommendation, 'fit persons'
to be members of a tribunal. The head chiefs were given the
right to convene their tribunals, and when the Commissioner
was absent from the district, to act as the head of a native court.
They were specifically prohibited from acting on their own
without the convening of a tribunal. All native laws in relation

to tenure of land, marriage, succession, and the like were to remain, and were to be enforceable by the native courts. Appeals from the decisions of the native tribunals to the Commissioners, removal of the case from the jurisdiction of the native tribunal, and appeals to the Supreme Court remained basically the same as in 1894. Reality extrudes through the theorizing in Section 24 where it stated that 'where the Commissioner is present, he shall preside, and the judgement of the Commissioner shall be the judgement of the tribunal'. Thus whatever the theoretical aspect of indirect rule, the Commissioners when they were present were, for all intents and purposes, the native tribunals. In addition they had the right to select those men who were to serve on the tribunals. All litigants before a native court had the right of appeal to the Commissioner either for a mitagation of a sentence or for the removal of the case from the jurisdiction of the native tribunal. Thus in reality the Commissioner was made the paramount chief of the area which he visited.

The duties of chiefs were further defined by a Protectorate Rule of 1905 which gave them added responsibility.[24] They were made specifically responsible for the upkeep of roads and bridges, and at the discretion of the Commissioner, they were authorized to build new ones. The up-keep of wells in a particular area, the maintenance of boundary pillars, and prevention of the accumulation of rubbish and other nuisances injurious to health and offensive to the public were specifically made the responsibility of the chiefs and head men. In addition, an area of approximately fifty yards was to be kept cleared around every town or village between the months of November and June of the following year. The Regulation of 1905 did not establish any new functions which the chiefs had not previously exercised, but simply made them, by law, definitely responsible under the tutelage of the Commissioner for carrying out specific tasks. The Regulation also clarified the form of summons to be used in native tribunals and also procedures to be followed in the operation of the tribunals. It authorized payment in cattle or produce for fines assessed by the courts and, at the discretion of the President, also authorized payment of fines on what could be considered an instalment plan. Very hopefully the Regulation also required the Commissioner to keep a record book of the proceedings of native tribunals. This was because previously no stipulation had been made for minutes of the trials to be kept. The Commissioners were to urge the chiefs and the tribunals to maintain a form of record book themselves so that the procedures utilized in a given trial could be reconstructed. This latter desire was not accomplished in the years immediately following. As late as 1960 there were only a minimum number of records kept by the native authorities.

In 1909 two Ordinances were passed which applied to the Protectorate. One ammended the section of the Ordinance of 1902 to give the native tribunals authority over all natives of West Africa who were resident within a district (providing they were not Christians), in matters relating to civil status, marriage, dowry, rights of parents, and guardianship.[25] The other Ordinance attempted to remedy one of the basic practical failings of the previous Protectorate Ordinances.[26] Under earlier Ordinances no thought had been given to the establishment of a constabulary for the Protectorate. This Ordinance gave the head chiefs and head men the right, with necessary permission, to appoint any number of 'badge messengers' that might be required to keep the peace in a given area. These badge messengers, so called because of a peculiar badge of authority which they wore, were to have all the rights, duties and liabilities of a police constable in the Colony area. Although the conditions in the Protectorate have altered radically in the past fifty years, these badge messengers are still the local constabulary who enforce the decisions of the chief or the native authority. Another Ordinance of May 1912 established fees to be paid to the native tribunals. For each court held, the President was to receive two shillings, and all the members of the court were to receive one shilling each.[27]

Ordinance No. 30 of 1913 was the last major legislation for the Protectorate for over twenty years.[28] This legislation added very little that was new to the total of previous Ordinances. However, it repealed all the previous Ordinances and correlated their various provisions into one Protectorate Ordinance which would be applicable throughout the Protectorate. This consolidation left undisturbed all the territory previously under the

Protectorate system and simply confirmed the Provincial and District boundaries which had been defined prior to the ordinance. Three points, however, were clarified by the Ordinance. One concerned defining cases that could be adjudicated before the native courts. Native courts were to be responsible in the main for jurisdiction over cases which would involve fines not exceeding £20 or a sentence of hard labour not exceeding six months. The Ordinance also introduced a new office of sub-chief between the head chief who had the responsibility for a district and the head man of a village or a town. And finally the Commissioner was given the power, at his discretion, to hold assemblies of any or all head chiefs belonging to the area under his immediate control.

An Ordinance of 1919 further refined the theoretical administration of the Protectorate by introducing the term of office of deputy head chief who would exercise control over a district upon the demise, absence, or sickness of a head chief.[29] Since there had been considerable difficulty in obtaining chiefs who would be at one and the same time honest and docile, the problem of removing a chief had come up from time to time and the Ordinance in 1919 specified in more definite terms the manner of appointing and removing all the officials of the Protectorate government. By far the most important item covered by this legislation was a new scale for the Yard Tax. The definition of a yard remained the same it had been before, but each yard that contained not more than four huts or houses was to be levied at the rate of four shillings per year. For each additional hut in the compound or yard, the tax was one shilling, and for every person residing in the yard other than a member of the family of the owner or the occupier, a fee of two shillings would be required.

Three Protectorate Amendment Ordinances of the 1920s further modified the system of indirect rule as it had been established by the composite Ordinance of 1913. An Ordinance of 1923 changed the jurisdiction of native courts to apply to civil cases where the fine was not to exceed £50, and in criminal cases where imprisonment did not exceed two years.[30] This compared to the old limits of £20 in civil cases and six months in criminal cases. An Ordinance of 1925 further increased the jurisdiction of native tribunals in that the Commissioner sitting alone or with one or more of the native members in a given district would have jurisdiction in civil cases for damage where the amount claimed was not over £200.[31] An Ordinance of 1928 changed a number of small details of the primary Ordinance of 1913 and consolidated the two above mentioned Ordinances into one. It provided in more specific terms the areas of appeal to the Court of Request, the Supreme Court, and the Supreme Court of Sierra Leone.[32] The Yard Tax for all those who lived within a given yard who were not members of the family or an occupier who cultivated the land was raised to six shillings per year. It further legalized what had already become practice of allowing the Commissioner or his assistant to pay the head chief, sub-chief, or head man a portion of the Yard Tax not exceeding half of what had been collected in a district, town, or village. Earlier in 1923 in the *Guide Book for Travelling Commissioners*, the various financial commitments of the Commissioners to the local authorities had been specified in more detail.

By 1930 these series of Ordinances had provided the Gambia with a theoretical structure of protected government based on the patterns of indigenous rule as the British understood it. Compromise had of necessity been made to bring this indirect rule into rough alignment with the overall concepts of British administration and British justice. British forms, however, had usually been granted reluctantly in many cases and certainly not with the idea of trying to force upon the chiefs and people of the Protectorate a stereotyped pattern of British rule. It should be noted that at no time did the government seriously attempt to determine the nature of the varying tribal systems in the Gambia. Although long association with one another, with Islam, and with Europeans had created similar patterns of land tenure and political structures, there were differences between a Wolof, a Mandingo, or a Fula area. Without exception Britain, in West Africa, assumed types of rule and their correlate social sanctions to be dominant in an area on only superficial knowledge. One must realize that indirect rule was not just the acceptance of institutions, but in many cases was an imposition of a type of rule that the administrators believed to be the indigenous system. This was particularly true when indirect rule ceased to be just the cheapest and most convenient manner of ruling large areas and became a system based upon definite philosophical concepts concerning the needs of the Africans and the eventual goal of colonial policy. This type of philosophizing came to the Gambia with the next major change in Protectorate government in the Ordinance of 1933. This Ordinance was more important for the ideological underpinning it provided for the system rather than for any change it effected in the basic forms already established.

It would be as well, before discussing this and subsequent Ordinanccs, to look carefully at the system that had been created over a period of forty years in order to see what, in fact, had been accomplished by the system of indirect rule and to discover how far the theories enunciated by the Ordinances had been put into effect in the Protectorate. The various Protectorate Ordinances had accepted the basic political institution of the Yard, which was operative in most of the native communities in the Gambia in the 1890s. The yard was one or a collection of several huts and their lands which at one time had been held by kindred groupings. Every yard had its own leader called the *Kordu Tiyo*. The yards were joined into quarters and the quarters into villages under the headship of a *Satiyo-Tiyo* or a village head. This village head was normally the eldest member of a family which was recognized as having titular right to this office. Although the justification for such office varied between different villages and among different tribes, it was normally based upon some kind of association with the founder of the particular village. His primary function was the keeping of law and order in the village and the adjudication of contrary claims between village members. These claims normally had to do with family affairs, or more often disputes concerning the occupation of land. In certain early documents describing this arrangement, the *Satiyo-Tiyo* was depicted as the owner of the land, and some European observers interpreted this in the Western sense to mean that he actually possessed the land. In reality all he did, with the aid of advisors, was judge claims and apportion the lands to members of the community. A group of villages were normally combined together in charge of a chief or *Alkali* who in most circumstances was chosen by quarter heads or family heads. Usually he was a *Satiyo-Tiyo* himself. As can be seen by the method of selection of leaders on all levels, they were not traditionally authoritarian rulers. Major decisions were reached by the chief in conjunction with a council composed of representative lesser authorities. Another restriction upon improper use of authority was the existence of age sets. The senior set, composed of the older unmarried and younger married men, had specific well defined duties to perform. They were in charge of much of the recreational life of a village as well as communal services such as repairing roads and digging wells. Rule on all levels had been based on a delicate balance of hereditary rights of certain persons belonging to certain families and election by lesser authorities. Much of this balance had been upset or totally destroyed in certain areas by the prolonged Soninki-Marabout Wars. This was particularly true of the major chieftaincies. Royal or *mansa* families that had shared the chieftaincies on a rota basis had been destroyed and their places taken by usurpers. Such a state of affairs was also noticeable on all the lower levels.[33]

Proclamation No. 7 of 1895 had recognized seventeen chiefs who exercised control over territorial subdivisions of the Protectorate.[34] The exact area of control had not been delimited, but no attempt had been made to create tribal divisions. Only a few of the chiefs appointed at that time and later were of *mansa* families; the others were creations of the administration. As such they were not 'of' the native system, but rather were imposed upon the districts. In many cases the exercise of the chief's authority was hindered by the appointive process, and the presence of the Commissioners was the only reason that a minimum of his orders were obeyed. This is indicated not only by the theoretical structure of the system, but by reports of the Commissioners themselves. One of these who had long service in the Gambia reported as late as 1926,

> Government in the person of the Travelling Commissioner now takes the place of the highest tribal authority, and his position and orders are unquestioned in all matters, except perhaps in things pertaining to witchcraft and the like, but

even there, if wrong-doing results, the Commissioner is run to at once. He is the father of the people.[35]

Throughout the forty year period of indirect rule to 1933 the Commissioners acted alone as administrators of territories which were larger areas than many English counties. Little money was expended in the Protectorate so even if the chiefs of an area or the Commissioner had been progressive, the funds were not available to carry out their projects.[36] Disease was an ever present menace, and this, combined with the necessary leave granted to the Commissioners, meant there was little continuity of authority in the major divisions of the Protectorate. Chiefs and people of a specific area would not have time to get adjusted to a Commissioner before he was transferred, invalided, or sent home. There was little co-ordination between Commissioners and few attempts were made to repost Commissioners for a number of tours in the same Division. Since the special system of indirect rule depended in large measure upon personal rule of the Commissioner who was a *de facto* paramount chief, no long range development plans were carried out.[37]

Important factors to consider in an analysis of the system are the economic disadvantages of the Gambia. The prevailing doctrine in the inter-war years was that a colonial territory had to live within its means and could not depend on the home government for grants. As will be detailed elsewhere, the Gambia, contrary to the widely held belief, was in excellent financial position until the early 1920s. This position was largely destroyed by the redemption of the French five-franc piece. From 1923 onward the Gambia with only one cash crop could not afford expensive development schemes. Most of the available money was expended in the Colony area. The Protectorate was considered to be functioning well if peace and order prevailed. Therefore no specific long range plans were ever formulated for Protectorate development. Even in the field of education, with the exception of the Chiefs' School at Georgetown, there were no great expenditures. Indirect rule, therefore, became a force not for slow political, social, or economic development, but for maintaining the *status quo*.

The various Ordinances had created a theoretical structure

of government. The philosophical basis of this system was that it was the continuation, with minor adjustments, of the indigenous system. Commissioner Hopkinson negated this idea when he reported in 1926 on the court system of the Protectorate. He wrote,

> Their [Seyfolu] powers in the courts should be supported, for now that is all the real authority a chief has, and the court members will replace the old Council of Elders, which was an integral part of the old Mandingo System of Government, where the 'King' unless an exceptional man was merely the ornamental head of the State, while the real power was in the hands of the 'Suma', elected from certain families (or towns) and his council of old men. They ran the King and got rid of him, if he went contrary to their wishes. Sumas seem to have much more rarely ended thus.[38]

Apart from misreading the indigenous systems, the Ordinances charged the chiefs with ministerial responsibility in areas where they previously had had no authority and also required them to do certain tasks which they could not accomplish. Keeping of records, collection of vital statistics, and efficient and honest handling of money were only a part of such responsibilities. By 1930 there were forty-five chiefs; they were almost all illiterate and had no trained administrative staff to carry out such details.[39] The better Commissioners aimed to carry out the provisions of the Ordinances for the efficient operation of the native tribunals. Hopkinson for one believed that if the tribunals were good they would be more effective than the Commissioners. However, he reported sadly, 'I only wish there were more tribunals I can really call good than there are . . .'[40]

Thus by 1933 the reality of administration was far removed from the theories contained in the Ordinances. These predicated a complicated system of indirect rule. The reality was a peculiar type of direct rule by the Commissioners channelled through what were believed to be the natural rulers of the hinterland. The Commissioners had little help, few facilities, and scant funds to carry out their major tasks of keeping law and order. However, the authorities had recognized that the system had been established to bring peace and quiet at a minimum expense, and there had been little theorizing concerning the ends of such a system. This was provided by the Ordinance of 1933.

In January 1933, the Governor, H. R. Palmer, believing in the need for reforms in the Protectorate administration, issued a work called *Political Memoranda for the Guidance of Commissioners and other Government officers Working in the Protectorate*. Certain citations show clearly the basis for the work and what it and the subsequent Ordinances would attempt to do. It stated,

> These Memoranda on 'Principles of Native Administration' and on 'Native Courts' are in essence an almost literal reproduction and in part an adaptation *mutatis mutandis* of the very lucid Memoranda issued by Sir Donald Cameron on these subjects in Tanganyika in 1926.[41]

This clearly tied Protectorate legislation in the future to the wider world of administrative theory developed by Lord Lugard and his chief colonial disciple, Cameron. Cameron's policy in Tanganyika became the model not only for the Gambia, but also for Nigeria. His rationale for indirect rule was presented clearly when he wrote of the goals for the Africans,

> Our desire is to make them good Africans, and we shall not achieve this if we destroy all the institutions, all the traditions, all the habits of the people, superimposing upon them what we consider to be better administration methods and better principles, but destroying everything that made the administration really in touch with the thoughts and customs of the people . . . "[42]

Palmer, a disciple of Cameron, enunciated in greater details his ideas of Protectorate rule.

> The future development of administration in the Gambia Protectorate can only follow one of two courses. It must either gradually become a form of direct administration by centralized Departments or it must, in some degree follow the general lines indicated in the memoranda.
>
> The deciding factor between these two alternative policies must necessarily lie in the ability of the Chiefs and Headmen under the guidance of Administrative officer, so to discharge

their functions that Government shall have increasing confidence in their integrity, competence, and judgement.[43]

Governor Palmer followed his *Political Memoranda* with a series of Ordinances in 1933. These did not establish indirect rule. That had already been accomplished forty years before. The Ordinances merely reconstituted that rule and redefined certain of its characteristics. Their further importance lay in the fact that the Governor and his advisors had rejected even a long term approach whereby the Colony and Protectorate would be served by the same administrative apparatus. Ordinance No. 3 was in reality an empowering Ordinance giving the Governor the right to establish administrative units called Native Authorities.[44] These Authorities could be either a chief or some other person or persons empowered by the Governor to act as the executive of a given district. Whereas all the previous Protectorate Ordinances had combined the native tribunals and executive authority, Ordinance No. 3 separated them. Section 9 specifically enumerated the areas of competence of the Authorities and the limits of their jurisdiction. Except for the wider range of responsibility in theory given to the executive, their tasks remained basically the same as stated in the Ordinance of 1913. Until 1944 the Native Authority remained the chief whose main function was to maintain order and collect the tax. The Governor and the Commissioners still retained the right to remove any or all members of an Authority and regulate the power of one or all of the Authorities created.[45]

The Native Tribunal Ordinance of 1933 did not add much to the rules that governed the courts under previous legislation. It confirmed in power all the native tribunals that were functioning at that time. The composition of the native tribunal was left ambigious so that future tribunals could be constituted as the Governor desired. The only real change effected was to make the native tribunals responsible for judicially carrying out the provisions of the Native Authority Ordinance No. 3. The tribunals had cognizance over native and customary law, the Mohammedan law relating to civil status, all rules created by a Native Authority, and rules, regulations, and Ordinances of the Governor in Council. A correlate piece of legislation established a provincial court for each of the Provinces for appeals from decisions of the native tribunals. This was really only a change in title for the Commissioner or Assistant Commissioner made up this appellate court. [46]

In 1935 two Ordinances relating to the Protectorate in the main only clarified points of the legislation of 1933. [47] The Ordinance of 1913 was finally repealed. This detail had been overlooked before, thus creating a situation where two major pieces of legislation were in force for almost two years. Protectorate Ordinance No. 2 of 1935 was the most important of the laws of 1935 because it established a new scale of Yard Tax to be collected by the chiefs and head men. For yards of not more than four huts the yearly rate was five shillings, and one shilling sixpence for each additional structure. In addition, for every inhabitant who was not a member of the family, the rate was two shillings and for every person who was a Strange Farmer, the tax was eight shillings per year.

As has been stated, the legislation in the 1930s, contrary to the views of certain observers, added very little to the Protectorate government. A point by point analysis of the various Ordinances show that a great amount of time and effort was given to the creation of these new Ordinances without basically changing what had been established in 1913. The major result achieved was the confirmation that the Native Authority system was to be the government of the Protectorate for the foreseeable future.

The major goal of Protectorate government up to the beginning of World War II had been the minimization of trouble and expense in governing. Despite the numerous Ordinances and Amendments, the structure of administration had remained basically the same as it had been at its inception. Most of the chiefs had been created by the central authorities and ruled in very specific areas prescribed for them by law or by the interpretations of the Commissioners. The extra work given to the Authorities was normally connected with gaining more revenue rather than being made responsible agents for the distribution of new social services. The bulk of administrative duties dealt with the carrying out of rules passed on from above or with the tribunals. Most of the money expended in the Protectorate went in emoluments for the chiefs and head men and not in improvements for the people. Commissioners still remained in charge of large territories and were overworked, with few assistants to aid them. Nor were the Authorities schools for learning the processes of local government. Educated Gambians were normally excluded from taking part in the government of the Protectorate. Thus by a misreading of the aims of indirect rule as established by Cameron, the Gambian government allowed an inflexible and archaic system to develop. This, combined with the conservative nature of the Protectorate population, meant that little initiative and few forwarding-looking ideas were forthcoming from the Authorities. The system saved money and was easy to administer, and as long as the Colony area was ruled directly by Crown Colony government, the method of indirect rule presented few administrative problems.

In the post World War II era concessions to the growing nationalistic movements in West Africa became necessary. Those applied to the Gambia created tensions which ultimately changed the whole nature of Protectorate government. In this period there have been two, at first parallel and then conflicting, series of improvements directed towards the Protectorate. The first was embodied in a series of Ordinances directed at making District government more responsible for the administration of the districts concerned. Although the role of the Commissioner was not minimized, the scope of activities to be undertaken by the Native Authorities was increased with the eventual aim that they should operate as effective units of local government. The second series of developments was an outgrowth of the liberalization of the central government. The pressure for more Gambian representation which began in the mid-'50s led to the granting of full internal self-government and this in turn has resulted in the gradual extension of direct franchise to the Protectorate. Although this was not at first conceived to be in conflict with the traditional pattern of Protectorate rule, it has worked to liberate the village Gambian from his older sense of alliegance to the *Seyfolu*. When viewed seperately, the various Protectorate Ordinances seem to be strengthening the chiefs by extending to them more responsibility, and by grouping the Native Authorities in larger units, making the government more

133

efficient. However, the extension of more freedom of choice to the Protectorate Gambian, combined with the antipathy of political leaders toward indirect rule, has created a situation where the chiefs exercise less actual authority then they did before 1945.

One of the first real moves to improve the efficiency of Protectorate administration was the appointment of a Senior Commissioner in 1944. Such a position had long been required to provide continuity and a type of centralized planning for the whole of the Protectorate. Until the creation of this office, individual Commissioners carried out their duties in their divisions with little reference to what had been done by previous Commissioners or to what was being attempted in the other segments of the Protectorate. With the rapid attrition rate due to health and a chronic shortage of personnel, lack of a co-ordinating official had meant that little continuity had been maintained anywhere in the government of the Protectorate.

Another advancement in the direction of a more standardized system of Protectorate rule was the institution in 1944 of an annual Conference of Protectorate Chiefs. In theory this gathering of the thirty-five chiefs was to provide a forum for them to make suggestions and to criticize programmes that had been instituted by the central government or the Commissioners. In actual practice the Conference became a convenient means whereby the government could annually introduce their proposals for development in the Protectorate. The Conferences were a composite of pomp and formalism together with semi-serious attempts to get the chiefs to express themselves on government policy. At the Conferences, after the message of greeting directed by the Governor, each central department presented a resumé of its activity of the past year together with the new projects that would be undertaken in the coming year. The responsibilities of the *Seyfolu* in these new plans would be outlined and they would be asked to comment upon them. Until 1958 the chiefs were totally passive, acting out a pre-set role. Few questions were asked and the government plans were accepted without protest. In essence the Chiefs' Conference became a rubber stamp for predetermined policy.[48] From 1958 onward the more dominant of the chiefs began to comment and question, sometimes bitterly, on the critical point of traditional representation in the Legislative Council. Nor were their later criticisms confined only to this, but tended to range over the entire government programme.[49] However, by this time other forces had replaced the Chief's Conference as the major force in the Protectorate and their newly found voice was that of an agency which had lost its major reason for existence.

Explicit in the earlier Protectorate Ordinances was the power to establish Native Authorities to replace the older dependence upon the chief and thus to widen the base of local rule. The government had also made clear its desire to establish District Treasuries which when functioning would supplement the Native Authority as an effective local government agency. However, little had been done by 1944 to put into effect either of these programmes. After 1944 it became the aim of the Gambia government to give practical effect to these goals that up to then had been theoretical only.

In the three years after 1944 a series of Ordinances redefined the term Native Authority and established these Authorities in place of the head chief acting alone.[50] These Native Authorities were to consist either of the district head as president and all the village heads and advisors, or the district head and only selected village heads and advisors. The process of change was not to be accomplished immediately, but on an evolutionary basis depending upon the receptiveness of the *Seyfolu* involved and the recommendations of the Commissioner. Thus even by 1960 there were still districts in the Gambia where the *Seyfolu* was still the Native Authority. Another restriction should be noted concerning the practical application of this broader type of Authority. The Authorities normally met only twice a year, and even then not all of the *Alkalolu* would attend. The every day administration of the districts still remained in the hands of the chief whose authority was restricted only by the activities of the Commissioner. So no matter what the Ordinances specified, the more that things changed in the Protectorate, the more they remained the same. This can be seen in the relatively slight use that the Native Authorities have made of their rule making powers. Many Ordinances enacted since 1945 have given the Authorities power to regulate land leases, prevent grass fires, establish groundnut stores, regulate cultivation of crops, issue orders for prevention of animal disease, and other minor legislation. With the possible exception of the groundnut stores regulation and livestock market rules there has been no uniform enactment by the separate Authorities on these subjects. In most cases the use of these rule making powers was a result of direct intervention on the part of the Commissioners. It is true that the policy of encouraging this type of subordinate legislation was new and was not pressed by the technical departments.[51] However, failure to utilize these powers more fully did not augur well for the independent development of responsible local government.

The basic Ordinance which established the Protectorate Treasuries had a more immediate effect upon the Protectorate.[52] Provisions were made for the establishment of District Treasuries, and Group Treasuries upon petition. The collection and disbursement of funds was to be the responsibility of a Finance Committee appointed by the group or Authority concerned. In case of an Authority this committee was to be composed of a chairman and not less than three members. In the formation of Group Treasuries there was to be a chairman and a sufficient number of members to see that each Authority was represented. A treasury scribe was to be provided and paid by the central government to keep the accounts. The Group Treasuries were to maintain separate account books for each component district whose representative would check the vouchers every month. In November 1945, the Governor had approved one District and four Group Treasuries, and by mid-1947 all the Gambia had been covered by the creation of one District and eleven Group Treasuries.[53] The Ordinance also made provision for the Treasuries to levy their own district tax. This supplanted the old Yard Tax which had previously been the main source of revenue for the Protectorate. The local annual rate at the inception of the programme was ten shillings for yards containing more than four dwellings, two shillings and sixpence for each additional hut or house, five shillings for every resident of a yard not related to the owner, and ten shillings for every

Strange Farmer. Although the district rate was the main source of revenue, the Treasuries' income was also supplemented by various license fees on land, markets, timber, and fees and fines from the Native Tribunals. In the first year of total operation the District tax for the entire Protectorate amounted to £23,998 while the incidental fees contributed only £7,555.[54]

As has been the case with so many of the plans constructed for the Protectorate, there was from the beginning a wide gap between what the Ordinances said and what was actually effected by them. The trained personnel necessary for the effective working of the system did not exist in the Protectorate. Thus one of the major purposes of the legislation, that of having the Authorities themselves lead in the implementation of the Ordinance, was defeated from the first. The preparation of estimates and the major responsibility of managing the Treasuries became almost entirely a function of the Commissioners' office. The actual functioning of the Protectorate Treasuries has been to strengthen the control of the central authority over the districts rather than to make the Native Authorities strong responsible local government units.

Another tendency in Gambia government can also be seen in the operation of the Native Authorities and Treasuries. No matter how inefficient the agency, multiplying its theoretical responsibilities increases the cost of administration. Much of the relatively small funds available for local improvements is taken up by the overheads of administration, This, coupled with the conservative nature of many of the chiefs, restricted the participation of the Native Authorities in providing more locally controlled dispensaries and Native Authority schools. The records of the Chiefs' Conferences show quite clearly how slow the establishment of such services was.

In this connection one should note the slow improvement in Protectorate education despite the many difficulties presented. In 1947 there had been only seven primary schools in the Protectorate, only two of which had been District Authority schools. By 1952 there were twenty-one Authority schools out of twenty-eight operative in the Protectorate. All of these operated on a semi-tuition basis and provided only four years of education.[55] Much of the difficulty in expanding the

137

educational facilities had its origins in finance and the hesitancy of the central government to provide large sums for expansion in all the districts. In all truth, the problem was not wholly financial, but was complicated by the reluctance of some Authorities to establish schools and by the lack of qualified teachers.[56]

The possible extension of more self-government to Gambians on the central level brought up the difficult problem of reconciling the semi-authoritarian system of indirect rule with the normal representative system then operative in the Colony area. The leaders of all political parties in the late 1950s demanded that the Protectorate should be treated in the same manner as the Colony. However, the British government was not prepared to sanction such a drastic change from the traditional system. They acted in line with the outspoken comments of the leading chiefs concerning this direct undermining of their authority.[57] The Constitution of 1960 did protect the traditional rulers in two ways. First the chiefs were allowed to select from their own group eight members of the new House of Representatives, a number equal to those directly elected by all the voters of the Protectorate. The second protection was the stipulation that no person not born in the Protectorate could stand for election there. This was aimed directly at the Colony politicians and the possibility that they would usurp control from the chiefs via the polls.[58]

The elections of 1960, nevertheless, did serious damage to the whole structure of Protectorate government. Some of the chiefs attempted to gain more than the reserved eight seats by having their sons enter the direct elections. In no case was the son of a chief elected. There is a great amount of truth in the observation that the people of a district, up till then inarticulate, rejected the entire scheme by which they had been ruled by voting against the chiefs' sons. The election did not represent a victory for any one political party. Therefore the indirectly elected chiefs held the balance in the House. Such a situation proved not only untenable for the Gambian politicians, but for the Governor and the Colonial Office.[59] The new constitutional instruments developed out of the conferences of 1961 did not reiterate the guarantees for the chiefs that were present in 1960. In a much increased House of Representatives, they have only a token four seats guaranteed by selection.[60]

The position of the chiefs in the Protectorate was also attacked from another direction. For some time the central government had been unsatisfied with duplication of effort in the thirty-five districts and the inability of the Native Authorities to take the lead in the formulation of plans and in guiding the Native Treasuries. The result of these deliberations was the creation of District Councils to take over many of the rule-making functions previously exercised by the Native Authorities. They were to be responsible for the collection of direct taxes, budgetary planning, and disbursement of funds. The chiefs would not be disturbed in their ceremonial functions, nor in their position relative to customary law and they would still act as executors of policy determined by the central government and the District Councils. Membership on the District Councils was by direct election. Chiefs or their advisors could be represented, but only if they were elected by the people of their district. The long range plan of the government was to have a District Council for the four Divisions. By the beginning of 1962 there had been elections for two such Councils, one at Brikama and the other at Basse. These institutions are too new to discuss in any but the most general terms, but it seems obvious that they, or some other similar agency, will be the keystone of the future local government of the Protectorate.

Concurrent with changes in the Native Authorities and Treasuries there were changes made in the Protectorate court system.[61] Although the system as established by the Native Tribunals Ordinance of 1933[62] was left basically unaltered, certain improvements were made. The Protectorate court system still remains the pyramidal type, with the High Court as the supreme authority, having the same appellate jurisdiction as the Supreme Court of the Colony. On the next level are British Subordinate Protectorate Courts with the Commissioners acting as *ex-officio* magistrates. On the lowest level are the Native Tribunals which administer the laws of the Gambia in both civil and criminal affairs as well as the customary law. The remodelling of the Protectorate Courts was concerned with creating two grades of native tribunals, the group and the district. There are thirty-five district tribunals with the district head as president aided by his elders. The group tribunals parallel the organization of the Group Authorities. The difference in the jurisdiction of the group and district courts concerns the seriousness of the crime. District Tribunals cannot make a sentence which exceeds a £10 fine and imprisonment for over six months for a criminal offence, or a fine of £25 in civil cases. The Group Tribunals have criminal jurisdiction up to fines of £25 and twelve months imprisonment, and in civil cases can assess a £50 fine. Crimes of a higher order are referred to the Commissioner Courts which have concurrent jurisdiction, or to the High Court. One further change was effected in 1954 which brought the Protectorate courts closer to the Colony model. The government finally allowed persons accused of a crime in the Protectorate to be represented by legal counsel.[63]

Similar difficulties to those encountered with the Native Authorities and Treasuries were also met in the reorganization of the courts on a group basis. However, much it seems on paper that the workings of Protectorate justice were changed by the Ordinances, in reality, few real changes have been instituted. Apart from small matters, the Commissioners who have direct access to the native courts and possess appellate jurisdiction remain the cornerstones of the Protectorate judicial system. The District and Group Tribunals serve primarily to take over the large burden of the unimportant cases, but even there primary responsibility does not rest with the chiefs, but with the Commissioners.

In retrospect the Protectorate government of the Gambia has followed the same pattern of development as in the other British West African areas. The institution of indirect rule was a pragmatic decision based upon the necessity of ruling large, semi-hostile areas with few officials and a minimum expenditure. The second phase saw the development of theories that gave an idealogical base to the established system. Concurrently, the Colonial Office and Treasury were following a policy of no unnecessary expenditure for the colonies, which meant a stagnation of social services and an attitude on the part of the administrators that was, in fact, the anti-thesis of the theories. In the post World War II era there were attempts by Britain to reach an accommodation between the outmoded system of rule by the chiefs and the rising demand by nationalists for a great amount of self-determination. The last period witnessed the failure of such compromise attempts because of the incompatibility of democratic institutions utilizing modern concepts and the system of traditional rule. The chiefs in the Gambia will remain, but only as figureheads with few real powers. The new central government will assume the real power to a much greater degree than ever practiced by the British.

Chapter Eight

THE ECONOMICS OF A MONOCULTURE

THE Gambia has been described as a classic monoculture. Unfortunately this is a true description since groundnuts comprise almost the whole of the export trade. All Gambian political and social development is tied to a one-crop economy since the largest portion of government revenue is obtained by a tax on imports and exports. In recent years increasing competition for world markets has resulted in a drastic fall in total income and a series of government budget deficits. These deficits have been masked by stringent economy measures and grants of aid from the United Kingdom. The present economic situation has led many persons to imagine that the riverine area has always been a monoculture. Concurrently the belief exists in the minds of a number of government officials that the Gambia has always been a drain on the Treasury of the United Kingdom. Neither of these assumptions is historically accurate. It seems necessary, therefore, for many reasons, to pause in the account of the political development of the Gambia and review, in a very general way, the economic factors that had such an important role to play in the devolution of the Gambia to its present non-viable condition.

It is true that the major agricultural export product of the area was groundnuts at the time of the assumption of British rule over the Protectorate. Groundnuts had first been exported to Europe in 1830 and had rapidly become the chief source of revenue to the farmers and small merchants. It is not correct, however, to assume that the Gambia area in the 1890s was a complete monoculture. Most of the peoples of the Protectorate had been forced by circumstances for centuries to be as self-sufficient as possible. This had meant the planting of certain compound crops and field crops to provide the necessary sustenence for the people of the villages. These compound crops varied with the tribe and with the geographic location of the villages. But generally the peoples of the Gambia cultivated lentils, cassava, yams, eggplant, bitter tomatoes, red peppers, and ocra as compound crops. On a very small scale they also maintained fruit trees. Citrus, particularly limes, grew well in the Western Division and in the Kombos. Other fruits of the Gambia were the pawpaw, mango and banana. Cereal crops were cultivated on a rather larger scale because they were the basic food supply for all the different tribes. The common cereals cultivated were millet, sorgham, maize, and most important of all, rice. Most of the tribes of the Gambia followed the Mandingo concept of differentiating between certain crops that were the responsibility of the women and products that were to be cultivated by the men. Under such a system all the work necessary for the provision of food for the compound came under the authority of the women. The men considered it a reflection on their masculinity if they were required to cultivate the so called women's crops. More will be said later about the interaction of government policy and the expansion of production of agriculture, but it should be pointed out here that the population of the Gambia after 1890 rose steadily, while the available land remained constant, and the means of production remained the same as in the nineteenth century. The failure to open up new lands or to experiment with new kinds of crops and production techniques by the 1930s produced a chronic shortage of food stuffs during a portion of the year. This time of the year came to be known as the hungry season and it was necessary for the government to import great quantities of cereals to tide large numbers of the people over until the new harvest.

In the self-sufficient subsistence economy that had existed in the nineteenth century there were crops apart from rice that had certain export potential. The main ones were cotton and rubber. Governor D'Arcy had been one of the first Europeans to note the possible potential of the Gambia for the production of cotton. He thought primarily in terms of providing the people of the areas adjacent to the Colony areas with a better quality of cotton for their own use. To this end he requested cotton seeds of a better variety and attempted to introduce these into the Gambia.[1] However, the time was not ripe for such an experiment since the Colonial Office did not want, even by inadvertence, to extend officially the political or the economic sphere. The Soninki-Marabout Wars were at their height, and therefore the disturbed conditions spelled an end to any attempt to better the type of cotton grown in the Gambia. The fact that cotton had a certain potential, at least for domestic use, on the North Bank was attested by Commissioner Ozanne in his first report. He stated, 'The cotton industry is almost as important as the groundnuts, and the people engaged in it work hard. In every town one comes across a row of cotton spinners' sheds, each containing a machine.'[2] Previously Administrator Carter had requested the Crown Agents to forward packets of Egyptian cotton seed from the Royal Gardens at Kew for experimentation in the Gambia.[3] Under Carter and later Llewellyn this experimentation took the form of giving the seeds to certain selected farmers and trying to encourage them to turn away from the culture of groundnuts to the growing of good cotton for exportation. The reports of the late '90s were rather optimistic about the possible success of such a scheme. The whole protect came to nothing because the Colonial Office refused to subsidize cotton culture until it could be well established as a full fledged competitor to groundnuts. The pilot farmers worked as hard on their plots as they would have done cultivating groundnuts, but were ready to drop the whole experiment, when they found that year after year, the returns for their labours were considerably less than if they had continued to plant groundnuts. The market price of groundnuts maintained a fairly high and steady average during this period, whereas the price that could be received on the open market for cotton was less. The Governors wanted to support the price of cotton by paying subsidies up to the level of an equivalent groundnut price. This was, however, vetoed by the home government. In 1904 a cotton expert travelled throughout the length of the Protectorate and reported, 'It is clear that the industry is dead'.[4] Gambian farmers, like their counterparts elsewhere, would not of themselves launch a new programme if it meant a decrease in the profits which they could expect. In subsequent years the increasing importation of cheap English and Far Eastern cottons soon destroyed the indigenous cotton spinning industry. Today cotton growing is a rarity in the Gambia with the exception of small crops still cultivated primarily by the Wolof and Fula.

Rubber was another product that for a time seemed to have a certain amount of potential for export. Had there been any type of long range plan or government control over the rubber culture and harvesting, this could have become, perhaps, a major source of revenue for the Gambia. In the 1890s wild rubber trees were localized in one province of the Protectorate. There was never at any time any thought giving to establishing rubber plantations to assure a continuing and growing supply of rubber. Harvesting the latex was left entirely to the initiative of local native units. In 1890 a total of 154,737 pounds with a value of £10,144 was exported. The exportation of rubber reached it speak in 1895 when 394,165 pounds with a value of £18,879 was harvested and exported. However, by 1903 the value of rubber exported was only £1,544 and the last report of any rubber being exported from the Gambia was in 1915 when only £31 worth was sold.[5] The reason for the demise of the domestic rubber industry in the Gambia is obvious. Rubber trees are delicate plants and the tapping of the trees must be done very carefully. The inexperienced native gatherers simply chopped the trees in the most convenient manner, gathering the harvest when they could and paying no attention to the destruction wrought on both old and young trees.

Early in the century certain officials believed that perhaps the Gambia might be a producer of certain kinds of exotic timber. However, a series of investigations reported,

The only timber fit to cut for export in the whole of the Gambia is obtained in Eastern Kombo, but in no great quantity. There is fair rosewood, but so far trial shipments made as experiments have resulted in a loss to the exporters; such timber as is at present cut is utilized merely for ship-building purposes at Bathurst.[6]

In 1908 samples or rosewood and mahogany grown in the Gambia were sent to the Imperial Institute for testing. The report of the Institute was that the Gambian rosewood did not have the colour and quality to pass as rosewood on the English market. Their analysis of the mahogany was even more devastating.[7] It is well to keep these early reports on the potential of Gambian timber in mind because, in the late '40s the over-emphasis upon the quality and amounts of timber in the Gambia was one of the major reasons why the Colonial Development Corporation scheme failed at Yundum.

If the Gambia lives or dies in a monetary sense depending on the production and sale of groundnuts, it literally lives or dies according to the amount of rice available in a given year. Rice is the staple food of all the peoples of the riverine area. Meat is at a premium, partly because most of the Gambia lies within the tsetse fly belt. Resistent strains of cattle are possessed by certain of the people in the Gambia, but these are relatively few in number and are owned by only the more affluent members of the society. They are also viewed more for their innate worth rather than for their potential for sale. Sheep and goats, in relatively large numbers, provide the basic meats of the Gambia, but in many cases the meat is so expensive that the average person in the Protectorate can only afford small amounts a few times a week. The Gambia River abounds in various kinds of edible fish, and in some places there are shell-fish, but the tribes of the interior with few exceptions have not attempted to realize this potential. Nor has the government been at pains to instruct them in methods of catching this readily available supply of protein. Rice is therefore the traditional food of most of the peoples and it serves as a base even when meats and other vegetables are present.

Until quite recently the basic types of rice grown were native varieties which had developed an immunity to rice blast. This was an inferior grade of rice and normally, under the best of circumstances, did not yield a great harvest. Earlier in the century attempts to introduce better varieties of rice had been unsuccessful because of disease, lack of sufficient funds, and the resistance of the native peoples to these new strains. Despite the fact that it has now been proved that all three kinds of rice varieties—swamp, flooded, and upland—do well in the Gambia, most of the tribes planted only the flooded varieties. The best native varieties of rice were of this type. There were few good strains of swampland rice, and the bush areas both in the swamps and in the uplands, had to be cleared before any large scale plantings of other types could be attempted. This is a laborious and expensive task. Left almost entirely to themselves, with little urging from the Department of Agriculture, the chiefs and Native Authorities attempted only a minimum effort to clear new rice lands. With the exception of a few drought years, the lands in the Middle River produced a sufficiency of rice for that area, and there was usually a local surplus. However, due to the poor road system until recent years, and the lack of any co-operative agencies, there were no available means to distribute these local surpluses to areas which had little rice, and were in fact for a large portion of the year without rice. The hungry season was considered by many to be a normal part of existence. This was particularly true in the upper river areas where the land is not naturally suitable for the cultivation of any but upland rice. Therefore to feed these people in the so-called hungry season it was necessary to import large amounts of foreign rice, generally of an inferior nature, at a relatively heavy cost to the Gambia.[8]

All this seemed likely to change in the latter part of the 1940s when, operating under the Colonial Development and Welfare Acts, the Colonial Development Corporation decided to attempt a large scale mechanized project to clear rice lands and to plant and harvest rice mechanically. This attempt at Wallikunda was a disaster, ranking second only to the abortive egg scheme of the same period. The Colonial Development Corporation invested a tremendous sum of money in what was believed would be a profitable venture. They soon discovered, however, that the necessary overheads were prohibitive. Mechanization called for the importation of large amounts of expensive machinery, operators for this machinery, a heavy outlay for native labour, and the expense of improved rice seed and seedlings. The overheads and difficulties thus encountered pushed the price per pound just far enough above the going world market price to make the scheme unprofitable. In 1952 the mission was reduced to an experimental farm concentrating on the techniques and economics of mechanized rice growing. In 1953 the Colonial Development Corporation withdrew as the operator of the experimental farm, and the Gambian government negotiated with the corporation a take-over of the facilities which were to be operated with financial assistance from Colonial Development and Welfare funds. The whole farm consisted of 4,700 acres of rice swamp irrigated by powerful pumps located at the eastern end of Sapu.[9] The fate of the experimental farm has yet to be decided. The rice produced there, while admittedly of a superior quality to other strains grown elsewhere in the Gambia, is too expensive for the average Gambian to purchase, even when a part of the selling cost has been written off by the government. It is doubtful whether the farm at Wallikunda would have been continued as long as it has, if it had not been that the Gambia government received Colonial Development and Welfare funds which enabled them to carry on the experiment.

The experiment of mechanized farming on a large scale at Wallikunda did have a secondary beneficial result. A very large amount of land was cleared by the equipment and later turned over to the villages. By 1950 the crucial nature of poor rice production had been recognized by a few people who were responsible for the administration of the Gambia. There were two factors involved: the clearing of large amounts of useable land by some mechanized means, and the development of new rice varieties and their acceptance by the natives. Governor Wyn-Harris realized very early the need to concentrate upon rice production. Under his guidance the aerial mapping of the Gambia was undertaken, ox ploughing schools established, a tractor ploughing scheme instituted, and new experimental stations, particularly at Jenoi, established under the direction of a rice expert. The rice expert, Mr. Ramaswami, first came to the Gambia in 1956 after a career of over twenty-five years in a similar role in the Madras Province in India.[10] The result of all these developments in the late '50s was to abolish the hungry season in all but a few villages of the Gambia. However, the real potential for rice production in the Gambia has never been reached. The root cause for this can be traced to lack of funds and lack of central planning. The Department of Agriculture has been experimenting for a long time with various forms of rice and synthetic and natural fertilizers. The French in Casamance and in Senegal have been even more successful in experimentation with varieties of rice. However, there has been little interchange between the French experiments and those that were being conducted in the Gambia. There was a reluctance, even after Mr. Ramaswami had arrived, to commit the government to a full scale attack upon the problem of educating the people of the Protectorate towards the utilization of new developments, and an equal reluctance to expend relatively large sums of money. By the close of the 1950s several blast resistant strains of rice had been discovered. The most promising of these had been developed by the French rice testing station in the Casamance, and although experiments were continued at the rice farm at Jenoi on this and other types, no serious attempt was made to introduce this form on a larger experimental basis into one of the districts of the Protectorate. Ramaswami believed that if there could be a wholesale substitution of this type of rice for the inferior native type, combined with the normal application of amonium sulphate fertilizer, the average return of swamp rice of about 1,000 pounds per acre could, at the very minimum, be doubled. In a long range forecast, ten years of active fostering of the new species together with the use of fertilizer would have provided the Gambia with an export potential in rice. This would have been accomplished without the clearing of one acre of new rice land.

The government was also dilatory in clearing bushland and mangrove land to increase the total acreage available to the native producers. Ox ploughing schools had been established in the late '30s, and under the Governorship of Wyn-Harris, a number of such new schools were opened. These have had beneficial effect upon some of the villages of the Gambia, but

149

not to any dramatic extent. The most forward-looking plan, aimed at opening up new acreage for production, was the tractor ploughing scheme. The government in 1953 decided to provide tractors which would be used at the discretion of the Native Authorities to clear bushland. This modest form of mechanized farming would have been particularly suited to the upper river areas which were chronically short of rice lands. The fees charged for the services of these tractors were minimum and it was expected that the government would, for a greater good, subsidize the clearing of lands. However, by 1961 most of the tractors were worn out and there had been little replacement either of parts or whole units. At this time the government proposed to raise the fees for tractor ploughing to such an extent that the tractor ploughing scheme is now all but a dead issue.[11]

The reluctance of the government to expend money on development projects, even on a small scale, can be seen not only with tractor ploughing, but also in their dealing with the problem of the education of the farmers and the sale of rice fertilizer. Except in the direct vicinity of Jenoi, there has been little change in the average Gambian's view that rice growing is women's work. In part of the middle river area Ramaswami and some of his assistants made a very deep impression on the chiefs and the people, and convinced a significant number of men to aid directly in the process of sowing and harvesting the rice. Yet this was only a side effect of Ramaswami's work. There was no organized government campaign to educate the people to plant better types or rice, to use rice fertilizer, or even to attempt to change the native attitude that rice cultivation was beneath the dignity of men. Without this change of attitude the result of attempting to sell ammonium sulphate fertilizer was a foregone conclusion. Even if the women had recognized the advantage of utilizing fertilizer, they could not have purchased it. Groundnuts are the only cash crop that the farmers of the Gambia have. The men plant, harvest, and sell the crop, and they retain the money from this production. The village women who are responsible for rice production do not have money, so therefore they could not buy the rice fertilizer. The authorities seem not to have recognized this situation and were bitterly disappointed when the fertilizer did not sell. Many of them concluded from this that the Gambians were unalterably backward and would not accept any new ideas pertaining to agriculture. As a result the major portion of the fertilizer that was imported to sell to the natives stayed in warehouses in the Colony area and presumably was used on the experimental farms.

All this is not to imply that great progress was not made in rice culture in the period of the 1950s. Agricultural development officers were brought out ostensibly to develop certain village projects in the various districts. There was to be an agricultural development officer for each one of the divisions for the Protectorate. Much of their time, however, was utilized for work totally unconnected with development purposes, usually in aiding the Commissioners. However, some great improvements were made in the direction of drainage of swampy areas, providing canals, and building rice buns.[12] The results of the development work in rice production in the 1950s, while falling far short of what could have been accomplished, were still dramatic enough to have removed the annual threat of the hungry season.

Before detailing the development and future prospects for groundnuts, it would be as well to survey briefly the various attempts made after World War II to provide a second source of export income. The first, and by far the most costly, experiment was the Yundum egg scheme which resulted in a financial disaster. The major reasons given for not attempting more economic and social plans had been lack of funds. Administrators in the '20s and '30s had been extremely reluctant to utilize reserve funds for even the most needed improvements. With the establishment of Colonial Development and Welfare Acts during the war, it appeared that the Gambia would receive the necessary money to begin a wide range of developments. The purpose of these funds was to enable a poor area to carry out necessary physical improvements in the form of schools, roads, and bridges which were beyond the financial capacity of the territory. There was no profit motive involved since these were outright grants to the territories. In 1948, however, the Colonial Development Corporation was formed. This organization was to devise development schemes for territories which would serve the dual purpose of providing necessary income for the areas involved and also a profit for the Corporation. The direction of the Corporation was the responsibility of a Board of Directors of eight members with Lord Trefgarne as chairman. Under the directors were two controllers, one for plans and one for operations. Field operations were the responsibility of area managers who supervised project managers. Theoretically the lines of control were well defined and almost self-policing. In actual fact, however, they were not as clear. This is particularly shown in the abortive Gambian egg scheme.[13]

The official under the controllers directly responsible for the Gambian egg scheme was Dr. Fowler, Manager of the Animal Products Division. Ostensibly under Dr. Fowler was the Project Manager, an American poultry expert, Mr. Millard J. Phillips whom Lord Trefgarne had met in January 1948 when he was employed in the management of a large poultry farm of approximately 75,000 birds in the Bahamas. Being suitably impressed with Mr. Phillips' qualifications, the Board authorized Lord Trefgarne on March 18, 1948, to offer him an appointment with the Corporation. His first duty was to visit the Gambia and to investigate and report on the practicability of establishing the production of poultry, eggs, and possibly hogs on intensive lines. After a visit of approximately twenty-two days, his party returned to England on May 17 and presented a brief report. They proposed to undertake the clearance of 10,000 acres of forest and bush, and to establish in the Gambia a large scale poultry farm capable of producing in two or three years, twenty million eggs per annum. This was to be followed by expansion if the results obtained justified it. A total capital outlay of £500,000 was envisaged under three main heads. The first involved the initial clearing of the land and the establishment of a saw mill to deal with the timber to be removed, the sale of which it was hoped would largely recoup the original capital outlay.[14] Mr. Hunt, the Forestry Officer of the Corporation, was not very impressed with the timber portion of the initial report. Secondly there was to be an agricultural farming site concerned with the production of coarse grain and legumes on the land cleared, which would provide a large portion of the feed for the laying flock. Finally the poultry farming site, which at maximum production, was ultimately expected to produce twenty million eggs and a million pounds of poultry per annum.

After considerable correspondence, Dr. Fowler, ostensibly Phillips' immediate superior, raised certain basic objections to Phillips' optimistic reports. Some of his criticisms were directed against Phillips' estimates of the amount of food required for the laying flock and the yield per acre of coarse grains proposed to be grown in the Gambia. Phillips' estimate had been that a total amount of about 7,700 short tons of food annually would be required, of which 5,000 tons would be grown on the land cleared and 2,700 tons imported. Dr. Fowler, however, considered that approximately 11,000 tons more would be required for the laying flock, a substantial difference bearing in mind that food was costing £20 per ton. He also calculated that the 5,000 tons to be grown on the land was an overestimation. Mr. Drenth, the Head of the Agriculture Division, concurred with Fowler. He expressed that view that the yield per acre would be in the neighbourhood of from 330 to 560 pounds per acre, whereas Phillips had assumed a figure of 900 to 1,000 pounds. Other criticisms made by Dr. Fowler were that the egg production of 200 eggs per bird per annum was too high and that the assumed price of eggs at two shillings and sixpence per dozen was too optimistic.

On July 15, 1948, Phillips was asked to prepare for the Board a report on the risk of poultry disease in the Gambia and the possibility of prevention and remedial measures. There is evidence that Phillips did not seek advice from any of the agricultural officers of the Gambia in preparing this and other reports. Whether by design or accident the moderating influence of men who had spent most of their working lives in the West African environment was lost. The later bad luck with fowl pest and other minor diseases might have been obviated had the Colonial Development Corporation worked in closer harmony with the Gambia government.

On July 16, a most important minute was circulated by Lord Trefgarne to the chief officers of the Corporation in which he said, 'This project appears to have become involved with various points of principle. I therefore decided to take direct charge of it from now on.' The Controller of Plans, Mr. Weeks, took this to mean that Lord Trefgarne had taken over the total responsibility for the project. Nevertheless, three days later he sent Lord Trefgarne further objections to the basic plan concerning estimated yields per acre, proposed death rates in culling losses, and degeneration which had been observed on exotic poultry in the tropics which led to smaller birds and smaller eggs after two or three generations. All the other senior officials of the Corporation stated later that they accepted the view that Lord Trefgarne was to be personally responsible for the project. Mr. Weeks, and Dr. Fowler particularly, regarded themselves as relieved of further functions concerning the project. By withdrawing from direct control of the project, Dr. Fowler removed the only man whose duty it was to tie up the loose ends, bring them into proper prospective, and act as a brake on Phillips. As Fowler did not exercise his normal functions as the head of a division responsible for the project, Phillips was permitted to deal directly with Lord Trefgarne and Sir Ernest Wood, the sub-chairman, on matters of policy and personnel without going through the ordinary channels.

By this time the initial £500,000 had been appropriated for the project and it was time for a revised schedule of costs and functions. On August 5 these revised programmes had been submitted to Lord Trefgarne on assumptions that timber reclaimed would be 640,000 cubic feet, and 32,000 cords of fire wood would be sold at seven shillings per cubic foot and ten shillings per cord; egg production would be 200 eggs per bird per annum; selling prices would be two shillings and sixpence for eggs per dozen, and poultry two shillings per pound dressed weight; feed consumption according to standards agreed substantially by Dr. Fowler and Phillips; and production of grain at 950 pounds per acre. On October 2, 1948, further revised estimates were circulated. This was to justify an additional expenditure of £200,000. The tentative figures given for expected annual profits were: timber production approximately £236,000; egg production, 200 eggs per bird at two shillings and sixpence per dozen; poultry two shillings CIF New York. It also noted that a five per cent increase or decrease in any of the above assumptions would mean on the part of the price of eggs a difference of £41,000; five per cent on egg production would increase or decrease the annual profit by £8,500, and a five per cent variation in production of grain per acre would mean an increase or decrease of £2,500. However, the additional £200,000 was approved.

The assumption that timber would realize £237,000 was 'hopelessly wrong'. In 1949, a further sum of £110,000 had to be appropriated to this scheme to cover the necessary capital expenditure to establish the project. According to the report, Lord Trefgarne was never informed of any of the doubts of the Forestry Officer, Mr. Hunt, and Sir Ernest Wood on the matter. Dr. Fowler had finally bowed to Phillips' experience in reference to the 200 eggs per bird, but the report of the investigating committee said owing 'to Mr. Phillips' failure to keep proper records, it has been impossible to establish whether the estimate was reached or not'. The projected selling prices of eggs was a substantial underestimate, and Phillips' estimate of 900 pounds grain yield per acre was a dreadful over-estimate. Up until October 1950 the crop reports indicate a yield of 207 pounds per acre.

Lord Trefgarne had great confidence in Mr. Phillips, and the Board in general shared this excessive confidence in the scheme. Sir Ernest Wood said in evidence, 'As a tropical poultry man, as a pioneer, as a man suited to the environment of creating in the African bush a tremendous enterprise, in that sense I felt then from the very beginning and I think now that he was quite outstandingly good.' He received this confidence from the board until early in 1950. Mr. Cable, one of the joint controllers, made an inspection early in 1950 and said,

A great job has been and is being carried out at Yundum. In barely a year a well equipped farm is practically completed with adequate housing accommodations, power house, shop, offices and club building; the best part of 10,000 acres has been cleared of timber and bush, and it is hoped that some 8,000 acres will be under cultivation by May; the breeding and laying flocks of poultry are being built up and it is expected that dressed chickens and eggs will be available for shipment in May and June.

155

This notable achievement is due to the ability, ingenuity
and drive of our Project Manager, Mr. Phillips . .

Phillips, however, had as early as January 1949 brought
attention to himself because of personnel difficulties at the site
and because some persons believed that the clearing of the land
was proceeding on the wrong lines. Instead of dividing the land
into fields of so many acres, all the trees were being removed
and there was no proper administration for the counting of
hens. Certain changes in personnel were made, a number of
officials removed, and this aspect of the matter was fully reported to the Board. In April 1949, Sir Ernest Wood wrote a
letter to Lord Trefgarne on the occasion of one of Lord Trefgarne's tours of the Gambia, which stated that Phillips had
two weaknesses which, however, Wood did not think would
detract from the success of the project. Phillips had nothing
good to say of anything British whether its personnel or equipment, and he was not a good organizer and administrator.
Wood believed that Phillips knew what he wanted, but did not
see clearly how to get it. In consequence, centralization was
carried too far, and his deputies had no clear cut responsibility;
thus anyone and everyone could go direct to him for orders.

In the autumn of 1949 Sir Ernest Wood and Dr. Fowler had
reason to express grave doubts as to the accuracy of Mr.
Phillips' monthly returns. These were quite important since it
was impossible in London to keep track of the project without
them, and Lord Trefgarne severely reprimanded Phillips.
After two years of operation, Sir Ernest Wood in the spring of
1950 expressed the view that Phillips, although a good pioneer
and poultry man, did not have sufficient experience as a
tropical farmer. Partly as a result of these alleged shortcomings,
the Colonial Development Corporation dispatched a man as
Phillips' farming assistant who was an experienced tropical
farmer. In October 1950, Lord Trefgarne approved a revised
plan for the scheme which involved Phillips' removal to another project. His proposed removal was not for mismanage-
ment, but because it was believed that his pioneering attributes
could be utilized better elsewhere.

By June 1950, the egg scheme had not been under way two

years and had cost £810,000. The timber which had been cleared from the land had not realized any profit. The actual production of grain in 1950 was 207 pounds per acre contrasted with Phillips' original expectations of 900 to 1,000 pounds. The birds, expensive Rhode Island Reds, had proved susceptible to fowl pest and great numbers had died. No one had expected the project to pay off the capital development immediately, but it was obvious by the fall of 1950 that the project was a liability. On July 12, 1950, another £100,000 had been appropriated to carry the project through the year. In October 1950, a detailed, revised plan for future administration of the project with revised estimates was prepared. Sir Ernest Wood and Dr. Fowler later admitted that they had no belief that the expectations for 1951 would be realized and that it would take other large sums to keep the project afloat that year. Even with such evidence of failure Lord Trefgarne, at the last meeting of the Board before his retirement, expressed his confidence in Mr. Phillips' ability as a manager. In February 1951, the decision was made to accept the losses in the Gambia and close down the project before it would cost more.

A thorough investigation of the egg scheme was conducted in 1951 and 1952 with the conclusion that although Lord Trefgarne was not to be held personally responsible, he had made certain errors in administration. He had either not investigated himself or adequately informed the Board of the pessimistic view held by some responsible officials concerning estimates. Nor did he and others who knew, make clear that most of the estimates accepted where those of Mr. Phillips and not supported by other experts of the Corporation.

In summary, the later investigation of this affair showed weak administration from the very top to the very bottom. It was true that the Corporation had many other projects under consideration at that time, but the fact still remained that this was a major scheme, the total expenditure being almost one million pounds. There did not seem to have been a very great sense of responsibility or knowledge on the part of those who were managing the project, leaving most of the decision making to Phillips who obviously, by the testimony of a number of officials, did not have very great administrative abilities. This was recognized at the time by those who were his superiors. Yet no check was put upon him, and presumably the men sent to aid him were either not of the best type, or Phillips ignored their advice. Thus from the very first, because of the administrative structure, the Gambia egg scheme was practically doomed to failure.

The failure of the egg scheme, combined with the Wallikunda experiment and losses incurred elsewhere in the Gambia, had far reaching effects on its future. These failures convinced private and government investors that little potential gain would accrue from development projects there. These failures also made the Governors and their advisors very wary of soliciting the type of capital investment necessary, not only to improve agriculture, but to effect the development of the harbour, airport, and land and water communications system. The Yundum scheme had lost almost one million pounds and all that was left to show for it was cleared ground, the chicken runs, and some large chickens in native compounds. It is not surprising that after this failure, investment tended to by-pass the Gambia.

However, two other attempts were made in the 1950s by private firms to discover and exploit any mineral resources of the area. It had long been believed, although there had never been a thorough survey, that there were no minerals of value in the Gambia. One exception to this long held belief seemed to be the discovery of Ilmenite deposits near Brufut. Explorations were begun by Gambia Minerals in 1954 because of the shortage of Ilmenite and the resultant high prices demanded by the major producers in India. Ilmenite ore is the source of rutile and also titanium oxide used in the manufacture of white paint. The Gambian deposits were found to be marginal, but notwithstanding this, work had begun on the selected sites in 1956. Gambia Minerals invested approximately £1,000,000 in building a railroad and a large electric dry mill. However, the deposits did not prove as extensive as first believed, having a maximum life of ten years. The plant was closed down in April 1959. The reason given was that over-production had caused a sharp fall in the world market price of zircon and rutile making it unprofitable to continue to operate the deposit.[15] In the late 1950s following the discovery of oil in the Sahara, a number of oil firms made exploratory drillings in the Senegal. Eventually British Petroleum ran a test well in Kombo in the same strata as that which had indicated some promise in Casamance. However, by mid-1961 the results were negative and it was obvious that the Gambia was not to recoup its financial fortunes by means of oil.

The closing down of Ilmenite mining and the negative results of oil exploration, following the catastrophic failures of Wallikunda and Yundum, meant that the Gambia economy would be based in the future totally upon groundnuts. Since the Gambia had long depended upon this crop, it would be well to examine in some detail the means of cultivation, local distribution, and export potential of this vital product. As previously related, the lands in the Protectorate are held in communal tenure, with the Native Authorities allotting lands to various family groups within their jurisdiction. This has precluded any large scale development scheme by progressive native cultivators. Almost all groundnut farms are quite small. There is no mechanization of groundnut farms; the methods of planting and gathering the harvest have remained relatively unchanged since the establishment of the Protectorate.

In April and May, before the rains, the ground is cleared preparatory to planting by using a small bladed axe or matchet. If there is considerable grass on the land, it is first burned off. Shrubs, timber, and other impediments are also burned. This method of clearing is common throughout West Africa and there are few differences to note between tribes. Some observers have indicated that the Wolof are more careful and less destructive of the bush than are the Mandingos. After the first heavy rain, the seed groundnuts, which have been selected from the previous year's crop and carefully stored, are planted. The Mandingos and Jola make ridges on which to plant while the Wolof plant on the flat. The planter holds in one hand a small narrow bladed hoe with which to make holes in the ground, dropping in the seed with the other hand. The holes are covered over by stamping the ground with the feet as the planted proceeds. After planting, the major task is combating the weeds. The groundnut land, whether it has been previously used or was secondary or primary bush, becomes quickly overgrown with grass and weeds in the rainy season so there is constant work clearing out this growth, generally with a broad shovel bladed hoe called an *iler*. When the plants have spread and the nuts are forming, all weeding must be done by hand to avoid damaging the plant. The fields also must be protected from baboons and monkeys. The depredations by baboons a few years ago were so extensive that a bounty was offered by the government for killing them. As a result they have ceased to be the menace they once were. However, the growing crops still demand watching.

Groundnuts are harvested usually in October by loosening the soil around the plant and then pulling it out of the ground. The plants are left to dry for a time on the ground and then gathered together for further drying. The final process occurs in December when the dried plants are threshed on a hard piece of ground by beating them with sticks. When the plants are threshed and the nuts separated, the stalks, dust, and other foreign matter are sifted by winnowing. The groundnuts thus harvested are placed in sacks and taken to the various trade centres for sale.[16]

From the start of the season this process takes over eight months of extremely hard work. One observer who spent a few days in the Gambia made much of the seeming laziness of the men who, to her, spent their time lolling under the *bantaba* tree. In all fairness the Gambian farmer works very hard on the groundnut crop which is considered men's work. For all this labour he is rewarded with an average crop yield of approximately 700 pounds to the acre, which amounts to a gross of less than £9. The price per ton given by the traders of the commercial houses is fixed by the Government Oilseeds Marketing Board, and has fluctuated from a high of £32 to a low of £22 per ton.

Traders licensed by the government, either natives or representatives of such large firms as United Africa Company or Maurel and Prom, purchase the raw groundnuts from the farmers and transport them to the decorticating centres or river ports. The major plants are at Kaur, Kuntaur, and Bathurst. The two former locations are the major up river ports, and the largest portion of the processed nuts from these plants is immediately shifted to ocean-going vessels. A large amount of the harvest is transported down river either to the storage areas or other decorticating plants. A growing amount of nuts for Bathurst is now transported by lorry, but much of the crop is still carried downstream by the picturesque, heavily laden groundnut cutters.

An analysis of the export figures shows clearly the traditional unhealthy dependence of the Gambia on the culture of the groundnut in the Protectorate. In 1830 the first recorded export of the crop was worth only £10 16s. 8d.[17] By 1889 the value of the crop had reached £140,086.[18] From this time until 1940 the value of the export increased steadily. The following table indicates this development and the total involvement of the Gambia with the success of the groundnut culture.[19]

	Tons exported	Value	Approx. price per ton
1890	18,262	£129,817	£7
1899	34,353	210,005	6
1910	58,456	387,943	6.10s.
1915	96,152	400,435	4
1925	48,700	693,097	14
1930	74,761	867,630	12
1935	45,110	368,887	8

These figures indicate the exteme fluctuations in the total harvest available for export and the wide range of the world market price. The basic unhealthiness of the situation was masked because bad harvests in the Gambia seldom coincided with low market prices. The boom period of the '20s, however, gave way to a generally lower, but more stable price in the '30s.

As has been noted already, Gambia groundnut farmers use no mechanization, and until the late 1940s very little fertilizer. There were also few attempts made to improve the quality of the crop. Growing competition from other African producers, as well as better quality nuts from American mechanized farms, gave rise, in the post-World War II period, to serious attempts to improve the quality and quantity of the export. Fertilizers began to be used widely and the government established the Groundnut Oil Seed Marketing Board in 1948.[20] This Board was given the responsibility for establishing grades for nuts and was empowered to purchase the whole of the crop for resale to buyers. Such an organization presumed a more reasonable approach to pricing of the crop. On a basis of the volume of the crop of the previous years, competition and the world price, the Board would set a standard price per ton for the crop. Any increase in the predicted price would result in a surplus which would be accrued in what was known as the Farmers' Fund. This Fund could be utilized to make up deficits when the predicted price was not obtained. A further development in marketing procedures was in the shipment of decorticated nuts. Decorticating plants at Bathurst, Kaur, and Kuntaur by the end of the 1950s were processing all but a few tons of the harvest.

Despite these changes, the Gambia was not able to cope with fluctuations in market prices which continued to fall during the 1950s.[21] The groundnut price in the early '50s had been established at £32 per ton, only slightly less than the price guaranteed by the French in Senegal. Due to a combination of a bad harvest, poor quality of nuts, and a fall in the world price, the government revenue for 1953 was in such a bad situation (a deficit of £150,000) that experts from the Colonial Office and Treasury were called in to investigate.[22] Following the recommendations of the experts, the government reduced expenditures and met the deficit from the reserves which were dangerously low. These reserves had been reconstructed by the end of 1954 by leaving incomplete certain projects that had been contemplated the previous year.

With great misgivings, the Groundnut Oil Seed Marketing Board announced at the beginning of the 1954-55 trade season that the price per ton would be maintained at £32. The world price continued to fall and G.O.M.B. had a net loss of £640,000 for the trading year. The bulk of the loss was absorbed by the Farmers' Fund. Fearing that a continued lowering of the world price and poor harvests would totally deplete the Fund, the Board set the price for the 1955-56 season at £25,10s.[23] A good crop (56,561 tons as compared to 46,000 the previous year) partially restored the government balances and the Farmers' Fund rose to £448,877.[24] This good season emboldened G.O.M.B. to set the price for the 1956-57 season at £31. The failure of a large portion of the Nigerian crop combined with a harvest of 77,396 tons indicated that perhaps the worst was over.[25] In 1957 the export tax was reduced to £1 5s. instead of the £2 of the previous year. To counteract this, G.O.M.B. planned to guarantee a payment of only £27 per ton. A record crop of 96,000 tons was harvested and the profit for groundnut farmers and the government exceeded that of the previous year.[26] However, beginning in 1958 the world price fell to new lows and the Board could only guarantee £22. This fall coincided with a mediocre crop of only 63,000 tons for the 1958-59 season, This meant that profits for the farmers were one and one third million pounds less than the previous year.[27] As will be detailed elsewhere, since 1956, government expenditure had exceeded income. This situation combined with the continued depressed groundnut market after 1958 forced the government to retrench in certain services and to approach the home government every year for grants to meet the government deficit. The budget deficit in 1962 was £575,000 and promises to continue to mount in future years. At the same time the reserve fund has been depleted to such an extent that only large scale grants can keep the Gambia financially viable even without an expansion of much needed services.[28]

Under the best of circumstances the Gambia with poor soil, and artificially constricted to its narrow boundaries, would have been in poor financial condition. The avowed governmental policy, which tried to maintain the *status quo* and effect a minimum expenditure on developing secondary agricultural products, left the area totally dependent upon one crop at mid-century. The later influx of large sums of money to provide other exports proved fruitless, and explorations for mineral wealth were not successful. Therefore the Gambia remains a non-viable monoculture. This financial fact was all important and remains so for the future. No major social change, economic development, or political arrangement can be contemplated without prior reference to the financial plight of the territory. Politically the Gambia is at the crossroads, having moved to the threshold of independence. No political leader could countenance a prolongation of colony status. Amalgamation with Senegal or Independence are the two alternatives. The success of each of these choices ultimately depends upon the precarious game of marketing groundnuts.

Chapter Nine

FISCAL ATTITUDES OF THE GOVERNMENT

ONE unifying theme in the modern history of the Gambia is the lack of resources of the territory. This has resulted in a minimum yearly government revenue. This situation, which at best would have limited the most enlightened colonial government, is even more pressing as the Gambia moves closer to Independence. Those responsible governments that have emerged since 1960 have discovered that manipulating the finances of a monoculture takes precedence over all other problems. Because the Gambia has been and will continue to be a prisoner of its poor economy, it is necessary to review carefully its financial history and the correlate lack of social and economic development.

The present economic impotence of the Gambia tends to mask the historical realities of British financial policy as it was applied to all colonial areas up to 1940. This basic policy was that each colony, however large or small, should be economically and financially self sufficient. A colony could not be a drain upon the Treasury of the mother country. Any capital developments that were to be instituted would have to be paid for out of the earnings of the colony itself. Such a policy, although understandable from the point of view of colonial administrators, was shortsighted. When applied to relatively rich areas in West Africa this dictum acted as a brake upon im-

165

portant developments which would have cost large sums of money in the initial stages. When it was applied, however, to an unwanted and basically backward area such as the Gambia, the results for the people were disastrous. The period from 1889 until 1914 was one of uncertainty. The attitude of a great number of important British and French statesmen was that the Gambia would soon be returned to its natural hinterland in exchange for adequate compensation elsewhere. Subsequently the four years of World War I saw Britain occupied with matters of far greater concern than the proper administration of colonial policy in backwater areas of the world. It is, therefore, in the period from 1918 until 1940 that one can see the damaging effects of the policy of no unnecessary investment or expenditure.

It has been stated so often that the Gambia is economically backward that the normal assumption is that it has always been a drain upon the British Treasury and has been an economically non-viable area. However, if the statistics for total imports and exports of the British West African colonies are compared for the years immediately after the war on a *per capita* basis, the Gambia is exceeded only by the Gold Coast.[1] The Gambia had always been self-supporting, and in the period of attachment to Sierra Leone in the latter nineteenth century had been the more prosperous of the two areas. With the exception of only a few years, the revenue of the Colony in the forty year period after 1900 had consistently exceeded expenditures. In 1912 the reserve assets of the Colony were £107,731 and by 1920 this amount had grown to £328,657 or twice as much as the actual expenditures of the Gambia for the year.[2] The size of the reserve fund is even more staggering when compared with the expenditures for key social services in this period Allocations for education in 1912 amounted to slightly more than £1,100.[3] In 1925 this had increased to only £3,500. The cost of financing the medical services in 1925 was £24,712.[4]

The Governors of the Gambia, partly influenced by the attitude of the British Treasury, followed most conservative financial policies. As can be observed by the expenditures on health and eduction, little attention was given to providing improved social services for the people of the Colony or the

Protectorate. Few major projects were undertaken in the inter-war period, despite the obvious need for better streets, roads, drainage systems, bridges, and electrification. This reluctance to expand and improve facilities was only partly based upon lack of funds to carry out development schemes. The restrictions placed upon colonial governments by the minimum expenditure dictum would have meant that at best the Gambia would have progressed slowly in any development plans. The unhealthy respect of the Gambia government for reserve funds was the major reason for the non-expansion of services and few capital expenditures in the inter-war period.

The most glaring example of the indifferent financial attitude of the British government concerning the needs of the Gambia was the demonetization of the French five franc piece. By an Order in Council in June 1843, this coin had been recognized as legal tender in the Gambia. The exchange rate for the piece had been fixed at three shillings and ten pence half penny. In 1880 when the five franc piece comprised approximately eighty-five per cent of the total circulation of money in the Colony, demonetization had been suggested, but the plan had been rejected at that time. The native Gambians knew and appreciated the coin. It was easily convertible and was very handsome. Many of the Wolof women utilized it for costume jewellery. During the first World War the stability of the French exchange was upset. In 1919 the world rate for the five franc piece was considerably lower than that which was still being paid in Bathurst at the legally accepted rate of conversion. The problem of the differential rates and loss of gold was noticeable immediately after the war, but nothing was done to make the official rate conform to the world rate. The British Treasury believed that the alloyed coins of the West African Currency Board which were issued in November 1920, would soon drive out the older currency. This proved a vain hope and the money crisis continued to develop. In March 1921, the banks in Bathurst refused to accept the five franc piece for transfer abroad except at the world rate. In the following month the importation of these coins was prohibited, but the number in circulation continued to increase since the Gambia was the only place in the world where such a favourable exchange of approximately one and three quarters to one could be effected. The Gambia, therefore, drew these coins like a magnet. By the end of 1921 the government had over 70,000 of these five franc pieces purchased at legal tender value which earned no interest and were of no use for transfers. Finally the pressure of the situation became so great that the government decided to demonetize in January 1922. The calling in of all the five franc pieces at the legal rate cost a total of £407,950 for approximately 2,100,000 coins. They were then shipped to England where they were melted down and realized slightly more than one half the cost of redemption.

The decision to continue the five franc piece in circulation long after other countries had followed the prevailing world rate was not one that the Gambia government, let alone the Gambian people, could make. This was a decision which had been made by Treasury officials of Great Britain. Their dilatory attitude in arriving at a reasonable conclusion was the primary reason for the continued existence of these coins as legal tender in the Gambia. Therefore it seemed logical to Gambian merchants, to many colonial servants, and to the Governor that the British government should assume the cost of demonetization. However, their pleas fell upon deaf ears and the Gambia which could not afford to expend more than £2,500 a year on education was saddled with the total burden of paying for the demonetization which cost them almost £200,000. To defray this, the West African Currency Board loaned a total of £177,893 at four per cent interest to the Gambian government. By 1930 this loan had been repaid. The result of the five franc fiasco was to reduce the excess funds available to the Gambian government for any type of development. The reserve fund that amounted to £286,396 in 1921 had been reduced to only £99,687 in 1922.[5] This is one of the most flagrant examples of lack of government responsibility towards the welfare of the colonial areas which they had appropriated. Even with the Gambia government refusing to spend extra money, it was not until the very eve of World War II that the Gambia again had a surplus of funds comparable in size to the amount of money they were forced to spend to cover the mistake of the Exchequer.

Demonetization came at an unfortunate time because the Gambia government had decided to begin modernization of the port of Bathurst. Their plans envisaged the electrification of Bathurst, drainage of a portion of Half-Die swamp, a slipway for larger ships, and a larger water reservoir. These long delayed measures were postponed for years due to the preoccupation with the five franc measure. They were eventually completed by 1930 at a cost of less than £100,000.[6] The policy of the Gambia government in the 1930s was not to continue such projects on a limited scale, but to retrench further because of world conditions. The current assumption that the Gambia was always a drain on the home government is totally false. There was always a substantial surplus fund which could have been wisely utilized to improve the Gambia. The government did not do so, and the attitude of economy and retrenchment predominated until the close of World War II. By then the administrative staff had grown, inflation had lowered the real value of the surplus funds, and the market for groundnuts had become increasingly more competitive.

The passage of the first Colonial Development and Welfare Act in 1940 gave promise of reversing the long established policy of self-sufficiency. The home government at last recognized that in areas such as the Gambia it had assumed a responsibility which could not continually be evaded. Looking towards a reasonable implementation of the Colonial Development and Welfare funds, the Colonial Office in February 1940, asked the Governors of all colonial areas to prepare detailed plans for the systematic development of their areas. Governor Southorn appointed a Development Committee under the chairmanship of Mr. K. W. Blackburne, an official of the West Indies who had been seconded to the Gambia. The local members of the Committee were the Colonial Secretary, the Senior Medical Officer, the Senior Agriculture Superintendent, and the Director of Education. The resultant report was a comprehensive survey of the Gambia and a forthright appraisal of the Gambia's economic and social needs.[7] This was the first time that the central government had ever attempted to set forth a planned programme for the future development of the country. All other developments had been accomplished almost as an afterthought, and many vital areas had been totally ignored. The Blackburne Report was accepted by the Colonial Office as the master plan to guide future government development.

During the war a number of short range programmes suggested by the Blackburne Report were put into effect. A senior Commissioner for the Protectorate was appointed, primary and infant schools in Bathurst were re-organized as government schools, and considerable funds were expended on health services. These latter plans called for the training of probationary nurses, dental technicians, and an additional medical officer and a Sanitary Superintendent. Also envisaged was the construction of a Health Centre at Basse, additions to the hospital at Bansang, and mosquito control in the area of Bathurst and Kombo.[8] However, an analysis of funds allocated under the 1940 Act shows that the government did not take advantage of the funds available to them. For example, two different schemes for medical and health improvement were in operation prior to 1945 with a total amount budgeted of £37,674. By the time that these plans lapsed, only £8,547 had been spent. Similar comparisons can be made concerning fund utilization by other departments.[9]

One of the most ambitious schemes recommended by the Blackburne Report concerned the improvement of Bathurst. There were few paved streets, an inadequate water supply, poor drainage, and the hospital facilities were woefully inadequate. The reconstruction of Bathurst, however, was overshadowed by another grandiose scheme which occupied much of the time of the government and in the end wasted great sums of money. The report had suggested that the government offices and a large segment of the population should be moved to a new location. In June 1943, £30,000 was made available for preliminary planning of this new townsite near Sukuta in Kombo. In November 1944, a Consulting Engineer and Architect arrived and it was announced in principle that a trunk airport would be constructed and maintained near Sukuta. In December 1944, the Town Planning and Development advisors agreed that the administrative centre should be moved to the healthier area near the proposed airport. The Colonial Secretary expressed great interest in the scheme and detailed planning began.

The basic plan called for the necessary improvements to Bathurst, the construction of the airport, a new bridge at Oyster Creek, a deep-water wharf at Bathurst, the purchasing of lands for the new site, construction of a brick and tile factory, drainage and levelling of the Sukuta area, and the construction of the necessary new roads and administrative buildings. The total expenditure was estimated at £691,002, and an application for a grant of this sum was made in February 1945. So certain was the Gambia government that this would be granted that the surveys of Bathurst had been completed and the clearing of land at the town site had begun. Suddenly the Colonial Office began to be less enthusiastic about the proposal. In May 1945, the plan to build a trunk airport at Sukuta was cancelled, possibly because of the wartime airstrip that would soon be available at Yundum. This caused a minor modification in the plans, but work continued at Sukuta and Bathurst. A further change of policy by the Colonial Office was declared in July 1945 when it was announced that the Gambia could not expect the full costs of the projects to be financed by Colonial Development and Welfare funds. It was indicated that perhaps between £500,000 and £750,000 would be available. Work on the projects was halted and the situation carefully reviewed. The Gambia government and its advisors prepared new individual plans for the proposed developments. They involved the expenditure of £1,014,660, and a grant of £514,660 was requested from Colonial Development and Welfare funds. The difference in the expenditure was to be met by a loan of £450,000 and the Gambia would provide £50,000. In October 1945, the Colonial Secretary replied that no loan would be considered and a maximum of £500,000 could be allotted for the completion of the projects. Again new plans and cost estimates were submitted to London along with a request for an interim grant for staff purposes of £282,740 which was received in March 1946. The Colonial Secretary visited Bathurst in January 1946, and informed the Governor that only £500,000 maximum could be expected from Colonial Development and Welfare funds, the remainder would have to be met locally or by borrowing.

Under these circumstances the Gambian authorities reluctantly gave up the idea of resettlement and returned £116,100 to Colonial Development and Welfare. The scope of development was to be restricted to the necessary improvements in the Bathurst area.[10]

In review of these complicated procedures, a number of factors stand out. The embryo plans in the Blackburne Report for the development of the Colony area were in the main very good. The Colony did need more water, electricity, paved streets, and better drainage. Drainage of the swamp areas around Koto stream and a new bridge were long overdue. A properly constructed tile and brick plant was a feasible project, and the proposed trunk airport in retrospect was perhaps even more important. The failure to build this or to improve Yundum meant that in the immediate post-war years, the major air-carriers by-passed Bathurst and made Dakar one of the great air travel centres of the world. The only questionable phase of the development plans was the building of a new administrative centre at Sukuta. This was a luxury which a poor area such as the Gambia could ill afford. But for a two year period the Gambia government was encouraged to believe that the Colonial Office completely approved of their plans and the method of financing them. Only after the expenditure of considerable sums and the preparation of a number of detailed development plans was the Gambia informed that the ambitious plans would have to be financed primarily by the Colony. This was a reversal of the previously stated position of the Colonial Office and a return in part to the philosophy of the inter-war period. The attitude was a negation of the warning of the Blackburne Report that the revenue of the Gambia was sufficient for recurrent expenditure but that 'financial assistance must be provided if any development is to be undertaken'.

The necessary improvements in the Colony that had been accepted in principle by the Colonial Office in 1943 were not really put into effect until the 1950s. From 1947 to 1957 a total of £1,058,800 was expended for Colony improvements. Of this sum, Colonial Development and Welfare grants accounted for £976,340, the remainder being a charge on the Gambia government. This was the period when the Colony acquired a new bridge, a high school, a better water supply, an adequate street drainage system, and paved streets for Bathurst. Discounting the Wallikunda rice development scheme, the Protectorate in this same period directly received £583,290, the major portion of which was to be expended in constructing a portion of the asphalt road from Brikama to Mansa Konko.[11]

The period since 1945 has been one of increased expenditures and increased services. Some of the funds were wasted in fruitless schemes, and certain ideas which held great promise were vetoed by the Colonial Office, but excepting at Wallikunda and Yundum, the money was wisely spent. The Gambia had been neglected for so long that even with this quickening of economic and social services, it remains very undeveloped and backward. A closer investigation of the various service areas will indicate the degree of improvement and the present inadequate level of the service departments.

The major service departments of the central government are Agriculture, Public Works, Marine, Education, and Public Health. The organization of all these departments is similar. Each has a director in charge of operations who until recently was appointed by the Governor and responsible to him. Since the constitutional reorganization of 1960 these department heads have been responsible to elected Ministers who in theory are in charge of policy making, but who in fact still depend very heavily for advice upon the heads of departments. All these service departments are headquartered in Bathurst and still focus much of their work and planning on the Colony. They have all been extremely handicapped by a lack of funds and have had difficulty in recruiting an adequate number of well-trained personnel to carry out their minimum functions. In the days of total colonial rule, the Gambia government was in competition for staff with the larger, more prosperous West African territories. Thus, there has been a chronic shortage on all levels of competent men, and in some cases in the 1930s the departments depended largely upon staff seconded from other areas of Africa. Another trait common to all departments was the failure to train Gambians to assume the middle and upper range positions. Although there were some exceptions, little progress had been made towards the Gambianization of the

Civil Service until the early 1950s. Agricultural experiments and developments have been discussed elsewhere. Thus, in the following pages attention will be given to the marine, public works, health, and finally education improvements that have been accomplished since 1945.

The Gambia River is the finest waterway in West Africa. This was taken for granted in the Blackburne Report, and part of the suggested development was to improve river communications by building deep water wharves in Bathurst and service wharves for up river ports, and by providing more and better river craft to link the Protectorate with the ocean. Much has been accomplished. Bathurst now has two deep water wharves, and the groundnut ports of Kaur and Kuntaur have been improved. A new river transport, 'The Lady Wright', was purchased and some new ferries, generally modelled on the Landing Craft of World War II, have been provided. In 1960, construction of a new landing stage at Barra to provide better cross river communications with Bathurst was begun. Despite all this, the state of river transport remains primitive. The 'Lady Wright' is the only large, safe government transport for the river. Major ports such as Basse are totally inadequate, even for the present level of service. The ferry system is not only poor, it is dangerous. Kerewan, through which all east-west road traffic on the north bank must pass, uses in part old hand operated cable ferries. The worst bottleneck is north-south traffic from Bathurst to Barra. The equipment is old and untrustworthy, and if all goes well, the trip across the river takes over one hour. At certain times in the day when there is a heavy incoming tide, the equipment in use is a menace to the traveller. In May 1957, one of the ferries capsized with the loss of over fifty lives.[12] Few new pieces of equipment have been added to the ferry service since that time.

The alternate communications system to that of the river is that of the Colony and Protectorate roads. Some improvement has been effected since 1955 with the construction of new asphalt roads and the bridge at Pakali Ba. Two major surfaced roads have been completed in the Protectorate. One is the trans-Gambian road, a north-south link of approximately twelve miles passing through Mansa Konko, which ties the

Casamance to Senegal. The other major completed project is the first part of the proposed system which will eventually provide the Protectorate with a good all-weather road on both the north and south banks. At present this segment has been completed just past Brikama. If the funds are available the entire system should be completed by 1966. Until this is accomplished the Protectorate roads are little more than dirt trails which are difficult to use even in the dry season. When the rains come they are impassable and many villages are isolated until the rains stop. Each Division of the Protectorate receives approximately £2,000 per year for upkeep of the roads. There is no mechanized equipment available to the Commissioners, and until the administration of Governor Windley there was not even a road grader for the Colony area. Under such conditions the Commissioners can do little with the available funds but repair the largest holes in the roads. Lack of adequate roads prevents movement of goods, surplus food, and adequate medical care.[13]

The medical and public health facilities of the Gambia are inadequate for a tropical country of its size even considering the large sums expended in the past ten years. Part of the reason for this can be explained by lack of money appropriated. In 1900 the Hospital and Medical Department was allocated £1,869.[14] By 1945 this had grown to £56,287,[15] and in 1958 to £154,487 or thirteen per cent of the total budget.[16] Before 1938 there were no hospital facilities for the entire Protectorate until the completion of the new hospital at Bansang. In 1953 the old hospital in Bathurst was replaced with Colonial Development and Welfare funds by a modern new facility, the Victoria Hospital. There are native dispensaries located at Basse, Kerewan, Kaur, Kuntaur, Mansa Konko, and Cape St. Mary. These are normally operated by Gambian medical orderlies. The Medical Officers in the Protectorate, as time allows, pay regular visits to these stations and nearby villages. In 1961, however, there were only two doctors in service for the entire Protectorate. The major dispensaries are provided with Land Rover ambulances. Seriously injured or critically ill patients in outlying villages often die before they can be brought to the medical centres, and during the rainy season it is often impossible to bring any type of medical services to them. In 1961 there were also two Red Cross sisters, one at Basse and the other at Mansa Konko, who in many cases were more effective in the villages than the ordinary medical officials. Since 1961 there have also been leprosy control officers in the Protectorate provided by the World Health Organization.

The medical position of the Colony is far superior to that of the Protectorate. Discounting the Chief Medical Officer whose functions are primarily administrative, in 1961, there were three doctors who were available for private practice as well as giving service in Victoria Hospital. They were hampered by shortage of many of the newer drugs and the unwillingness of many Gambians to seek medical advice from European trained physicians. In addition, the Public Health Service was quite active in Bathurst in trying to control the mosquito menace and eradicate the large rat population. The Medical Research Council staff, located at Fajara, although primarily concerned with research into tropical diseases, do hold dispensaries and as such are good adjunct to the medical facilities of the Colony area.

The paucity of medical staff and health care for one quarter of a million people is highlighted by a consideration of the types of medical problems present. The greatest of all the potential killers is the mosquito. Although the Bathurst area has been rendered relatively safe, the Protectorate has been almost untouched by the massive preventive measures necessary to control the danger of the mosquito. Few studies have been made concerning mortality rates in the Protectorate, but preliminary investigations have indicated that infant mortality rates in certain parts of the Protectorate exceed five hundred per thousand. Most of these deaths are connected with malaria.[17] Apart from the deaths, malaria has a debilitating effect upon most of the population because few persons know of or can afford malarial suppressives, Yaws, intestinal and skin worms of various kinds are a continuing cause of poor health and discomfort. Malnutrition is one of the greatest threats. The average Gambian has little protein in his diet, eats few vegetables, and his staple food, rice, is so polished that little of food value is left. Milk is an extreme luxury that only a very few persons in the Colony area can afford. Sleeping sickness is endemic and

176

leprosy is a continuing menace. One Leprosy Control official estimated that there were over six thousand untreated cases of leprosy in the Gambia. If true, this means that over two per cent of the population is afflicted by it. With such outstanding health and medical problems, even the growing government expenditure and increase in staff and facilities only serve to indicate how much has been needed.

In the area of education, the long standing policies of little expenditure and support of indirect rule meant that the educational facilities available in 1945 were little better than at the turn of the century. The Gambia government decided in the nineteenth century to leave education entirely in the care of the missionaries. In 1888 an education expert from Sierra Leone visited the schools of the Colony and found them to be totally inadequate. In his report he made certain recommendations that were not put into effect for almost fifty years.[18] Even before the government assumed responsibility for the Protectorate, Administrator Llewellyn was aware of the need for some more active participation in the field of education. The Roman Catholic schools in the Colony were attended primarily by Wolof and children of French descent. The immigrants from Sierra Leone (Akus) who were Christian sent their children to the Wesleyan and Church of England schools. The Mohammedan citizens, who were the bulk of the population and taxpayers, had no schools other than the very poor informal Mohammedan ones. There, the learning opportunities were restricted to being taught the Koran and the ability to write and recite a few phrases of imperfect Arabic. The Governor concluded by stating, 'It is, I think, indubitable that this is a lamentable condition, and injurious at once to the best interests of the people and of the government.'[19]

The major change regarding government participation in education that was authorized in the 1890s was a grant in aid to mission and Mohammedan schools. In 1900 this grant for all the schools of the Gambia amounted to only £416.[20] By 1925 when the total expenditures of the Gambia government reached almost £275,000, education still received a trifling sum of £3,460.[21]

Governor Armitage established in 1923 a school for the sons of chiefs at Georgetown which after a shaky start has grown, particularly since World War II, to be the major educational facility in the Protectorate. It was not intended to be this, and for a long time catered only to the Protectorate aristocracy, trying to give them the rudiments of reading and writing English. The other main educational facilities in the Protectorate in this period were the Wesleyan elementary school at Georgetown and the Catholic mission schools at Basse. There was only one secondary institution in the Colony, the Wesleyan High School which had fifty pupils on its rolls in 1920. Despite the previous statements by Governor Llewellyn and others concerning the poor educational facilities available for the Mohammedans, the government gave a total grant of only £151 to such schools in the Colony. In 1921 another education expert arrived in the Gambia at the invitation of the government. In a classic understatement, the report said that the system of subsidization of education 'leaves much to be desired'. The expert drafted a new education code which called for more government intervention in educational affairs and a larger expenditure of funds. The code was not implemented because as the government stated, 'its adoption will necessitate an expenditure which cannot be incurred at the moment'.[22] This expression of lack of funds coincided with the expenditure of £200,000 for demonetization.

In 1930 a Teacher Training Institute was opened in Georgetown, but in 1938 only six persons were attending the school. In this latter year, apart from the Training Institute and Armitage School, there were only six elementary schools in the Protectorate—one Wesleyan, two Anglican, and three Roman Catholic. In Bathurst educational facilities, although not good, were in much better condition than in the Protectorate. There were six elementary mission schools with a total of 1,698 pupils on the rolls including 544 girls. However, the average attendance was only 1,277 pupils. In addition there were four secondary schools—two Wesleyan and two Catholic. The Catholic schools were ungraded and smaller than their Protestant counterparts. The Wesleyan Boys and Girls High Schools were the most important secondary schools in the Gambia and later became the nucleus of the government High

School. In 1938 there was a total enrolment in all of these secondary schools of 69 boys and 128 girls. The budget allocation for education had grown to be £5,528 by 1940. This, however, included the salary for a newly created post of Director of Education, who with a board of missionaries to advise him, was placed in charge of the educational plant. In addition there was a Mohammedan school with 238 pupils in Bathurst and one at Georgetown with 56 enrolled, where rudiments of English and Arabic were taught.[23]

Thus, until World War II, the government had almost totally disassociated itself from educating the people. For fifty years the government had expended an average annual amount in grants to schools of less than £2,000. No standardized textbooks were utilized, nor was there any real attempt to set a common standard of performance for either students or teachers. The education given was a duplication of that given to English students on the same level although conditions in the Gambia were far from being like those of England. Little attention was paid to vocational or agricultural training, the aim of all of the schools being the classic liberal arts programme. Thus, many students were over-educated, having proceeded far enough to be unsatisfied with traditional life, and not far enough to enable them to get and hold clerical positions with the government or private firms. There was no advanced education beyond the secondary level possible in the Gambia. Those students who could afford it went to the United Kingdom or to Fourah Bay College in Sierra Leone. Many of these became professionals and some have never returned to the Gambia. Thus teacher recruitment continued to be as great a problem as the necessity to invest more money in education.

Compared with the lethargy which prevailed before World War II the years since have seen tremendous progress in education under the direct support and encouragement of the government. There is today a Minister of Education responsible for development and planning, who is assisted by a Director of Education. This administrative structure has evolved from the initial stage where there was a Director of Education who was assisted by an Education Officer for the Colony and one for the Protectorate. The central and local government authorities have taken over directly the administration of almost all the mission schools. In the Colony the Wesleyan Boys and Girls High Schools have been merged into the Gambia High School under the guidance of a principal. Under a Colonial Development and Welfare grant, a new High School is being completed on the outskirts of Bathurst, which is a great improvement over the old, cramped structure in central Bathurst. The Roman Catholic boys and girls secondary schools continue as separate schools. In 1960 the total enrolment in all these schools was 388 boys and 235 girls. In addition a new post-primary school, constructed at Crab Island with Colonial Development and Welfare funds, was attended in 1960 by over five hundred pupils. On the primary level in the Colony area there were twelve government primary schools and three private elementary facilities with a total of over 3,700 students on the rolls.

It has been in the Protectorate that the most dramatic improvement has taken place. In 1940 there were only six primary schools offering four years of schooling. In 1960 this number had grown to thirty-seven village primary schools, twenty-five of which were owned and controlled by district authorities. Most of these schools had been upgraded to give education to standard six, and were largely staffed by government teachers. There were over 2,200 pupils in attendance.[24] Armitage School at Georgetown remained a post-primary boarding school with a limited enrolment, but by 1961 it had been enlarged to accommodate over two hundred students.

In post-secondary education the government has also assumed a position of leadership. The buildings at Yundum which were abandoned after the abortive egg scheme were purchased and turned into Yundum College for Teachers with the first class entering the school in 1952. It provides a three year course, reduced to two years for certificate holders, designed to train men and women teachers for the elementary levels.[25] To provide more advanced training, the government began to grant scholarships to Gambians for overseas training. In 1960 there were forty-four Gambians in training overseas on such grants. In addition over one hundred private students were studying in the United Kingdom.[26]

This rapid growth of education in the Gambia has taken place against the concerted opposition of many of the traditional rulers in the Protectorate. In some areas the district schools still have very small enrolments, and in others, particularly in the upper river, schools have been closed because of lack of support by the Native Authorities. It has also cost the government an ever increasing amount of money to finance education. In 1948 the expenditure was less than £30,000. By 1958 it amounted to over £124,000.[27]

Only the most optimistic observer would pronounce the Gambian educational system good. Money alone does not create a good educational facility. There is still an appalling lack of well trained teachers at all levels. The school at Yundum, while better than what existed before, does not measure up to the better training institutions in other parts of West Africa, and certainly does not compare with its counterparts in the United Kingdom. Too many of the students trained in overseas universities either go into the professions or stay away from the Gambia on completion of their training. The enrolment of 2,500 students in primary schools out of a total population of one quarter of a million means that great improvements are still necessary. An adequate survey of the potential needs of the Gambia still remains to be done so that the educational plant can begin to approximate these needs. Except in few instances the system is still geared to turning out white collar workers with little attention being given to agriculture or the vocations. However, with all these shortcomings, the past fifteen years has witnessed a revolution in education in the Gambia.

Before concluding this eclectic discussion of Gambian financial affairs and the services performed by the central government agencies, it is necessary to survey briefly the problem of general administrative costs. One of the major reasons for establishing indirect rule in West Africa had been to minimize the cost of administration. The institution of this system into the Protectorate of the Gambia did make most of the cost of maintaining law and order there minimal. However, the insistance upon a complete system of Crown Colony government for the Colony meant from the outset the expenditure of large sums to administer a very small population. In effect this small enclave supported two overlapping systems of government, one for the

181

Protectorate and one for the Colony. A very great portion of the cost of the Gambia went into paying salaries of the administrative staff, mostly European. It is almost impossible without a detailed analysis of each yearly budget to state exactly what percentage of the budget was devoted to pure administrative costs. However, a mean figure of seventy per cent would be relatively accurate. The Protectorate cost very little to maintain. In 1950 out of a budget of over £1,000,000, the Protectorate administration received less than £37,000.[28] Thus a disproportionate sum was spent to administer less than 30,000 people in the Colony area.

Many critics of the government, both Gambian and European, pointed out that the Gambia was too small and too poor to afford such administrative expenditure and still have funds to carry out needed services. One scheme that would have acted as a brake upon unnecessary staff was suggested in the early 1940s. This envisaged the government of the United Kingdom guaranteeing to pay a large portion of the cost of maintaining the redundant staff of the Colony, thus releasing to the government a large portion of the yearly budget to carry out necessary improvements in the Gambia. Such a plan would have had a secondary effect of proving to the Gambians that their ever increasing taxes were being utilized for something besides the maintenance of a large European staff. The plan was rejected, and to the present time the major charge of the Gambia budget is for administration.

Correlate with this problem of a large administrative staff was the slowness of Gambianization of the government. Part of the problem was undoubtedly the fact that there were few trained Gambians to fill the necessary posts. However, the government did not have an avowed policy of training and then employing qualified Gambians for important positions until after World War II. Considerable improvement in this direction in all levels of the Civil Service has been achieved. In 1948 in Super scale and Categories I and II of the Civil Service there were only seventeen Gambians in Categories I and II as compared to seventy-nine expatriate officers. In 1959 there were fifty-three Gambians in all three categories as compared to sixty-seven expatriates. Four Gambians qualified for the Super scale category. This most favourable improvement is somewhat misleading since at the same time there were fifty-four additional expatriate overseas officers who normally held the highest government posts.[29] The attitude of a large segment of articulate Gambian opinion was that they were being taxed to maintain an inefficient government structure that they did not want and which was staffed by non-Gambian personnel. These charges, partly true, became particularly vocal with the grant of more political freedom to the Gambia.

In retrospect the Gambia, small and poor as it was after 1889 has had to contend with the additional burden of a large administrative staff, a lethargic economy minded Colonial Office, and a local government which did not attempt to expand the economic and social facilities until the post World War II period. Independence for the Gambia in the near future means that the new state will enter this world with only minimal facilities provided by the seventy year colonial administration of Great Britain.

Chapter Ten

THE DEVELOPMENT OF POLITICAL PARTIES AND SELF-GOVERNMENT

THE central government of the Gambia has been called upon to perform many different functions. First it is the chief legislative and executive authority for both the Colony and Protectorate. Subsidiary departments such as the Agricultural Department and Public Works have responsibilities in both segments of the territory. The Governor and Council, and since 1962 the Premier and the Ministry, have the primary function of making and enforcing the laws for the Colony and Protectorate. The central government also has specific functions which it exercises only in the Colony, since the Protectorate in theory is governed by the instrumentality of indirect rule. Finally, because the city of Bathurst and the Kombo Rural Authority were created very late and exist with only restricted funds, the central government provides most of the major services normally reserved for a municipal government. In the period since 1945, as the Gambia moved closer to independence, the tendency has been for the central government to assume more of the burden for governing the whole territory. This trend was inevitable and was late in being asserted for the Gambia is too small to afford the luxury of two overlapping systems of govern-

184

ment. The Gambian politicians, not the official administration, are primarily responsible for the breakdown of indirect rule in the Protectorate. Due to their influence, the chiefs in the past five years have been reduced dramatically to mere spokesmen of the Central Authority.

The development of the Central Authority will be considered under two separate sections, although in recent years both have been closely intertwined. The first is the slow movement, actuated largely by the Colonial Office, from classic Crown Colony government to the present state where the Gambians have full internal self-government. The second is the historic development of Gambian political parties from a rather indefinite Colony-oriented intellectual group to the present situation where the political parties are the natural form through which central power is exercised.

In the late nineteenth century the government of the Gambia was a modified form of a Crown Colony with the Administrators, however, responsible for their actions to the Governor of Sierra Leone. When the Gambia was made dependent upon Sierra Leone in 1866, the Gambia Executive and Legislative Councils were abolished. In their place a small council composed of the Administrator, Collector of Customs, and the Chief Magistrate was created.[1] This advisory group was expanded until in 1887 it contained five officials and four unofficial members of whom two were African. Anticipating a satisfactory boundary settlement with France, the administrative link with Sierra Leone was severed in 1888 and the Gambia was created as a separate colony.[2] The office of Administrator was not upgraded to Governor until 1901, but the Gambia was immediately given its own Executive and Legislative Councils, and in 1893 the government of the Colony was empowered to make the necessary rules and orders for the government of the Protectorate.[3] In 1915 the Legislative Council was enlarged to contain the Governor and Colonial Secretary as *ex-officio* members, four Official, and three unofficial nominated persons. Of the three unofficial members, one was to represent the business community while the other two posts were to be filled by African Christians from Bathurst. In 1921 Governor Armitage appointed a Bathurst Mohammedan to the Council in place

185

of one African Christian. He also gave some attention to the appointment of one Protectorate chief to the Council, but did not pursue this because no chief could be found who could read and speak English sufficiently well. A further change was effected in 1932 when the size of the Council was increased by one additional African member nominated by the Bathurst Urban District Council and by one of the Commissioners of the Protectorate.[4] This was the first time that the Protectorate had been represented in the central government. However, these modifications did not upset the basic format established by the original legislation. The Legislative Council still acted primarily as an advisory group and did not initiate legislation, and all members were nominated. The Council was dominated by the official element. Those unofficial appointees were Bathurst residents who reflected, however imperfectly, the ideas of only one seventh of the population of the Gambia.

The end of World War II brought new political factors to prominence in West Africa. In Nigeria and Ghana, national movements were becoming better organized and the Colonial Office responded with more liberal constitutions that permitted the nationals to assume a more active role in the central government. No such pressures from organized political groups were present in the Gambia. Nevertheless, Britain reorganized the Legislative Council in 1946.[5] The new Council provided for three *ex-officio* members, three nominated government officials, six unofficial nominated members, and one elected member representing Bathurst and the Kombo rural area. The election was from a common roll with no property or income qualifications. Electors qualified by meeting only age and residence requirements. Two of the unofficial members were specifically to represent the Colony, one the commercial interests, and the other was appointed from either the Muslim or non-Muslim community, depending upon whether the elected member was a Muslim, in which case the appointed member would be non-Muslim, and vice versa. The Protectorate was represented by the other four unofficial appointees with the hope that these would be appointed by the Protectorate chiefs. This latter wish proved premature due to the low level of literacy of the chiefs. Apart from introducing the elective

186

principle at the central government level, the new constitution was important only because it gave, in theory, a parity of unofficial and official representatives in the Council.

The Executive Council was also revised to reflect a non-official viewpoint.[6] In 1947 the Council was composed of the Governor, the Colonial Secretary, three nominated official members, and three nominated unofficial members. These unofficial representatives were chosen from the official element of the Legislative Council and normally included the elected representative for Bathurst. In the immediate pre-war years few people considered that the Gambia would ever have a relationship other than one of dependency upon Great Britain. Therefore no provision was made for the members of the Executive Council to be responsible for government departments, and the Executive Council remained only an advisory body for the Governor.

At a lower level of government, there had been formed in 1931 an Urban District Council whose main function was to act as a liaison between the people of the Colony and the central government. The Council was composed of six members who were nominated by the Governor, usually from the ranks of the Rate Payers Association. In 1935 the name of the organization was changed to the Bathurst Town Council.[7] It was still primarily advisory, although it was empowered to act in maintaining markets and caring for the cemeteries. It was, however, not until 1946 that the Council was given an elected majority and authorized to act as a municipal Authority in specified areas.[8] The Council still operates under this Ordinance and is composed of the Colony Commissioner, four nominated members, and fifteen elected officials. The amount of authority that is exercised by the Council is very limited since the central government departments are in charge of electricity, education, public works, and health. The Council oversees the cleaning of the streets and drains and the maintenance of markets, playgrounds, buildings, and cemeteries. Apart from these small duties the prime function of the Council has been to provide some training for Gambian politicians and to act as a stepping stone for them for higher public office.

In 1946 another lesser government organization, the Kombo

Rural Authority, was created.[9] Until then the Kombo area, although a part of the Colony, had been administered by the Protectorate government. The Authority is a purely nominated body under the direction of the Colony Commissioner. It has three *ex-officio* members who are heads of government departments. The remainder of the board are nominated. The Authority is composed of over twenty-five members and would be, under the best of circumstances, an unwieldly instrument. However, the duties of the Authority are minimal because most of the functions that would normally be performed by the agency are handled by the central government. The money available to the Authority is so small that no major task could be undertaken. The Authority was and is primarily a paper experiment in local government.

In 1951 a further step in the development of the central government was taken. The constitution was revised to provide for an additional elected member for the Bathurst-Kombo area.[10] The elections for the two seats on the Legislative Council were from a common roll. This constitution was but a logical continuation of that of 1947 and did not grant ministerial responsibility to members of the Executive Council. The heads of departments, who were all British Civil Servants, continued to act directly under the control of the Colonial Secretary and the Governor. However, the election of 1951 marked the real beginning of political parties and organized pressure upon the Gambia and home governments for revision of the governmental system. Partly because of increasing Colony dissatisfaction with the Constitution of 1951 and partly due to the increased tempo of political advance elsewhere in West Africa, the Colonial Office approved in principle a major revision of the Gambia Constitution in 1953. In May, Governor Wyn-Harris invited thirty-four ex-members of the Legislative and Executive Councils to meet, discuss, and formulate proposals for the establishment of the new government. All except two of these delegates were Africans. After six long meetings they submitted their suggestions which, with minor modifications, became the substance of the Constitution of 1954.[11]

The Legislative Council was composed of the Governor, five *ex-officio* official members, two nominated official members, and persons elected from the Colony and the Protectorate. Of the fourteen elected members, seven would be from the Colony, while an equal number represented the Protectorate. The election procedure was quite complicated. Three persons for Bathurst were to be chosen from a common roll by direct suffrage of adults over twenty-five years old. One member was to be chosen by the same method from Kombo. The seven representatives from the Protectorate were to be chosen indirectly. Four were to be elected by the Divisional Councils from names submitted by the District Authorities while three were to be selected by the chiefs. The remaining three representatives from the Colony and Kombo were selected by the members already elected from a list of nine names submitted by the Bathurst Town Council and the Kombo Rural Authority. The Executive Council was also reorganized to contain five *ex-officio* official members and not less than six unofficial members chosen by the Governor after consultation with the elected element of the Legislative Council. From these unofficial members, three persons would be chosen to head ministries. They were not in charge of the departments concerned, but were to evolve policy and co-ordinate work with the European heads of departments.

The Constitution of 1954 was most important because it established a number of precedents. It was the first instrument of government to be drawn up on the basis of the recommendations of the Gambians rather than created by the Governor and his staff. This was the first time that the Protectorate had really been represented in the central government, and it is most significant that its representatives had been chosen by election, however indirect. Of equal significance was the admission of elected members in theory to a share in running the government departments. Although the ministers were not really responsible and leaned heavily upon the Civil Service, the prospect of ministerial responsibility had been admitted.

Although the government instituted in 1954 was a great improvement, it left many areas of potential conflict unresolved. In the following years all political parties agreed in demanding that Gambian ministers should have more responsibility. The indirect method of election in the Protectorate gave the Commissioners and thirty-five chiefs the equivalent voting power

189

of all the voters of Bathurst and Kombo. Some Gambians were not pleased that almost one quarter of a million persons in the Protectorate should have their representatives chosen by men they suspected to be amenable to government pressure. The worsening of the economic position of the Gambia, combined with the growing demands of the Gambians for better social services, soon indicated that the Constitution of 1954 would have to be modified if there was not to be serious trouble. Toward this end a conference composed of leading citizens and representatives of the political parties met in March 1959, and after deliberation presented their proposals to the government.[12] In June the Colonial Secretary, Mr. Lennox-Boyd, arrived in Bathurst for a two day official visit. He met with delegates of the political parties and assured them that there would be elections under a new Constitution by May 1960.[13] By September 1959, the final details of the new Constitution had been completed.

The chief legislative authority for the Colony and Protectorate was to be a House of Representatives of thirty-four persons. The official point of view was to be reflected by four *ex-officio* and three nominated members. The Colony area was to choose seven members by direct election based upon wards. The Protectorate for the first time was divided into electoral districts and twelve representatives were to be chosen from these on the basis of universal suffrage. Although most parties and the government had by this time agreed that indirect rule in the Protectorate had to be modified, the chiefs could not be totally ignored in any system which represented the Protectorate. Therefore they were given the right to choose eight representatives for the new House. The elections for the new legislature were held in May 1960. The Executive Council was also revised to admit the principle of ministerial government. It was to contain the Governor, four officials, and not more than six ministers. Four of these ministers would be directly responsible for government departments, and in theory the previous Civil Service heads of these offices were to function under the direction of the ministers in charge.

As will be detailed more thoroughly elsewhere, dissatisfaction with the new Constitution began almost immediately.

This arose primarily because no political party won a clear cut majority at the polls. Thus the ministry and the Legislative Council was an uneasy coalition. The fault for this was alleged to lie in the indirect method whereby the chiefs selected more representatives than the Colony area. A further source of contention was the lack of a co-ordinating or chief minister. Governor Windley announced late in 1960 his intention of appointing such an official. Again personalities intervened and the chiefs were responsible for shifting the balance of power in favour of one candidate. The ensuing political difficulties, combined with the deterioration of finances, labour disturbances, and the granting of independence to Nigeria and Sierra Leone, convinced the Governor and Colonial Office that full internal self-government to the Gambia should be granted.

Once again constitutional delegations were chosen and two meetings, one in Bathurst and another in London, were held with Colonial Office officials. The resultant Constitution gave the Gambia full internal self-government with a House of Representatives of thirty-six members.[14] The Colony area's representation was seven elected representatives, no increase over the number which had been assigned them by the Constitutions of 1951 and 1954. The Protectorate received a more equitable representation by being given twenty-five representatives chosen by direct election. Although the ability of the chiefs to influence the balance of power was removed, they still retained the right to choose four of their number. This gave the Protectorate twenty-nine representatives as compared with only seven for the Colony, thus shifting the focus of the election into the hinterland. The Constitution provided for a responsible government of eight ministers controlled by a chief minister. The only reservations in the powers of the Premier and his ministers lay in the conduct of affairs of a non-domestic nature, and also in theory the Governor retained the ultimate power of disallowance.

Thus by May 1962, in less than ten years, the central government of the Gambia had shifted from a typical Crown Colony form, with minimum participation by the Gambians, to one where the principle of universal suffrage determined the composition of the governing agencies. Instead of appointed, primarily European officials, there are today Gambian politicians who are responsible for formulating and carrying out government policy—this at a time when the finances of the country are in a state of collapse and the major problem is the choice between independence or re-unification with Senegal.

To complete the historical picture of the central government, a survey of political parties and an indication of how they fit into the quickened pace of post-World War II reform, is necessary. Political parties in the formal sense have only recently begun to develop in the Gambia.[15] In this sense the area is far behind her West African neighbours. Among the reasons for this slowness one can point to the Gambia's small geographic area and its economic non-viability, which in turn made the Gambia more dependent upon Britain, and thus the twin system of Crown Colony government and indirect rule continued in force long after it had been abandoned or radically modified in the other British West African territories. Neither method of government is really conducive to the formation or operation of political parties. However, the successful nationalist movements throughout Africa following World War II have had an emancipating effect upon the quiescient Gambian political scene. First they have created a more malleable attitude in the minds of the colonial officials, and secondly these political movements elsewhere have been examples to those Gambians who now wish to control their own affairs. The reversal of previous colonial policy in this respect is particularly apparent in attitudes toward independence. Many colonial officials now view this as a more desirable end than do the conservative Gambians.

The first quasi-political movement in the Gambia was the Bathurst Trade Union formed in 1928. This was not a large body and its influence did not extend beyond the Colony area. Nevertheless, it was strong enough to conduct the first successful strike in Gambian history in 1929. The Union was the handiwork of Edward Small, the father of modern Gambian politics. He was one of the organizers of the British West African National Congress and continued to play an important role in non-Gambian political movements until his death. In the early 1930s he organized the Rate Payers Association whose main function was to act as a liaison between the people and the colonial government and to provide a pool of interested men to stand election for the Urban District Council. These are isolated examples of indigenous political activity in the inter-war period and are relatively unimportant. Any change in the political direction of the Colony and Protectorate areas was dictated by the Governor in Council.

It was in the milieu of quickened political development over the past fifteen years that Gambian political parties came into being. They were formed to meet a specific election need created by the colonial government's decisions to approximate the advance in other West African areas. One must note that it is only since 1960 that political parties have exercised the function of pressure groups attempting to force the rate of political advance. Before this they were content merely to react to changed situations designed and dictated largely by non-Gambians.

Before discussing the formation of the present political parties there are some general comments that should be made. First there are very few real differences between the parties, either as regards programmes, organizations, or group representation within the parties. The actual economic and political problems demanding solutions have called forth almost the same general-ized responses from all parties. They all follow the same loose organization pattern. There is a central committee of varying size composed of the most important contributors and sup-porters of the party located in Bathurst. The dominating figure is the party leader who determines the selection of those who are on the central committee. The Gambia is divided into districts. In the Protectorate these largely correspond with the Native Authority Divisions. Each district in theory has a District Committee which is supposed to organize political activity in that particular area. Below the District Committee are the village committees whose main function is to carry out the planned activities decided upon by the District and Central Committees. This brief description should not be taken to mean that the Protectorate is organized as well in fact as in theory. Politics is a new 'fad' for most of the people and, therefore, there are many gaps in the actual political organization. But all parties follow this organization form. The party leaders resident in Bathurst keep in contact with the outlying districts by making frequent trips into the bush. This is done more to keep the people familiar with the figure of the leader, than to expound programmes or to check on the efficiency of the organization. No party is narrowly based upon one religious or tribal grouping. Support comes from all sections of the community. Thus for discussion purposes, one can consider Gambian political parties, with the exception of the personalities of the leaders, as a unity rather than as discrete entities.

The first Gambian party was the Democratic Party, formed in February 1951, by Reverend John C. Faye to contest for one of the Bathurst seats under the revised Constitution of that year. Reverend Faye had long been associated with the government as a member of the Bathurst Town Council and had been a nominated member of the Legislative Council since 1947.[16] The formation of the Democratic Party was simply the logical culmination of his public and personal ambitions. As far as can be ascertained, the members of the party executive were a few influential Bathurst citizens who agreed with Reverend Faye in his conclusions concerning the future of the Gambia. Thus the Democratic Party from the first was personality oriented.

Soon afterwards in January 1952, a second party, the Muslim Congress Party, was created. Superficially it differed in nature from the Democratic Party in being a fusion of the Bathurst Young Muslim Society with a number of similar Muslim organizations in the Kombos and the Protectorate. Actually the Muslim Congress depended as much upon the personality of its leader, I. M. Garba-Jahumpa, as the Democratic Party learned upon the popularity of Reverend Faye.[17] Garba-Jahumpa had held many positions in the Gambia from clerk to teacher. He had been a member of the Bathhurst Town Council since 1942 and had been elected to the Legislative Council as the second member for Bathurst in the elections of 1951. At the time of the formation of the Congress he was probably the most articulate and politically influential Muslim in the Gambia. The Congress was designed to link religious affiliation with political activity. The majority of the population of the Gambia is Muslim. Therefore if the new party could successfully appeal to this sectarian feeling, future political control of the Gambia would be a foregone conclusion.

The third political party was also formed as an outgrowth of the 1951 elections. It, too, was an organization built around one man. Unlike the other two organizations, the United Party was created because of the failure of its leader, P. S. N'Jie, in the 1951 elections.[18] Although a well known barrister in Bathurst, he had only returned to the Gambia in 1948, and prior to the elections had taken little interest in government matters. It was decided in October 1951, that if he and his followers, lacking the political background and following of Faye and Garba-Jahumpa, were to be successful in future elections, a political vehicle able to project the image of P. S. N'Jie was needed. In the three year period that elapsed before the 1954 elections this was dealt with so well that N'Jie was elected to the Legislative Council in 1954 at the head of the poll.

The last of the major Gambian parties to be created was the Progressive Peoples Party which was formed for the 1960 election. The centrum of this movement was David Jawara, an ex-veterinary officer.[19] The Progressive Peoples Party took advantage of the extension of the franchise to the Protectorate, Jawara's Protectorate origins, and a more thorough organization, to become in a few months the dominant party in the Gambia. It is controlled fairly rigidly by Jawara, but is less dependent upon personality than are the other parties. From the first it stressed the Protectorate whereas the older parties had been Colony oriented. In addition the P.P.P. had been more radical in their proposed programmes and more aggressive in their actual electioneering tactics. The success of the Progressive Peoples Party in the Protectorate was shown by their winning eight of the twelve elected seats in 1960 and seventeen of the twenty-five seats in the elections of 1962.

There were attempts in the period from 1954 to 1962 to create other parties. The most important were the formation of the National Party, the merger in 1960 of the Democratic Party and the Muslim Congress, and the formation of the Gambia National Union in 1962. In the first case, the National Party was purely Colony oriented. It operated on a limited scale for four years and broke apart because of internal dissension on the eve of the 1960 elections. The merger of the two older parties was caused by the recognition of the falling popularity throughout the country of the leaders, Faye and Garba-Jahumpa. By merging the parties into the Democratic Congress Alliance, the leaders hoped to offset the growing strength of the United Party and the Progressive Peoples Party. To accomplish this merger the Muslim Congress admitted the failure of their appeal to the Muslim community, and the need to come to terms with non-Muslim elements. As will be shown, the merger failed in its objectives since neither of the leaders was returned to the House of Representatives in 1960 or 1962. The Gambia National Union was a combination of persons who had belonged to the now defunct National Party and politicians dissatisfied with the Progressive Peoples Party. In the 1962 elections its leaders campaigned for the United Party and its defeat can be measured by the larger defeat suffered by the United Party at the polls. The Gambia National Union hardly developed past the planning stage since its leaders decided to campaign under the United Party while still maintaining a freedom of action not allowed to regular United Party candidates.

The rapid disintegration of a party's influence is a common factor in Gambian politics. One reason for this is because the role of the leader is over-emphasized. Personal activities and rumours concerning possible behind-the-scenes manoeuvring are quickly magnified by political opponents. What, in more mature political systems, would be passed off by opponents and the public as permissible indiscretions are seized upon in the Gambia, and the largely illiterate electorate quickly move from one favourite to another. Another factor is the association of political leaders with the necessary business of managing government departments. The political tag of 'government man' has been attached to all the important politicians. This signifies that he is easily managed by the Governor and the senior Civil Servants. The government of the Gambia since 1947 has necessarily represented a series of compromises between the Crown Colony system and the ultimate aim of self-government. Any politician, no matter how pure his motives, who occupied a ministerial post for long, was associated in the public eye with being a pawn of expatriate interests.

These two conclusions are borne out by events since 1954, P. S. N'Jie, whose United Party was so successful in the elections of that year, remained a minister for less than a year. His resignation was precipitated by a public disagreement with the Governor. Instead of limiting his popularity, this incident created the image of the United Party standing for the rights of Gambians against a stubborn, inefficient colonial government. That this image was largely a fabrication does not alter its real meaning. While Garba-Jahumpa, Faye, and their followers continued to co-operate with the Governor and serve as ministers, N'Jie and the United Party disassociated themselves entirely from government responsibility and could charge their opponents with being supine government servants. Such a policy resulted in the United Party sweeping the Colony seats in the elections of 1960 and there is little doubt that their position in the Protectorate would have been more favourable if the Constitution of that year had not prevented Colony born men standing for election in the Protectorate. By assuming office in 1961, the United Party ceased to have this favourable position and was forced to act in conjunction with the Governor. It is impossible to state to what degree this affected the results of the 1962 election. In the Gambia, however, the effect of being an office holder is normally detrimental.

David Jawara and the Progressive Peoples Party were also saved by not being associated directly with previous semi-ministerial functions. In the electioneering in 1960 and 1962, the Progressive Peoples Party stressed the inadequate attention that had been shown in the past to the Protectorate. The bad roads, poor health facilities, inadequate schools, and the primitive state of agriculture in the Protectorate were blamed upon the inactivity of the government and the alleged preference for the Colony areas. All politicians who had been associated in the management of Protectorate affairs were made to seem equally guilty.

The political affiliations of the elected portion of the House of Representatives after the 1960 election were: eight chiefs, eight Progressive Peoples Party, six United Party, three Demo-

197

cratic Congress Alliance, and two independents.[20] These figures should be considered approximate, since in the year following some representatives shifted their affiliation. The ministers in the Executive Council reflected the groupings in the lower house with the exception that P. S. N'Jie was not offered a full ministry, but only one without portfolio. On these terms he preferred to remain outside the government. The United Party was represented on the Council of Ministers only by a new-comer to politics.

Soon after convening the 1960 House, the Governor an-nounced his intention of naming a co-ordinating minister, or as he came to be called, a Chief Minister. Statistically, the spread of representatives from the parties seemed to make this a relatively easy move. Actually it was a most difficult decision. The economic situation, labour unrest, and general disaffec-tion of the population meant that if he did not want continued disturbances he must choose a man who could effect a concilia-tion between his party and one of the other groups in the House. During the campaign the Progressive Peoples Party had so alienated the feeling of the chiefs that there could be no mutual support between them. This meant that neither Jawara or the chiefs' spokesman, Seyfou Omar M'Baki, could secure effective support. The Governor went outside the Executive Council and P. S. N'Jie, who in the autumn of 1960 had not been proffered a full ministry, became Chief Minister in March 1961, with the full support of the chiefs.[21] Jawara and the other Progressive Peoples Party minister resigned and began to demand a revision of the constitutional instruments. Realizing the need for such a change, the Governor and the United Party agreed and new constitutional talks were held in Bathurst in May and in London in July 1961.

The political situation after March 1961 created new political alignments. The Progressive Peoples Party, who had considered it only a matter of time before it held the political future of the Gambia, was quite shaken by the appointment of N'Jie as Chief Minister. This caused a re-evaluation of the party and a *rapprochment* with the Democratic Congress Alliance. Reverend Faye and Garba-Jahumpa reconsidered their bad opinions of the Progressive Peoples Party, and although no merger took place, the Democratic Congress Alliance worked in conjunction with the Progressive Peoples Party throughout the 1962 campaign. No Democratic Congress Alliance sponsored candidate stood for election in opposition to a Progressive Peoples Party candidate in the Protectorate, and the Progressive Peoples Party reciprocated in the Colony contests.

Apart from personalities, two issues were paramount in the campaign of 1962—tribalism and the role of the chiefs. The Progressive Peoples Party continued to stress the unequal distribution of funds and services to the Protectorate, particularly to the predominate Mandingo population. The United Party were left with no rebuttal to this charge except denial, which tended to convince Mandingo voters that the allegations of the Progressive Peoples Party were correct. In dealing with the future of traditional rulers, the Progressive Peoples Party, although modifying its more radical statements of 1960, still stressed the debilitating effects that indirect rule had had on the Protectorate. They stressed the consistency of their opposition to the chiefs and took considerable credit for the area councils and the modified influence of the chiefs in the new government. The United Party, due to its close relationship with the chiefs in the past government, again was forced into defending the *status quo*. As mentioned previously, the United Party was also compromised by being the party then in power. Thus all the long standing, unsolved issues could be attributed to the lethargy of the United Party. In the Gambia there is no defence against such a charge. In the campaign of 1962, both major parties campaigned vigorously in all areas of the country. Although there were cases of tempers getting the best of reason, the campaign was no more violent or tribally oriented than that of 1960.

The election results of 1962 appear to be a complete vindication of charges by the Progressive Peoples Party that the appointment of P. S. N'Jie as Chief Minister in 1961 was in violation of the will of the majority of the Gambians.[22] The Progressive Peoples Party contested all twenty-five constituencies in the Protectorate and won seventeen, gaining over sixty-four per cent of all votes cast. In the Colony the Progressive Peoples Party entered two contests, adding one seat to their

199

Protectorate total, Their partners, the Democratic Congress Alliance, however, were unable to destroy the United Party control of the Colony area. Even the one victory of the Democratic Congress Alliance can be considered as a personal, rather than a party, victory. The United Party and its allies, despite controlling five of the seven Colony seats, had only thirteen members in the new House.[23] Thus, even if the appointed chiefs supported the United Party, they would still be at a disadvantage in the House by two votes. The new government majority in the House was secure and would presumably allow Jawara to instigate any changes he felt necessary for the Gambia.

With this general framework of rapid political extension in mind, one can begin to analyse the relationship between social factors and the political parties. The most important of these factors is the relationship between traditional rulers and political parties, religion, tribalism, and the economic environment. There is a rough unanimity of view among all political leaders about the position the chiefs should occupy in the government. No responsible leader wants the complete abolition of the chiefs. Rather they want them to be relegated to local government heads under the overall direction of the central authorities. However, only one party, the Progressive Peoples Party, has repeatedly stated this publicly. All the other parties realize the power of the chiefs and have refrained from expressing any concrete plans for Protectorate reorganization. The United Party was called to form the first ministry primarily because of the support given by the chiefs. Therefore it would have been highly inexpedient for it to have expounded any radical change in the status of the chiefs. Under the Constitution of 1961, the chiefs have only four seats in the House as compared with eight in the previous House. Although this reflects their diminishing official influence, they are still powerful enough not to be regarded lightly by any politician wishing to be successful.

The second social factor to consider is the influence of religion upon politics. The majority of the population of the Gambia are professed Muslims. This proponderence has not been reflected politically. The Muslim Congress failed to gain the support of the Muslims, while the United Party and the Progressive Peoples Party led by Christians have had considerable success in all elections since their inception. There are three reasons for this odd separation of religion from politics in the Gambia. Politics have so far been personality oriented and thus the popularity of the leader has been far more important than his religion or his political platform. Secondly, the extended family system over-rides religious differences. One can change his beliefs and still retain his position within the group without loss of popularity or prestige. Thirdly, there is little connection between Gambian Muslims and any outside pan-Islamic movement which equates Islam with political goals. Whether this tolerance of religious differences will remain as the level of education and westernization increases in the future is unknown, but at the present, religious affiliation is a very minor issue in Gambian politics.

Tribalism, until recently, had not been an important factor, although the boundaries of the Gambia cut through five major tribal areas. The reason for this is the lateness of Gambian political development. The system of indirect rule, while ostensibly fostering tribal identity, restricted the ways in which differences could be manifested. This, aided by Islam, gave the people a superficial identity as Gambians. However, since 1960, there have been indications of a resurgence of tribalism. Since all politics prior to that time were Colony centred, all successful politicians had been Wolof. The largest tribal group, the Mandingos, are located in the Protectorate and are generally less educated than the Bathurst Wolof. Much the same can be said of the Jolas, Seres, and Fulas. The Progressive Peoples Party has campaigned in the past on tribal lines, stressing that the Colony has been given everything and the Protectorate neglected, particularly the Mandingo population. The other party leaders deplore this type of emotional appeal and point to its obvious dangers. However, a close examination of the election results of 1962 shows how complete was the victory for the Progressive Peoples Party using these tactics. This is particularly noticeable for the Lower River and Western Districts, and confirms pre-election speculation that the source of strength of the Progressive Peoples Party lay in their control of the Mandingo voters. Although no really accurate statistics exist for population distribution of tribes, these two districts are primarily Mandingo. In contrast, the United Party elected four members from the six contested areas of the predominently Fula and Serahuli Upper River Division.

The economic situation is perhaps the most important single factor for the future of the Gambia. As such, it has a great latent influence upon the political parties. The Gambia dependence upon groundnuts in the face of falling prices has meant since 1954 a series of unbalanced budgets, price supports, and aid from Great Britain. The political parties have of necessity concentrated their attacks upon the colonial administration, accusing them of inadequate planning, expensive over-staffing of departments, and a lack of an intelligent agricultural development programme. So far no Gambian political leader has been in any position to change established policy. With the arrival of full internal self-government, all this should change. In future elections, whatever party wins will be responsible for implementation of its own programme of economic development and will no longer be able to use the excuse of colonial exploitation to explain economic distress.[24]

The political leaders still speak in generalities about the economic future. They rightly believe that under proper conditions rice, citrus fruit, kola, and oil palms can be productively grown in the region. However, no party has the benefit of good economic advisors, and apart from the conviction that things could be better, they have no positive detailed plans for economic betterment. All hopes for a better economic future rest upon securing large amounts of public and private capital. The politicians naïvely hope for large scale financing from Great Britain, the United States, and international agencies without realizing the need for detailed investigation and pilot schemes before approaching these agencies. This optimism is likely to be rudely shattered when a Gambian government faces the extremely difficult task of managing the Gambia.

One important side aspect of the economic situation is the growing importance of the one effective trade union. The Gambian Workers Union led by M. E. Jallow was only formed in 1959, but in this short period it has established itself as a powerful influence.[25] Its leader is a very effective tactician and has never called a strike without achieving results. He has succeeded, particularly in the groundnut ports, in creating a picture of the Union as the one agency which has no interest except the betterment of wages and working conditions. The Union has no compunction against continued strikes during the groundnut season until it has achieved the goal of considerably higher wages for its members. In the elections of 1960 and 1962, the Union stood aloof from the present parties. Jallow has stated many times that none of the political leaders of the parties really understands or appreciates Gambian problems, and therefore none is deserving of the Union's political support. However, there are indications that his attitude is changing. For example, Jallow was included in the two constitutional delegations in 1961. It is too early to say whether he will be content to support one of the parties, or whether he will attempt to form yet another party. But in a small country, such a decision by an organized group could be vital. Although all the political leaders will deny it, they are concerned with the Union and have made various overtures to gain the Union's support in the future.

Two other factors in the Gambia make any prognostication extremely difficult. One is the presence of the uncommitted 'intelligentsia' on the outskirts of politics. The other is the necessity of some type of reconciliation between the Gambia and its natural hinterland, the Senegal. There are comparatively few well educated or well trained Gambians. The majority of these have refused or been constrained from entering politics. The small number of professional men, despite many overtures from the political leaders, are suspicious of the present parties and have refrained in the past from directly supporting any party. A much larger group belong to the Civil Service and by the nature of their positions could not commit themselves. There is no way of knowing how their 'élite' and respected people will align themselves in the future. All that can be said is that they will soon be forced to choose. If there is approximate block support from these people for any one party, then, because of the paucity of educated men in the Gambia, that party will dominate the Gambian scene.

Of more immediate importance is the question of future relations with Senegal. Economically and tribally the Senegambia is one area. But the interposition of colonial rule has created two cultural blocks. Except in the high bush of the Protectorate, the Gambians are English. Their cousins in Senegal are French. The problems of joining these groups even in a loose political federation are immense.

Britain and Senegal, for different reasons, are eager for such a political *rapprochement*. Gambian politicians, while recognizing the inevitability of closer economic ties, are not prepared to discuss political amalgamation except in very general terms. This is only partly due to their realization of the difficulties involved. They do recognize that large groups in the Gambia are opposed to any move that would effect their positions. The chiefs do not wish to become mere figureheads and fear that this would happen under Senegal. The professional people are not certain of their future status under any new arrangement, and conclude that the Gambia, once in such a federation, would always be the 'tail of the dog'. The groundnut farmers with an assured subsidy are not clear on the actual methods and amount of support they would receive from Senegal. These are some very good reasons for the wariness of all political parties when discussing what seems to be the obvious solution. Any premature strong stand in favour of amalgamation could react unfavourably against a political party. There is also another reason for the politicians' reluctance to contemplate a quick union. They recognize that they are amateurs by comparison with the Senegalese politicians. It is better for them to be the leaders of a small state than to be shuffled to one side by their more experienced northern neighbours.

In summing up the Gambian political scene there are a few salient points to reiterate. Political parties and the direct electoral system are very new. All parties are personality oriented and the political programmes of the parties are almost identical. The parties suffer from lack of experienced and educated men in the second echelon of party leadership. The mechanics of party organization and the functions of government are imperfectly understood even by the leaders. And the precarious economic position of the Gambia does not admit of a long period of education and adjustment by the leaders.

For these reasons the Gambian political system can be considered as more important than its size suggests. The Gambia is a microcosm, containing all the political problems which bedevil any new African state, no matter what its size. It is particularly interesting for the political observer because here the birth of real political parties and democratic electoral principles almost coincide with the advent of self-government. With the present economic situation and the closeness of independence, political maturity must come to Gambian politics quickly. There can be no long period of apprenticeship for the politicians as in other West African states. If the Gambia is to survive as a political entity, this maturity will have to be gained much quicker than should reasonably be expected of such a long neglected, economically non-viable area.

Conclusion

THE FUTURE—A
PROGNOSTICATION

IT seems necessary to depart from the historical approach to the Gambia and discuss briefly the current status of the enclave and its probable development. Any type of prognostication concerning the future is not only non-historical, but because of the quick silver nature of African politics, it is likely to be incorrect. Nevertheless no history of the Gambia would be complete without some indication of its present problems and their possible solutions.

There is one over-riding area of difficulty from which all other problems arise. The finances of the would be country are fixed to the export of one crop. There is nothing else of comparable value to the groundnut in the territory, although with long range plans and sufficient money, other tropical agricultural products could be developed. But here is the vicious circle which is almost impossible to solve. Groundnuts at present bring only minimum prices on the world market. Increasing competition from more efficient producers will probably continue to lower the price per ton of this crop. Government revenues in such an eventuality will continue to drop, making it extremely difficult to maintain even the current level of government activity and services. This fact precludes the expenditure of large sums of money for the necessary agricultural programme which could possibly alleviate the total dependence of the government on this one crop.

The Gambia government for the past three years has encountered budget deficits which even with monetary assistance from Great Britain, have all but destroyed any Treasury surplus. Premier Jawara's attempts in 1963 to arrive at a satisfactory solution with the home government to the long range question of recurring shortages was unsuccessful. Thrown back on its own meagre resources the present Gambian administration has been forced to reconsider a speedy merger with the now foreign hinterland of the Senegal. A decade ago association with the Senegal was only one of the possible political courses of action which responsible leaders considered for the Gambia. The favourite, and from a strictly logical viewpoint, the best political arrangements had been the Malta solution. This plan would have had the various small non-viable British colonial possessions throughout the world associated with the home government in a type of federal alliance which would assure their continued protection by Britain, but allow them a large measure of independence. With the grant of independence to many of these territories, the Malta plan is now no longer feasible for the Gambia. Another seriously considered amalgamation was the re-association of the Gambia with Sierra Leone. However, few Sierra Leone politicians wanted such an arrangement because of the many practical difficulties. Independence for Sierra Leone also removed this as an even remote possibility.

The two courses of action left to the Gambia are independence or association with the Senegal. Most influential Gambians prefer immediate independence with a long range approach to eventual amalgamation with their neighbour. There is implicit in this attitude the recognition that the two areas have grown apart in the sixty years of colonial rule and considerable readjustment would be necessary before any meaningful union could be achieved. Even before the Constitution of 1962 the Gambia government had instituted discussions with their Senegalese counterparts concerning a readjustment of tolls, customs, and other financial matters. Correlate with this was the beginnings of teacher exchanges on the secondary level to improve the teaching of languages in each area. Before association of any type, there are numerous hitherto untouched problems to solve. Some of the major questions are the relative status of professional persons, the official language, the type of criminal and civil law to be followed, currency, and perhaps most important of all, the status of the Gambian enclave in a future political association. Any sudden precipitous move before such complex matters have been thoroughly considered would see the Gambia once more as a dependency of a larger and stronger nation.

The second alternative is complete independence without association. This largely depends upon the financial health of the Gambia. At present the enclave is at the immediate pre-independence stage with an elected government responsible for all internal affairs. However, even the negotiations with the Senegal are circumscribed by the present colonial position. Equally the present financial plight can only be solved by Britain since the normal channels of negotiation with foreign governments, if not in theory, at least in practice, are closed to the Gambia. Independence of the territory could work, at least as a transitional stage, if the recurring budgetary deficits could be met by either British or foreign loans. However, the current attitude of the Colonial Office seems to be one of financial retrenchment and an overt desire to see the Gambia reunited with the hinterland, a wish denied them by the Convention of 1889, without the preliminary step of independence. Such an attitude is forcing the present Premier, David Jawara, into a hurried attempt to resolve differences between the Senegal and the Gambia because of finances. To this end he has invited a United Nations investigating team to survey the Gambia and make recommendations concerning such a *rapprochement*. These investigations have just begun, but it is doubtful whether a report, no matter how logically constructed, which does not recommend speedy association, has a chance of being adopted in the face of the economic realities.

It is difficult for an observer of the Gambian scene to be optimistic concerning the social, medical, and educational future of the territory. The present services which have been partly described in the preceding chapters are woefully inadequate. To expand these facilities further, however, would mean an increased expenditure and the Gambia does not possess enough capital to drastically increase these services. The political and economic uncertainty has, if anything, caused a decrease both in the quantity and quality of the social services. Thus at the time when the Gambia needs well educated, trained personnel, large numbers of Gambians either remain in Great Britain following their training or accept positions elsewhere in Africa. This is but a continuation of a pattern already discernable in the mid-'50s. Shortages of really well educated persons, combined with a lack of government and private funds, can only mean continued stagnation for the Colony as well as the Protectorate areas. These critical shortages suggest that the easiest method of solving the Gambia's dilemma is a speedy integration with the Senegal. This could be only a superficial betterment. The Senegal, although healthier and more viable than the Gambia, is far from having solved its own critical social, medical, and educational problems. One might suggest that the average Gambian would not necessarily be in a more favourable position under Senegalese rule than he is at present.

One of the underlying themes of the second portion of this book has been to show how the decision to accept the boundary solution of 1889, combined with chariness and lethargy, created the current serious financial and political situation. There will be solutions to the manifold difficult conditions of the Gambia, but they will be of the compromise variety which will not provide, in the foreseeable future, great changes in the present situation. The Gambia has been stunted in its political, economic, and social development for so long that any easing of its burdens may be considered by government leaders as a major victory. The future, however, of this oldest British West African possession, from any point of view seems indeed gloomy.

APPENDICES

Appendix I: Governors and Administrators of the Gambia

1829	Lieutenant-Colonel Alexander Findlay	*Lieutenant Governor*
1830	George Rendall	,, ,,
1840	Sir Henry Huntley	,, ,,
1843	Captain H. F. Seagram, R.N.	*Governor*
1843	E. Norcott	,,
1844	Commander G. Fitzgerald, R.N.	,,
1847	Sir R. G. Macdonnell	,,
1852	A. E. Kennedy	,,
1852	Colonel L. S. O'Connor	,,
1859	Colonel G. A. K. D'Arcy	,,
1866	Admiral C. G. E. Patey, C.M.C.	*Administrator*
1871	T. F. Callaghan, C.M.G.	,,
1873	Sir C. H. Kortright, C.M.G.	,,
1875	Sir Samuel Rowe, K.C.M.G.	,,
1877	Dr. V. S. Gouldsbury, C.M.G.	,,
1884	Sir C. A. Moloney, K.C.M.G.	,,
1886	Sir J. S. Hay, K.C.M.G.	,,
1888	Sir Gilbert T. Carter, K.C.M.G.	,,
1891	Sir R. B. Llewellyn, K.C.M.G.	,,
1901	Sir G. C. Denton, K.C.M.G.	*Governor*
1911	Lieutenant-Colonel Sir H. L. Galway, K.C.M.G., D.S.O.	,,
1914	Sir Edward J. Cameron, K.C.M.G.	,,
1920	Captain Sir C. H. Armitage, K.B.E., C.M.G., D.S.O.	,,

1927	Sir John Middleton, K.B.E., C.M.G.	*Governor*
1928	Sir Edward Denham, K.C.M.G., K.B.E.	,,
1930	Sir H. Richmond Palmer, K.C.M.G., C.B.E.	,,
1933	Sir Arthur Richards, K.C.M.G.	,,
1936	Sir Wilfred T. Southorn, K.C.M.G., K.B.E.	,,
1942	Sir Hilary Blood, K.C.M.G.	,,
1947	Sir Andrew B. Wright, K.C.M.G.	,,
1949	Sir P. Wyn Harris, K.C.M.G., M.B.E.	,,
1957	Sir Edward Windley, K.C.M.G., C.B.E.	,,
1962	Sir John Paul, M.C.	,,

Appendix II: List of Seyfolu (Chiefs) by District and Division from Sessional 4/58

WESTERN DIVISION:

Landing Omar Sonko	Upper Niumi
Landing Sonko	Lower Niumi
Abu Khan	Jokadu
Lang Jammeh	Foni Jarrol
Famara Koli	Foni Bondali
Landing Sanyang	Foni Kansala
Seyni Bwiaji	Foni Bintang-Karenai
Fabakari Sanyang	Foni Brefet
Ture Sanyang	Kombo East
Landing Bojang	Kombo Central
N'Jundu Ture	Kombo South
Fansu Bojang	Kombo North

CENTRAL DIVISION:

M'Famara Singhatey	Lower Baddibu
Silla Ba Dibba	Central Baddibu
Tamba Jemmeh, O.B.E.	Upper Baddibu
Ali Ture	Lower Saloum
Matarr Sise	Upper Saloum
Soru Dabo	Jarra East
Afamara Kumba Damphi	Jarra Central
Sekuba Jarjussy	Jarra West
Karamo Kabbah Sanneh	Kiang West

MAC CARTHY ISLAND DIVISION:

Haruna Meta Chami	Nianija
Sader Maneh	Niani
Omar M'Bake	Sami
Mariba Kurubally	MacCarthy Island
Koba Leigh	Fulladu West
Ismaila Sise	Niamina East
Musa Sawane	Niamina West
Lamin Baro M'Boge	Niamina Dankunku

UPPER RIVER DIVISION:

Yugo Kasse Drammeh	Sandu
Kanda Kasse Juwara	Wuli
Manjang Sanyang	Kantora
Jwuru Kurubally	Fulladu East

Appendix III: Tonnage of Groundnuts Exported and Value

Year	*Tons*	*Value*
1890	18,262	£129,817
1893	25,218	172,765
1899	34,353	210,005
1905	29,499	169,426
1910	58,456	387,943
1915	96,152	400,435
1920	84,037	2,322,032
1925	48,700	693,097
1930	74,761	867,630
1935	45,110	368,887
1938	46,981	246,691
1945	41,094	493,128
1950	58,791	2,107,000
1955	57,995	1,854,750
1956	54,857	1,398,853
1957	77,396	2,399,276
1958	62,931	3,723,000
1959	40,568	2,433,000

Appendix IV: Yearly Gross Income and Expenditure

Year		Gross Revenue	Gross Expenditure
1899		46,840	30,405
1908		57,898	61,097
1909		72,675	56,237
1910		82,880	63,301
1911		86,454	71,390
1912		96,221	81,340
1913	(no record)		
1914		86,071	120,921
1915		92,253	89,028
1916		103,075	83,217
1917		117,977	94,519
1918		133,323	88,703
1919		180,585	143,451
1920		268,788	171,160
1921		183,201	225,461
1922		204,244	*430,312
1923		407,851	211,316
1924		208,613	203,635
1925		189,086	271,836
1926		214,181	213,643
1927		252,419	277,625
1928		255,385	250,596
1929		235,265	289,506
1930		216,739	253,228
1931		184,825	227,487
1932		206,132	196,015
1933		231,787	180,061
1934		221,564	174,663
1935		245,485	194,669
1936		257,180	209,000
1937		285,204	243,323
1938		166,749	263,199
1939		151,744	205,889
1940		203,753	198,633
1941		247,197	208,453
1942		407,753	295,311

*Reflects devaluation of 5-franc piece.

213

1943	475,910	425,940
1944	523,908	526,023
1945	587,004	430,729
1946	616,328	545,854
1947	693,774	633,272
1948	866,900	1,014,097
1949	964,155	1,170,190
1950	999,216	1,062,312
1951	1,144,825	1,171,028
1952	1,431,495	1,424,213
1953	1,201,068	1,085,693
1954	1,420,356	1,168,309
1955	1,493,146	1,423,310
1956	1,405,006	1,646,900
1957	2,128,107	1,817,931
1958	1,895,006	1,961,539
1959	1,457,467	1,754,396

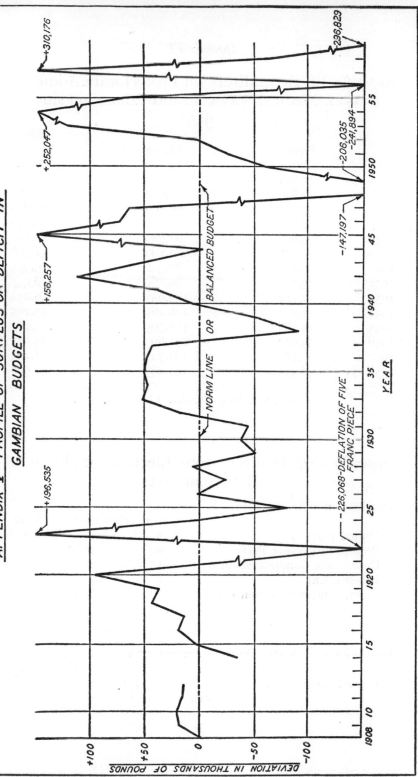

APPENDIX V – PROFILE OF SURPLUS OR DEFICIT IN
GAMBIAN BUDGETS

Appendix VI: Expenditure on Protectorate Administration, Medical Services, and Education since 1945

Year	Protect. Adm.	Medical Services	Education Dept.
1945	21,645	47,635	22,863
1946	32,850	55,033	19,785
1947	37,903	68,396	27,694
1948	67,041	70,045	29,539
1949	39,806	83,999	41,888
1950	41,447	80,163	51,388
1951	35,468	80,502	53,994
1952	35,450	89,860	58,947
1953	34,112	103,051	59,651
1954	24,211	108,269	73,265
1955	24,586	117,509	85,165
1956	32,980	131,605	84,941
1957	36,782	154,735	101,203
1958	38,345	154,487	130,960

Compiled from Colonial Office Reports.

Appendix VII: Results of 1960 Election for House of Representatives

Distribution of Seats:

	Colony	Protectorate	Total
United Party	5	1	6
Peoples Progressive Party	0	8	8
Democratic Congress Alliance	1	2	3
Independent	1	1	2
Chiefs—indirect election		8	8
			27

Distribution of Popular Vote in Percentages:

	Colony	Protectorate
United Party	47·1	11·4

Peoples Progressive Party	17·2	38·9*
Democratic Congress Alliance	17·5	11·2
Others	18·2	38·5

Note: For the first general election only, 50·9 per cent of the registered electorate voted in the Protectorate.

*Does not include Kombo where P.P.P. candidate was returned unopposed.

Appendix VIII: Results of 1962 Election for House of Representatives

Distribution of Seats:

	Colony	Protectorate	Total
United Party	5	8	13
Peoples Progressive Party	1	17	18
Democratic Congress Alliance	1	0	1
Chiefs*		4	4
			36

*Election of these members by the Protectorate Chiefs.

Distribution of Popular Vote in Percentages:

	Colony	Protectorate
United Party	53·5	35·7
Peoples Progressive Party	13·5**	64·3
Democratic Congress Alliance	33·0	0**

**Because of agreement, the D.C.A. and P.P.P. did not contest against each other.

Distribution of Popular Vote in Percentages cast by Districts:

	Upper River	MacCarthy Island	Lower River	Western	Colony
U.P.	49·6	42·2	32·2	19	53·5
P.P.P.	50·4	57·8	67·8	81	13·5
D.C.A.	0	0	0	0	33

BIBLIOGRAPHY

GOVERNMENT CORRESPONDENCE

Foreign Office Files:

F. O. 27/2418
F. O. 27/2614
F. O. 27/3771
F. O. 367/6

Colonial Office Files:

C. O. 87/98	C. O. 87/134	C. O. 27/2414
C. O. 87/98B	C. O. 87/135	C. O. 27/2415
C. O. 87/99	C. O. 87/136	C. O. 27/2614
C. O. 87/130	C. O. 87/137	C. O. 267/42
C. O. 87/131	C. O. 87/138	C. O. 537/12
C. O. 87/132	C. O. 87/143	C. O. 806/301
C. O. 87/133	C. O. 87/144	C. O. 806/304

Bathurst Archive Files:

1512/1904
694/1905
1752/1905
131/1926

A. O. F. Archive Files:

1F11

1 F22
1 F24
P-93

GOVERNMENT PUBLICATIONS

Great Britain, Colonial Office:

Annual Reports up to 1960
Colonial Office Paper No. 52
West African Pamphlet No. 1, 1870
*Papers Relating to the Recent Outbreak of Cholera in the Settlement of the
  Gambia, 1869*
*Correspondence Respecting the Recent Expedition to the Upper Gambia,
  1881*
Further Correspondence Relating to the Gambia, 1892
Correspondence Relating to the Gambian Expedition, 1901

Great Britain, House of Commons:

Reports of the Select Committee on the West Coast of Africa, 1842
House of Commons Paper No. 170
Report of the Select Committee on Africa, 1865
House of Commons Paper No. 444

Great Britain, House of Commons, Papers by Command:

C 1409	Cd.	2383
C 1498	Cmd.	2744
C 1827	Cmd.	3340
C 3065	Cmd.	6175
C 4978	Cmd.	8560
C 5001	Cmnd.	1469
C 6701		

Gambia Government:

Blue Books
Gazettes
Cession of Territories and Treaties with Native Potentates, 1887
Travelling Commissioners Conference Report, 1926
Development and Welfare in the Gambia, 1943

Bibliography

Ordinances:

No. 11, 1894	No. 7, 1919	No. 18, 1944
No. 1, 1895	No. 1, 1923	No. 19, 1944
No. 7, 1895	No. 16, 1924	No. 13, 1945
No. 6, 1896	No. 10, 1925	No. 1, 1946
No. 4, 1897	No. 3, 1933	No. 15, 1946
No. 4, 1901	No. 4, 1933	No. 5, 1947
No. 7, 1902	No. 5, 1933	No. 21, 1948
No. 11, 1909	No. 2, 1935	No. 29, 1948
No. 13, 1909	No. 3, 1935	No. 7, 1954
No. 30, 1913	No. 34, 1939	No. 14, 1954

Sessional Papers:

No. 1, 1945	No. 2, 1953
No. 14, 1946	No. 7, 1955
No. 8, 1951	No. 4, 1958
No. 5, 1952	No. 8, 1959

BOOKS

M. Adanson, *Voyage to the Senegal, the Isle of Goree and the Gambia in the Year 1750* (London: 1759).

James E. Alexander, *Narrative of a Voyage of Observation Among the Colonies of West Africa* (London: 1853).

F. Bisset Archer, *The Gambia Colony and Protectorate* (London: 1906).

Thomas Astley, *A New General Collection of Voyages and Travels* (London 1745).

Sarah Biller, *Memoir of Hannah Kilham* (London: 1837).

E. W. Bovill, *Caravans of the Old Sahara* (London: 1933).

Prosper Cultru, *Histoire du Senegal du XV Siecle à 1870* (Paris: 1910).

K. G. Davies, *The Royal African Company* (London: 1957).

J. D. Fage, *A Short History of West Africa* (Cambridge: 1961).

John W. Fortesque, *The History of the British Army*, Vol. XI (London: 1911).

William Fox, *History of the Wesleyan Missions on the Western Coast of Africa* (London: 1851).

David P. Gamble, *The Wolof of the Senegambia* (London: 1957).

John M. Gray, *The Gambia* (Oxford: 1940).

William Gray, *Travels in Western Africa in the Years 1819-1821* (London: 1825).

Lord Hailey, *Native Administration in British African Territories*, Vol. III (London: 1951).

Bibliography

Richard Hakluyt, *Principal Navigations of the English Nation*, Vol. IV (London: 1927).

Hakluyt Society, *The Voyages of Cadamosto and Other Documents on Western Africa in the Second Half of the 15th Century* (London: 1937).

Hardinge, *The Fourth Earl of Carnarvon* (London: 1925).

Edward Hertslet, *Map of Africa by Treaty* (London: 1894).

J. F. Napier Hewitt, *European Settlements on the West Coast of Africa* (London: 1862).

B. Holas, *L'Homme Noir D'Afrique* (Dakar: 1951).

H. Regional Jarrett, *A Geography of Sierra Leone and the Gambia* (London: 1954).

Richard Jobson, *The Golden Trade* (London: 1932).

Sir Harry Johnson, *History of the Colonization of Africa* (Cambridge: 1930).

Jean Baptiste Labat, *Nouvelle Relation de l'Afrique Occidentale* (Paris: 1728).

Henri Labouret, *Les Mandings et leur langue* (Paris: 1934).

M. Le Maire, *Voyage to the Canaries, Cape Verd and the Coast of Africa under the Command of M. Dancourt, 1682* (Edinburgh: 1887).

Eveline Martin, *The British West Africa Settlement 1750-1821* (London: 1927).

Otto Heinz Mattiesen, *Die Kolonial und Uberseepolitik der kurlandischen Herzöge im 17 und 18 Jahrhundert* (Stuttgart: 1940).

Francis More, *Travels in the Inland Part of Africa* (London: 1738).

H. R. Palmer, *The Carthaginian Voyage to West Africa* (Bathurst: 1931).

H. R. Palmer, *Political Memoranda for the Guidance of Commissioners and other Government Officers Working in the Protectorate* (Bathurst: 1933).

Mungo Park, *Journal of a Mission to the Interior of Africa in the Year 1805* (London: 1815).

Mungo Park, *Travels in the Interior Districts of Africa* (London: 1899).

E. G. Parrinder, *West African Religion* (London: 1949).

Henry F. Reeve, *The Gambia* (London: 1912).

R. Robinson, J. Gallagher and A. Denny, *Africa and the Victorians* (New York: 1961).

Lady Bella Southorn, *The Gambia* (London: 1952).

Eliot Warburton, *Memoirs of Prince Rupert and the Cavaliers* (London: 1849).

ARTICLES

'The Gambia's Amiable Example', *West Africa*, 30 Aug. 1952.

'The Gambia's First Minister', *West Africa*, 12 Dec. 1953.

'Portrait, Gambia's Rice Expert', *West Africa*, 23 Nov. 1957.

'Portrait, P. S. N'Jie', *West Africa*, 3 May 1958.

'Portrait, David K. Jawara', *West Africa*, 21 Jan. 1961.

'New Men in the Gambia', *West Africa*, 9 June 1962.

H. A. Gailey, Jr., 'Gambia Chiefs' Question', *West Africa*, 11 March 1961.

H. A. Gailey, Jr., 'The Gambia Moves Forward', *West Africa*, 1 April 1961.

H. A. Gailey, Jr., 'Portrait, Gambia's Labour Leader', *West Africa*, 27 May 1961.

H. A. Gailey, Jr., 'European Rivalry and Diplomacy in the Mella-courie 1879-1882', *Sierra Leone Studies*, No. 15, Dec. 1961.

D. P. Gamble, 'Infant Mortality Rates in Rural Areas of the Gambia Protectorate', *Journal of Tropical Medicine and Hygiene*, July 1952.

Robin Hallett, 'The European Approach to the Interior of Africa in the 18th Century', *Journal of African History*, Vol. IV, No. 3, 1963.

D. B. Harden, 'The Phoenicians on the West Coast of Africa', *Antiquity*, Sept. 1948.

H. Reginald Jarrett, 'Population and Settlement in the Gambia', *Geographical Review*, Oct. 1948.

H. Reginald Jarrett, 'The Strange Farmers of Gambia', *Geographical Review*, Oct. 1949.

R. Rousseau, 'Le Senegal d'autrefois second étude sur le Cayor', *IFAN Bulletin*.

Lady Bella Southorn, 'The Wandering Fulbie', *West African Review*, June 1938.

NOTES

CHAPTER ONE: THE LAND AND PEOPLE

[1] For correspondence concerning the difficulties of establishing boundaries see F.O.367/6.

[2] As estimated for 1957 in Great Britain, Colonial Office, *Annual Report, 1956-1957*, p. 12.

[3] The most detailed geography of the Gambia is H. Reginald Jarrett, *A Geography of Sierra Leone and the Gambia* (London: 1954).

[4] A Mandinka term for areas above river levels that remain arid in the dry season and become swamps in the rainy season.

[5] H. Reginald Jarrett, 'Population and Settlement in the Gambia', *Geographical Review*, Oct. 1948, p. 639.

[6] *Ibid.*, pp. 634-635.

[7] For a detailed discussion of Gambian agriculture see Chapter VIII.

[8] B. Holas, *L'Homme Noir d'Afrique* (Dakar: 1951), pp. 36-69.

[9] For a good, brief synthesis of religions of the area see E. G. Parrinder, *West African Religion* (London: 1949).

[10] E. W. Bovill, *Caravans of the Old Sahara* (London: 1933), pp. 67-81.

[11] *Ibid.*, pp. 82-113.

[12] Hakluyt Society, *The Voyages of Cadamosto and other Documents on Western Africa in the Second Half of the 15th Century* (London: 1937), pp. 29-30.

[13] For a concise discussion of the various theories see David P. Gamble, *The Wolof of the Senegambia* (London: 1957), p. 14, and R. Rousseau, *Le Senegal d'autrefois, second étude sur le Cayor*, (IFAN Bulletin: Dakar), pp. 79-144.

[14] M. Le Maire, *Voyage to the Canaries, Cape Verd and the Coast of Africa under the Command of M. Dancourt, 1682* (Edinburgh: 1887), p. 46.

[15] Francis Moore, *Travels in the Inland Part of Africa* (London: 1738), p. 19 and 22. Richard Jobson in *The Golden Trade* (London: 1932), p. 65, had called the ruler the King of Bursall.

[16] Henry F. Reeve, *The Gambia* (London: 1912), pp. 173-174.

[17] Population figures for the Gambia are only approximate due to the length of time between census reports and the rapid changes in population.

All figures quoted are based on the latest census returns of 1951. Great Britain, Colonial Office *Annual Report, 1956-1957,* pp. 12-13.

[18] John Milner Gray, *The Gambia* (Oxford: 1940), footnote p. 325.

[19] Gamble, 1957, p. 15.

[20] For early notes on the Mandingos see M. Adanson, *Voyage to the Senegal, the Isle of Goree and the Gambia in the Year 1750* (London: 1759), pp. 162-163; Jobson, 1932, pp. 51-83; and Moore, 1738, p. 29; and for later elaboration concerning the Mandingos see Henri Labouret, *Les Mandings et leur langue* (Paris: 1934).

[21] Jobson, 1932, p. 51.

[22] Moore, 1738, p. 36.

[23] J. Gray, 1940, pp. 325-329

[24] Great Britain, Colonial Office, *Annual Report, 1956-1957,* p. 13.

[25] Jean Baptiste Labat, *Nouvelle Relation de l'Afrique Occidentale* (Paris: 1728), Vol. V, pp. 30-34.

[26] Moore, 1738, p. 36.

[27] S. M. X. Golbery's translated account of his travels in Francis Blagdon, *Travels in Africa* (London: 1802), Vol. I, p. 70.

[28] J. Gray, 1940, p. 326.

[29] Reeve, 1912, pp. 200-201. An interesting account of the Fula is that of Sultan Bello in H. R. Palmer, *The Carthaginian Voyage to West Africa* (Bathurst: 1931), and also Lady Southorn, 'The Wandering Fulbie', *West African Review,* June 1938, pp. 30-31.

[30] Bovill, 1933, pp. 69-100.

[31] Sir Harry Johnson, *History of the Colonization of Africa* (Cambridge: 1930), p. 201.

[32] Jobson, 1932, pp. 47-48.

[33] Great Britain, Colonial Office, *Annual Report, 1956-1957,* p. 13.

[34] For a full discussion of the 'Strange Farmers' see H. Reginald Jarrett, 'The Strange Farmers of Gambia', *Geographical Review,* Oct. 1949, pp. 649-657.

CHAPTER TWO: EARLY EUROPEAN CONTACTS

[1] The best treatment of these early references in Herodotus, Appian, and Strabo is in Bovill, pp. 16-49. For Hanno's investigations see Palmer, 1931. See also D. B. Harden, 'The Phoenicians on the West Coast of Africa', *Antiquity,* Sept. 1948, pp. 141-150.

[2] Hakluyt Society, p. 27.

[3] *Ibid.,* p. 52-62.

[4] *Ibid.,* pp. 66-82.

[5] For a description of the character of Portuguese settlements see Le Maire, p. 47.

[6] J. Gray, 1940, pp. 10-15.

[7] Jobson, 1932, pp. 37-38.

[8] Richard Hakluyt, *Principal Navigations of the English Nation* (London: 1927), Vol. IV, p. 45.

[9] *Ibid.*, Vol. IV, p. 286.

[10] *Ibid.*, Vol. IV, pp. 264-265 and 285.

[11] Or as Thomas Astley put it in *A New General Collection of Voyages and Travels* (London: 1745), Vol. II, p. 159, 'They were so injured in their Trade by Interlopers that they were soon greatly tired of it.' Also see Jobson, 1932, pp. 9-10.

[12] Jobson, 1932, p. 123.

[13] Eliot Warburton, *Memoirs of Prince Rupert and the Cavaliers* (London: 1849), Vol. III, p. 361.

[14] Hakluyt, Vol. IV, pp. 39 ff, and Vol. V, p. 45.

[15] J. Gray, 1940, p. 200.

[16] *Ibid.*, p. 29.

[17] The best account of the Courlander's experiment is Otto Heinz Mattiesen, *Die Kolonial und Uberseepolitik der kurländischen Herzöge im 17 und 18 Jahrhundert* (Stuttgart: 1940), pp. 236-331 and 518-548.

[18] A raid by Prince Rupert on Bintang was important in convincing English traders of the fabulous wealth of the Gambia. According to Warburton, Vol. III, p. 361, Rupert got possession of a document which claimed that up river was a 'firm rock of gold of great bigness which might countervail the greatest charges as may be expended in finding it'. Jobson, p. 123 also reported that a respected chief had told him of a 'great Towne above, the houses whereof are covered only with gold'.

[19] Jobson, 1932, p. 120.

[20] J. Gray, 1940, p. 53.

[21] Astley, 1745, Vol. I, p. 159.

[22] J. Gray, 1940, p. 86.

[23] The Royal African Company by Letters Patent of 1672 was given as its concession the whole of the West Coast of Africa, extending as far south as the Cape of Good Hope. The Gold Coast was the most profitable area in West Africa and the company concentrated most of its interest there. The Gambia was a secondary area of trade and remained subsidiary to the more profitable stations in the south throughout the period.

[24] Astley, 1745, Vol II, p. 3.

[25] Reeve, 1912, pp. 54-57.

[26] J. Gray, 1940, p. 100.

[27] *Ibid.*, pp. 102-106.

[28] K. G. Davies, *The Royal African Company* (London: 1957), p. 272.

[29] For the economic effects of the War of the League of Augsburg upon the company see *Ibid.*, pp. 205-221.

[30] 9 and 10 Wm. III C. 26.

[31] Labat, 1728, Vol. IV, pp. 198-331.

[32] Davies, 1957, p. 273.

[33] Labat, 1728, Vol. IV, pp. 347-349.

[34] J. Gray, 1940, pp. 152-160.

[35] Eveline Martin, *The British West Africa Settlements 1750-1821* (London: 1927). p. 7.

[36] J. Gray, 1940, pp. 152-160.

[37] This attitude can be partially explained by the loss incurred in the long wars with France. See Davies, pp. 205-210.

[38] J. Gray, 1940, p. 164.

[39] Some exeptions to this were the voyages of Captain Hodges in 1681 and 1688. Hodges reported that the only favourable way to the interior was via the Senegal. A special expedition was outfitted in 1721 to look for the lost mines and a number of Cornish miners were engaged for the task. The ship taking them to the Gambia, however, was lost at sea. Gray, 1940, p. 185.

[40] Moore, 1738, pp. 235-297.

[41] Labat, 1728, Vol. I, pp. 156-210 for the continuation of trade, and Edward Hertslet, *Map of Africa by Treaty* (London: 1894), Vol. II, p. 544-546.

[42] J. Gray, 1940, pp. 187-197.

[43] Moore, 1728, p. 41.

[44] *Ibid.*, p. 42.

[45] *Ibid.*, p. 43.

[46] Prosper Cultru, *Histoire du Senegal du XV Siècle a 1870* (Paris: 1910), p.199.

[47] Astley, 1745, Vol. II, p. 160, and Davies, p. 152.

[48] Commons Journals XV, p. 958, and XXVIII, p. 274.

[49] 23 George II, C 31, and Martin, 1927, p. IX.

[50] Martin, 1927, p. 12.

[51] Commons Journals XXVI, p. 146. Also Martin, pp. 12-14 for the fortunes of the company and difficulties arising from the dual control.

[52] J. Gray, 1940, pp. 221-226.

[53] 23 Geroge II, C 31.

[54] Martin, 1927, pp. 57-59.

[55] 4 George III, C 20.

[56] See Martin, 1927, pp. 59-64 for the manoeuvres on the part of the merchants to regain their rights and especially the details of the abortive Act of 1764 which invested all rights to trade in the area in a Company of Merchants Trading in Africa. Before the royal assent was given to the act the Board of Trade decided to vest the government of the Senegal and the Gambia in the Crown.

[57] *Ibid.*, pp. 66-69.

[58] For a detailed account of the rivalry between Lt. Governors Pryrer and MacNamara and Governors O'Hara and Clark see J. Gray, pp. 235-265, and Martin, pp. 76-96.

[59] Martin, 1927, p. 93.

[60] *Ibid.*, p. 99.

[61] Hertslet, 1894, Vol. II, p. 539.

[62] 23 George III, C 65.

[63] J. Gray, 1940, p. 276.

[64] *Ibid.*, p. 280.

[65] *Ibid.*, p. 281-283, and Robin Hallett, 'The European Approach to the Interior of Africa in the 18th Century', *Journal of African History*, Vol. IV, No. 3, 1963, p. 204.

[66] For a complete description of this journey see Mungo Park, *Travels in the Interior Districts of Africa* (London: 1899).

[67] For an elaboration of this plan of action see J. Gray, 1940, pp. 288-289.

[68] Mungo Park, *Journal of a Mission to the Interior of Africa in the Year 1805* (London: 1815).

[69] J. Gray, 1940, pp. 295-296.

[70] *Ibid.*, p. 306.

[71] 1 and 2 George IV, C 28.

CHAPTER THREE: THE SONINKI-MARABOUT WARS

[1] J. Gray, 1940, p. 391.

[2] The best lengthy account of the conditions of the hinterland is found in Travelling Commissioner Ozanne's first report of August 1893 in C.O. 87/143.

[3] Kortright to Carnarvon (Confidential), 19 June 1874, C 1409.

[4] Salisbury to Hicks-Beach, 22 Nov. 1879, F. O. 27/2418; Minute Paper by Meade, 14 May 1888, C. O. 87/132; and C. O. to Carter, 27 Nov. 1888, C. O. 806/304 are selected examples of such statements.

[5] For the full narrative development of the early phase of the war in the vicinity of Sabaji and Gunjur see J. Gray, Chapter 26, pp. 388-398.

[6] Hertslet, 1894, Vol. II, p. 17.

[7] J. Gray, 1940, p. 391.

[8] Hertslet, 1894, Vol. II, p. 79 and 82.

[9] For the details of Maba's activities in the early '60s see J. Gray, 1940, pp. 418-424.

[10] Hertslet, 1894, Vol. II, p. 101.

[11] J. Gray, 1940, p. 423.

[12] Great Britain, Colonial Office, *Annual Report, 1866.*

[13] Great Britain, House of Commons, *Report of the Select Committee on Africa (1865).*

[14] *Ibid.*

[15] J. Gray, 1940, p. 427.

[16] For these disturbances see *Ibid.*, Chapter 28, pp. 416-430.

[17] For example, there is contained in Great Britain, *Colonial Office No. 52* a veiled implication by D'Arcy in a letter to the C. O. of July 1861 that he could take the large kingdom of Saloum merely by showing the proper interest.

[18] H. St. George Ord, *House of Commons Paper No. 170, Report on the Conditions of the British Settlements on the West Coast of Africa, 1865.*

¹⁹ Great Britain, Colonial Office, *Papers Relating to the Recent Outbreak of Cholera in the Settlement of the Gambia, 1869.*

²⁰ J. Gray, 1940, p. 449.

²¹ *Ibid.*, p. 450.

²² *Ibid.*, p. 450.

²³ *Ibid.*, p. 451.

²⁴ Great Britain, Colonial Office, *Further Correspondence relating to the Gambia, 1892*, pp. 74-76.

²⁵ Details of Fodi Kabba's activities in the late '70s are given in Gouldsbury to Herbert, 27 May 1880, Misc. Records, Bathurst Archives, and his activities in the '80s are detailed in C. O. 87/135.

²⁶ Carter to Antrobus, 23 April 1889, C. O. 87/135.

²⁷ Great Britian, Colonial Office, *Annual Report, 1880.*

²⁸ Report Kortright to Berkeley, 26 June 1875, C. 1409.

²⁹ Chief of Brikama to Kortright, 5 May 1874, and Report of Kortright to Berkeley, 26 June 1875, *Ibid.*

³⁰ J. Gray, 1940, p. 455.

³¹ Gouldsbury to Rowe, 28 May 1880, in Misc. Records, Bathurst Archives, and Lyons 'verbal note', 31 Oct. 1881, F. O. 27/2614.

³² Rowe to Colonial Office, 2 March 1887, C. O. 87/130.

³³ Carter to Colonial Office, 4 May 1887, and telegram 5 May 1887, C. O. 87/130. For earlier treaties with Bairam Sisi, 7 Feb. 1887 and Said Matti, 11 Feb. 1887 see Hertslet, 1894, Vol. II, pp. 18-19.

³⁴ Great Britain, *Parliamentary Debates, Commons,* New Series, V. 316, Col. 56 and V. 317, Col. 1149. See also numerous letters concerning the state of the Gambia in 1887-1888, C. O. 87/130.

³⁵ Particularly statement by Knutsford, 31 Dec. 1888, concerning French activity, C. O. 87/134.

³⁶ These treaties are reproduced in full in Gambia, *Cession of Territories and Treaties with Native Potentates, 1887.*

³⁷ C. O. 87/138.

³⁸ J. Gray, 1940, p. 467.

³⁹ Hertslet, 1894, Vol. II, p. 20.

⁴⁰ Great Britain, Colonial Office, *Correspondence Relating to the Gambian Expedition, 1901.*

CHAPTER FOUR: THE GAMBIA COLONY IN THE EARLY NINETEENTH CENTURY

¹ C. O. 267/42.

² James E. Alexander, *Narrative of a Voyage of Observation among the Colonies of West Africa* (London: 1853), Vol. I, pp. 70-71.

³ Lady Bella Southorn, *The Gambia* (London: 1952), p. 156.

⁴ John W. Fortesque, *The History of the British Army* (London: 1911), Vol. XI, pp. 370-371.

[5] William Gray, *Travels in Western Africa in the Years 1819-1821* (London: 1825), p. 365.

[6] Southorn, 1952, p. 157.

[7] 1 and 2 George IV, C 28.

[8] Southorn, 1952, p. 165.

[9] 6 Victoria, C 13.

[10] Hertslet, 1894, Vol. 1, pp. 7-8.

[11] J. Gray, 1940, pp. 335-336.

[12] Hertslet, 1894, Vol. I, p. 11.,

[13] *Ibid.*, pp. 8-9.

[14] *Ibjd.*, pp. 11-12.

[15] *Ibid.*, p. 10.

[16] *Ibid.*, p. 11.

[17] For the details of this war see J. Gray, 1940, pp. 344-353.

[18] F. Bisset Archer, *The Gambia Colony and Protectorate* (London: 1906), p. 35.

[19] J. Gray, 1940, p. 346.

[20] Confidential Despatch, Cooper to Gov.-in-Chief, 6 Jan. 1876, Misc. Records, Sierra Leone Archives.

[21] C. O. 87/143.

[22] As an example of numerous such despatches see Gouldsbury to Herbert, 27th May 1880, Misc. Correspondence, Bathurst Archives.

[23] For the early efforts of the Society of Friends see Sarah Biller, *Memoir of Hannah Kilham* (London: 1837).

[24] William Fox. *History of the Wesleyan Missions on the Western Coast of Africa* (London: 1851).

[25] An F. R. G. S. (Richard Burton), *Wanderings in West Africa* (London: 1863), Vol. I, p. 152.

[26] Gambia Government, Proposed Gambian Budget 1900, *Ordinance No. 4, 1901.*

[27] Gambia Government, Proposed Gambian Budget 1940, *Ordinance No. 34, 1939.*

[28] Ord, *Report.*

[29] In 1886 the Gambia contributed £1,900 towards a steam launch for the Governor-in-Chief despite the fact that he had not even visited the Gambia in three years. This was in addition to the £500 per year contributed towards the salary of the Governor-in-Chief. Letter dated Dec. 29 1886, Bathurst, in C. 4978.

[30] Great Britain, House of Commons, *Report of the Select Committee on the West Coast of Africa* (London: 1842), p. vii.

[31] Great Britain, Colonial Office, *Correspondence Respecting the Recent Expedition to the Upper Gambia (1881).*

[32] Moore 1738, p. 108.

[33] Southorn, 1952, p. 184.

[34] Great Britain, Colonial Office, *Annual Report, 1889.*

[35] Hertslet, 1894, Vol. I, 11. 13-14.

³⁶ *Ibid.*, pp. 17-18 and *State Papers*, Vol. XLVIII, p. 899.

³⁷ Hertslet, 1894, Vol. II, pp. 716-718 and *State Papers* XLVII, p. 36.

³⁸ J. F. Napier Hewitt, *European Settlement on the West Coast of Africa* (London: 1862), pp. 55-56.

³⁹ Southorn, 1952, p. 157.

⁴⁰ Hewitt, 1862, pp. 70-71.

⁴¹ An F. R. G. S. (Burton), Vol. I, p. 156.

⁴² Biller, 1837, pp. 196 and 198.

⁴³ Hewitt, 1862, pp. 283-285.

⁴⁴ Ord, *Report.*

⁴⁵ Great Britain, House of Commons, *Report of the Select Committee on Africa (West Coast) (1865).*

⁴⁶ Letters Patent, 19 Feb. 1866, *State Papers*, Vol. LIX, p. 1194 and Letters Patent, 17 Dec. 1874, *State Papers*, Vol. LXVI, p. 948.

⁴⁷ For a picture of the depressed financial conditions of Sierra Leone in the 1870s see the Report of a Departmental Committee on the subject in F.O.27/2414.

⁴⁸ The official opinion regarding MacCarthy Island and the up river areas in the decade from 1866-1876 is in Carnarvon to Kortright, 24 Nov. 1876, C 1827.

CHAPTER FIVE: THE LURE OF EXCHANGE

¹ For French activity in West Africa in this period see G. Hanotaux and A. Martineau, *La Colonisation Française* (Paris: 1931), Vol. IV, pp. 112-194.

² Foreign Office note, 22 Jan. 1870, C. O. 87/98B.

³ Carnarvon to Lyons, 11 Feb. 1870, *State Papers*, Vol. LXI, p. 1107.

⁴ F. O. to Napoleon III, 22 May 1868, C. O. 87/98.

⁵ F. O. Memo, 22 Jan. 1870, C. O. 87/98B.

⁶ Kennedy to Granville, 29 April 1869, *House of Commons Paper No. 444.*

⁷ *Ibid.*

⁸ Kennedy to Standford, 23 Sept. 1869, *Ibid.*

⁹ Patey to Monsell, 1 Oct. 1869, *Ibid.*

¹⁰ F. O. Memo, 22 Jan. 1870, and Clarendon to Lyons, 11 Feb. 1870, C. O. 87/98.

¹¹ Lyons to Clarendon, 31 March 1870, *Ibid.*

¹² Great Britain, House of Commons, *Parliamentary Debates, Commons,* 3rd Series, Vol. 201, Cols. 1842-43.

¹³ Great Britain, *Parliamentary Debates, Lords,* 3rd Series, Vol. 203, Cols. 339-42.

¹⁴ Petition H. Finder *et. al.* to Granville, April 1870, *House of Commons Paper No. 444* and Kennedy's opinion of this to Granville, 10 May 1870, C. O. 87/98. The second petition dated 6 May 1870 and Acting Adminis-

trator Bravo's comments, 13 May 1870 are also in *House of Commons Paper No. 444.*

[15] Bravo to Kennedy, 6 June 1870, *House of Commons Paper No. 444.*

[16] Lyons to Foreign Office, 5 July 1870, C. O. 87/98.

[17] Tomani Bojang to Administrator, 23 May 1870, *Ibid.*

[18] Foster and Smith to Granville, 4 July 1870, *Ibid.*

[19] Brown to Granville, 12 July 1870, *Ibid.*

[20] Examples of this type of correspondence in 1870 are the meeting of Manchester Chamber of Commerce, 1 July; Memorial Quin and Brown to Kimberley, 21 July; and also Memo. 30 July from Chown & Co. in *House of Commons Paper No. 444.* Also see Colonial Office, *West African Pamphlet No. 1,* 1870.

[21] Granville to Lyons, 20 July 1870. C. O. 87/98.

[22] Kimberley to Kennedy, 23 July 1870, *House of Commons Paper No. 444.*

[23] Herbert To Otway, 4 Aug. 1870, *Ibid.*

[24] Kennedy to Kimberley, 3 March 1871, C. O. 87/99.

[25] Kortright to Gov. Berkeley, 27 June 1874, C 1409 and policy statement by Carnarvon, 9 March 1877, C 1827.

[26] Memo. M. Gavard to F. O. and Derby to Lyons, 11 April 1874, C 1409.

[27] Kortright to Carnarvon (Confidential), 19 June 1874, *Ibid.*

[28] Strahan to Carnarvon, 23 March 1875, *Ibid.*

[29] Kennedy to Carnarvon, April 1875, *Ibid.*

[30] Memorandum (Confidential) Derby to Carnarvon, 25 June 1875, *Ibid.*

[31] The most important of these communications are Brown to Colonial. Office, 24 Sept. and 7 Oct. 1875; petition of Brown and 151 others, 7 Oct.; petition from 388 Gambians, 31 Dec.; and memorial from Gambia Committee, 2 Feb. 1876, *Ibid.*

[32] Great Britain, *Parliamentary Debates, Lords,* 3rd Series, Vol. 227, Col. 374.

[33] Hardinge, *The Fourth Earl of Carnarvon* (London: 1925), Vol. II, pp. 144-145.

[34] Great Britain, *Parliamentary Debates,* 3rd Series, Vol. 228, Cols. 264 and 272.

[35] Memo. to Derby, 24 April 1876, C. O. 806/301.

CHAPTER SIX: DRAWING THE BOUNDARY

[1] *Journal Officiel,* Senate, 12 Nov. 1884.

[2] The proceedings and results of the Berlin Conference are in France, Ministry of Foreign Affairs, *Documents diplomatiques des affaires du Congo, Inde et Est Afrique* (Paris: 1885), pp. 55-292 or C 4361.

[3] Bismarck believed that 'if the English and French locomotives collide somewhere', Germany would benefit. Edward A. Fitzmaurice, *Life of Lord Granville* (London: 1905), Vol. I, p. 273.

[4] For the best discussion of the meaning of Egypt in this diplomatic scramble see R. Robinson, J. Gallagher, and A. Denny, *Africa and the Victorians* (New York: 1961), pp. 76-158.

[5] J. D. Fage, *A Short History of West Africa* (Cambridge: 1961), p. 153.

[6] H. A. Gailey, Jr., 'European Rivalry and Diplomacy in the Mellacourie, 1879-1882', *Sierra Leone Studies*, No. 15, Dec. 1961.

[7] C. O. 87/134.

[8] *Ibid.*

[9] Quoted in General Brackenbury's Intelligence Report, C. O. 537/12.

[10] Minute dated 1 Oct. 1887, C. O. 87/131.

[11] Lyons to Salisbury, 11 June 1879, C. O. 27/2415.

[12] Memorandum by Pauncefote, 30 Aug. 1879, F. O. 27/2414.

[13] F. O. 27/2614 and C. O. 87/132.

[14] Gouldsbury to C. O., 10 Feb. 1882, F. O. 27/2614.

[15] Carter to C. O. telegram, 5 May 1887, C. O. 87/130; Carter to C. O. 25 Oct. 1888, C. O. 87/133.

[16] Memorandum by Knutsford, 31 Dec. 1888, C. O. 87/134.

[17] There are many examples of these orders. See for example Minute Paper by Meade, 1 Oct. 1887, C. O. 87/131 and Knutsford to Carter, 27 Nov. 1888, C. O. 806/304.

[18] Minute Paper, 1 Oct. 1887, C. O. 87/131.

[19] Minute Paper, 3 Aug. 1888, C. O. 87/133.

[20] Minute Paper, 1 Oct. 1887, C. O. 87/131.

[21] Minute Paper, 3 Aug. 1888, C. O. 87/133.

[22] Brackenbury's Intelligence Report in C. O. 537/12, and Memorandum by Hemming in C. O. 806/301.

[23] The correspondence concerning the entire Conference is in C. O. 537/12.

[24] Egerton to Salisbury, 10 May and 29 May 1889, *Ibid.*

[25] Brackenbury to Commissioners, 18 May 1889, *Ibid.*

[26] Hemming to C. O., 5 May 1889, *Ibid.*

[27] Hemming to Meade, 2 July 1889, *Ibid.*

[28] Hertslet, 1894, Vol. II, pp. 729-734 and C 6701.

[29] Hemming to Meade, 2 July 1889, C. O. 537/12.

[30] Hertslet, 1894, Vol. II, p. 734.

[31] Hemming to Meade, 2 July 1889, C. O. 537/12.

[32] F. O. to C. O., 26 Nov. 1889, C. O. 87/136.

[33] Hemming to Meade, 2 July 1889, C. O. 537/12.

[34] Letters Patent, 28 Nov. 1888.

[35] Gambia Protectorate Ordinance *No.* 11, 1894, *Gambia Gazette*, 1895.

[36] Llewellyn to C. O., 3 April 1893, F. O. 87/143, and Roseberry to Llewellyn, 18 July 1893, F. O. 87/144.

[37] The details and correspondence of these boundary teams are found in F. O. 367/6 and Bathurst Archives, Minute Paper Files 1512/1904, 694/1905, and 1752/1905, and in A.O.F. Archives, Dakar, Files 1F22 and 1F24.

[38] Various Minutes concerning Fodi Kabba and the boundary Commissioners are in C. O. 87/139.

[39] Cd. 2383.

[40] Llewellyn to Chamberlain, 14 June 1899 and Chamberlain to F. O., 24 Aug. 1900, F. O. 27/3771.

[41] F. O. 27/3771.

[42] C. O. to Denton, 22 Feb. 1902, F. O. 27/3771.

[43] Hemming to Meade, 2 July 1889, C. O. 537/12.

[44] Confidential Memo. by Carter, 5 July 1889, *Ibid.*

[45] Llewellyn to Hemming, 12 April 1893, C. O. 87/143.

[46] Confidential Despatch, Monson to F. O., 28 Nov. 1901, F. O. 27/3771.

[47] Cambon to F. O., 4 Dec. 1901, *Ibid.*

[48] Bathurst Archives, Minute Paper Files 1512/1904 and F. O. 367/6.

[49] *United Empire*, Vol. 15, Jan. 1934, p. 35.

[50] Roseberry to Dufferin and Ava, 27 Dec. 1893, C. O. 87/144.

[51] The text of this agreement is in F. O. 27/3771.

[52] Confidential Denton to C. O., 28 Oct. 1905, F. O. 27/3771.

[53] F. H. Villiers to C. O., 12 Jan. 1906, F. O. 367/6.

[54] Minute Paper by Hurst, 8 May 1906, *Ibid.*

[55] Crowie to Landsdowne, 28 Feb. 1905, F. O. 27/3771.

[56] Report by M. Hardel, 25 Oct. 1910, A.O.F. Archives, Dakar, File P-393.

[57] Memo by Chef du Cabinet and M. Roume, Feb. 1907, A.O.F. Archives, Dakar, File 1F11.

[58] *Ibid.*

[59] For confirmation of this thesis see *Note relative à La comparison entre Gambie, considerée comme voie de penetration au Soudan et le Chemin de Fer du Thies au Kayes Niger,* undated but in dossier marked April 1915 in A.O.F. Archives, Dakar, File P-393.

CHAPTER SEVEN: GOVERNING THE PROTECTORATE

[1] Enclosure No. 5 to despatch from Llewellyn to Col. Office, 23 Mar. 1893, C. O. 87/143.

[2] Lllewellyn to Ripon, 3 Nov. 1893, C. O. 87/144.

[3] Great Britain, Colonial Office, *Annual Report, 1893,* p. 4.

[4] Commissioner Ozanne's First Report, July 1893, C. O. 87/143.

[5] Great Britain, Colonial Office, *Annual Report, 1894,* p. 9.

[6] Great Britain, Colonial Office, *Annual Report, 1895,* p. 4.

[7] Great Britain, Colonial Office, *Annual Report, 1896,* p. 5.

[8] Order in Council dated 23 Nov. 1893.

[9] Despatch Llewellyn to Colonial Office, 23 March 1893, C. O. 87/143.

[10] Gambia Government, *Ordinance No. 11, 1894.*

[11] Gambia Government, Protectorate Yard Tax *Ordinance No. 7, 1895.*

[12] Gambia Government, *Ordinance No. 1, 1895.,*

[13] Gambia Government, *Ordinance No. 7, 1895.*

[14] Great Britain, Colonial Office, *Annual Report, 1904,* p. 39.

[15] Proclamation *No.* 7, May 1895, *Gambia Government Gazette Supplement,* May, 1895.

[16] Gambia Government, *Ordinance No. 6, 1896.*

[17] Gambia Government, *Ordinance No. 4, 1897.*

[18] Regulation by Governor Denton in Council, 31 July 1905.

[19] Gambia Government, Protectorate (Public Lands) Regulations, 1915.

[20] Great Britain, Colonial Office, *Annual Report, 1903,* p. 38.

[21] Great Britain, Colonial Office, *Correspondence Relating to the Gambian Expedition, 1901,* and Great Britain, Colonial Office, *Annual Report, 1900,* pp. 16-17.

[22] *Ibid.*

[23] Gambia Government, *Ordinance No. 7, 1902.*

[24] Gambia Government, *The Protectorate (Procedure) Rules, 1905.*

[25] Gambia Government, Protectorate (Amendment) *Ordinance No. 11, 1909.*

[26] Gambia Government, Protectorate (Amendment) *Ordinance No. 13, 1909.*

[27] Regulation by Gov. Galway in Council, *Gambia Government Gazette,* 18 May 1912.

[28] Gambia Government, Protectorate (Amendment) *Ordinance No. 30, 1913.*

[29] Gambia Government, Protectorate (Amendment) *Ordinance No. 7, 1919.*

[30] Gambia Government, Protectorate (Amendment) *Ordinance No. 1, 1923.*

[31] Gambia Government, Protectorate (Amendment) *Ordinance No. 10, 1925.*

[32] Gambia Government, Protectorate (Amendment) *Ordinance No. 10, 1928.*

[33] An excellent treatment of the standardized indigeneous system is Lord Hailey, *Native Administration in British African Territories* (London: 1951), Vol. III, pp. 334-335.

[34] Proclamation *No.* 7, *Gambia Government Gazette (Supplement),* 7 May 1895.

[35] A memorandum prepared by E. H. Hopkinson for the Colonial Secretary, 11 Feb. 1926, Bathurst Archives, File 131/1926.

[36] It is difficult to arrive at a composite figure for money expended in the Protectorate in this period for there are no good financial breakdowns available. One knows, for example, that in 1925 out of a total budget of £273,284, only £13,996 was budgeted directly for Provincial Administration. However, some funds for education, police, and public works were devoted to the Protectorate. How little would be mere guesswork.

[37] This was a consensus opinion obtained by interviewing a number of present and former officials of the Protectorate. For corroboration see Gambia Government, *Development and Welfare in the Gambia* (Bathurst: 1943), p. 3.

[38] Memo. by Hopkinson, 11 Feb. 1926.

[39] Gambia Government, *Travelling Commissioners Conference Report, 1926* (Bathurst: 1927).

[40] Memo by Hopkinson, 11 Feb. 1926.

[41] Introduction to H. R. Palmer, *Political Memoranda for the Guidance of Commissioners and other Government Officers Working in the Protectorate* (Bathurst: 1933).

[42] Sir Donald Cameron, *The Principles of Native Administration and their Application* (Lagos: 1938), p. 1.

[43] Palmer, *Political Memoranda*, 1933.

[44] Gambia Government, Native Authority *Ordinance No. 3, 1933.*

[45] Gambia Government, Native Tribunal *Ordinance No. 4, 1933.*

[46] Gambia Government, Subordinate Courts *Ordinance No. 5, 1933.*

[47] Gambia Government, Protectorate *Ordinance No. 2, 1935,* and Native Tribunals (Amendment) *Ordinance No. 3, 1935.*

[48] This is confirmed by the record of any Chiefs Conference. See particularly the Second Conference of Protectorate Chiefs, Gambia Government, *Sessional No. 6, 1945.*

[49] H. A. Gailey, Jr., 'Gambia Chiefs' Question', *West Africa,* 11 March 1961.

[50] Gambia Government, *Ordinance No. 19, 1944,* and *Ordinance No. 7, 1954* contain the most important revisions of the Native Authorities.

[51] Lord Hailey, 1954, Vol. III, p. 340.

[52] Gambia Government, *Ordinance No. 13, 1945.*

[53] Lord Hailey, 1954, Vol. III, p. 338.

[54] *Ibid.,* p. 339.

[55] Gambia Government, *Sessional Paper No. 5, 1952.*

[56] Gambia Government, *Sessional Paper No. 8, 1951; No. 5, 1952; No 7, 1955;* and *No. 4, 1958* all treat of the various problems of Protectorate education.

[57] See statement by Sefu Tambeh Jammeh, the chiefs' major spokesman at the 15th Conference of Protectorate Chiefs in March 1958, *Sessional Paper No. 4, 1958.*

[58] Draft of Letters Patent amending Gambia Colony Letters Patent. 8 April 1960.

[59] H. A. Gailey, Jr., 'Gambia Moves Forward', *West Africa,* 1 April 1961.

[60] Cmd. 1469 and Order in Council, 18 April 1962.

[61] Gambia Government, Protectorate Courts *Ordinance No. 5, 1947.*

[62] Gambia Government, Native Tribunal *Ordinance No. 4, 1933.*

[63] Gambia Government, Protectorate Courts (Amendment) *Ordinance No. 14, 1954.*

CHAPTER EIGHT: THE ECONOMICS OF A MONOCULTURE

[1] In 1843 the Gambia area exported 68,978 pounds of cotton. In 1862 on the request of the Governor, 1 ton of good Egyptian cotton seed was shipped to the Gambia. Gambia Government, *Annual Report, 1903.*

[2] Commissioner Ozanne's first report, C. O. 87/143.

[3] Gambia Government, *Annual Reports, 1903* and *1904* give excellent accounts of these attempts to introduce cotton.

[4] Gambia Government, *Annual Report, 1904.*

[5] Gambia Government, *Annual Reports, 1890, 1895, 1903* and *1915.*

[6] Great Britain, Colonial Office, *Annual Report, 1904.*

[7] Great Britain, Colonial Office, *Annual Report, 1909.*

[8] The observations on rice culture and the potential for this crop are based upon personal observations and a number of long conversations with Gambian Agricultural experts.

[9] Great Britain, *Colonial Office Report, 1952-53,* p. 23. It is noteworthy that there is little mention of the objects, procedures, and development of this scheme in the *Reports* of the years immediately preceeding its failure.

[10] 'Portrait', *West Africa,* 23 Nov. 1957.

[11] The original fees charged by the Department of Agriculture were 30s. per acre for ploughing and 25s. per acre for discing. In 1953 less than 200 acres had been cultivated. By 1955 the total acreage was 1,500 acres, mostly in the middle river areas.

[12] These Development Officers were financed by the Farmers' Fund of the Government Oilseeds Marketing Board. See Gambia Government, *Sessional No. 5,* p. 19.

[13] The discussion of the Yundum egg development plan will be considered in some detail since its failure, more than any other event, since the boundary demarcations determined the economic future of the Gambia. Because of the controversial nature of the project, the figures and conclusions drawn here are extracted from the official report of the investigating committee, Cmd. 8560. Unless otherwise noted, all quotations and figures in this section are taken from the report. Considerable other evidence is available to form a more serious judgement of the officials involved. This is not alluded to in the following pages. It should be stated, however, that the Gambian officials had little to do with the failure. They, particularly the Governor and the Commissioner of the Western Division, were so happy that the home government had decided to aid the Gambia that they did everything possible to assure the success of the venture. When the advice of Gambian officials was ignored or not requested, they merely stepped aside and hoped for the best.

[14] The early devastating report on timber resources as shown in Great Britain, *Colonial Office Report, 1909,* was totally ignored.

[15] *West Africa,* 25 Oct. 1958. In a private conversation in 1961, I was assured by one member of the group responsible for liquidating the Ilmenite equipment that the sole reason for beginning the project had been to help drive down the world price. As soon as this had been accomplished the marginal Gambian operation was closed.

[16] A more detailed description of groundnut culture is in D.P. Gamble, 1957, pp. 30-33.

[17] Southorn, 1952, p. 184.

[18] Great Britain, Colonial Office, *Annual Report, 1889.*

[19] These figures are extracted from the Government *Blue Books* and Colonial Office *Reports* for the years involved.

[20] Gambia Government, *Ordinance No. 29, 1948.*

[21] Values and prices are taken from the Colonial Office *Reports* for the years involved.

[22] S. D. Light and H. C. Barker, 'Report of the Treasury/Colonial Office Mission to the Gambia 1953', dated Nov. 1953, mineographed copy in Colonial Office. It is noteworthy that the experts placed their hope of a stable budget in the success of the Ilmenite mining.

[23] Great Britain, Colonial Office, *Annual Report, 1956-57,* p. 5.

[24] The amount of loss sustained by G. O. M. B. in this three year period can be seen in the decrease of the Farmers Fund from its high level of £2,000,000 in 1952. See Gambia Government, *Sessional No. 5, 1952,* p. 19.

[25] Great Britain, Colonial Office, *Annual Report, 1956-57,* p. 6.

[26] Great Britain, Colonial Office, *Annual Report, 1958-59,* p. 3.

[27] *Ibid.*

[00] *West Africa,* 19 Jan. 1963.

CHAPTER NINE: FISCAL ATTITUDES
OF THE GOVERNMENT

[1] Lord Frederick Lugard, *The Dual Mandate in Tropical Africa* (London: 1922), p. 45. The figures for income per head are Gold Coast 238s. 3d.; Gambia 200s. 3d.; Sierra Leone 54s. 5d.; and Nigeria 28s. 11d.

[2] Great Britain, Colonial Office, *Annual Report, 1912* and *Annual Report, 1920.*

[3] Great Britain, Colonial Office, *Annual Report, 1912.*

[4] Gambia Government, *Ordinance No. 16, 1924.*

[5] For a full discussion of the problems of demonitization see Minute Paper File 441/1921, Bathurst Archives.

[6] Great Britain, Colonial Office, *Annual Report, 1930,* p. 13.

[7] Gambia Government, *Report on Development and Welfare in the Gambia* (Bathurst: 1943).

[8] Gambia Government, *Sessional No. 14, 1946, Memorandum on Development.*

[9] Gambia Government, *Report on Development and Welfare, 1947* (Bathurst: 1948).

[10] *Sessional No. 14, 1946* and *Ibid.* give full details of these plans.

[11] The figures for expenditures are abstracted from Great Britain, Colonial Office, *Reports* from 1952 to 1957.

[12] Gambia Government, *Commission of Inquiry into the Accident to the Bathurst-Barra Ferry on 9 May 1957* (Bathurst: 1957).

[13] A government Entomologist, Robert W. H. Campbell, published a *Report on Protectorate Conditions* (Bathurst: 1949) and made a number of valuable suggestions concerning road building, particularly for utilization

of brush rafts similar to those in use in Canada to provide a firm, yet porous roadbed.

[14] Gambia Government, *Ordinance No. 4, 1901.*

[15] Gambia Government, *Ordinance No. 18, 1944.*

[16] Great Britain, Colonial Office, *Annual Report, 1958*, Appendix III.

[17] One of the few surveys made of infant mortality is D. P. Gamble, 'Infant Mortality Rates in Rural Areas of the Gambia Protectorate', *Journal of Tropical Medicine and Hygiene*, July 1952.

[18] C. O. 87/133.

[19] Gambia Government, *Blue Book, 1886*, p. 45.

[20] Gambia Government, *Ordinance No. 4, 1901.*

[21] Gambia Government, *Ordinance No. 16, 1924.*

[22] Great Britain, Colonial Office, *Annual Report, 1921.*

[23] Great Britain, Colonial Office, *Annual Report, 1938* and Great Britain, Colonial Office, *Colonial Office List, 1940*, p. 316.

[24] All statistics on school enrolment are taken from Great Britain, Colonial Office, *Colonial Office List. 1960*, p. 97.

[25] Gambia Government, *Sessional Paper No. 2, 1953.*

[26] Great Britain, Colonial Office, *Colonial Office List, 1960*, p. 97.

[27] *Ibid.*

[28] Gambia Government, *Ordinance No. 21, 1949.*

[29] Gambia Government, *Sessional Paper No. 8, 1959, Progress Report on Gambianization of the Civil Service.*

CHAPTER TEN: THE DEVELOPMENT OF POLITICAL PARTIES AND SELF-GOVERNMENT

[1] Letters Patent, 20 Feb. 1866.

[2] Letters, Patent, 28 Nov. 1888.

[3] Order in Council dated 23 Nov. 1893.

[4] The development of Central Authority from 1893 to 1943 is covered adequately in Gambia Government, *Development and Welfare in the Gambia, 1943*, Chapter 3, pp. 2-4.

[5] Gambia Legislative Council, Order in Council 1946.

[6] Letters Patent, 29 Nov. 1946, Amended by Royal Instructions, 26 Nov. 1947.

[7] Gambia Government, Bathurst Advisory Town Council Ordinance (1935).

[8] Gambia Government, Local Government (Bathurst) *Ordinance No. 1, 1946.*

[9] Gambia Government, Kombo St. Mary Division *Ordinance No. 15, 1946.*

[10] Amendment to Gambia (Legislative Council) Order in Council, 1946 dated June 1951.

[11] The proposed Constitution is in *Gambia Gazette No. 27*, Vol. 70, 3 July

1953. The final Constitution was approved by Gambia (Constitution) Order in Council 1954.

[12] Gambia Government, *Record of the Constitutional Conference, 6-11 March 1959.*

[13] For the disturbances in Bathurst at the time of Lennox-Boyd's visit see *West Africa*, 20 June 1959, p. 580, and 22 Aug. 1959, p. 634. For Constitution of 1960 see Draft Letters Patent 1954, 8 April 1960.

[14] Cmd. 1469 and Order in Council, 18 April 1962.

[15] The substance of the following discussion of political parties was gained by personal observation and lengthy interviews with all the political leaders of the Gambia.

[16] For more detail concerning the Rev. Faye's career see 'The Gambia's Amiable Example,' *West Africa*, 30 Aug. 1952, p. 803.

[17] Garba-Jahumpa's background is detailed in 'The Gambia's First Minister', *West Africa*, 12 Dec. 1953, p. 1157.

[18] 'Portrait, P. S. N'Jie', *West Africa*, 3 May 1958, p. 411.

[19] 'Portrait, David K. Jawara', *West Africa*, 21 Jan. 1961.

[20] See Appendix VII.

[21] For a discussion of these events see H. A. Gailey, 'The Gambia Moves Forward', *West Africa*, 1 April 1961.

[22] 'New Men in the Gambia', *West Africa*, 9 June 1962, p. 619.

[23] See Appendix VIII.

[24] As an example of the magnitude of the financial problem and Jawara's attemps to solve it, see Appendix V and Appendix IX.

[25] H. A. Gailey, 'Portrait, Gambia's Labour Leader', *West Africa*, 27 May 1961.

INDEX

240

Index

Index

Kennedy, Sir Arthur (Gov. in Chief) 51, 83, 84, 85
Kerewan, 174
Kiang, 54, 58
Kilham, Hannah, 68, 75
Kombo, 22, 36, 43, 44, 48, 55, 56, 59, 65, 67, 73, 79, 87, 101
Kordu Tiyo, 126
Kortright, C. H., (Adm.), 91
Kuntaur, 3, 160, 162, 174, 175

Lagos, 47
Lennox-Boyd, Alan, 190
Leopold II, (King of Belgium), 98
Llewellyn, R. B. (Adm.), 105, 106, 111, 112, 114, 115, 118
Lugard, Lord Frederick, 112, 119
Lyons, Lord, 86, 100

Maba, 46, 47, 48
M'Baki, Omar, 198
MacCarthy, Sir Charles, 37, 61, 63
MacCarthy Island (Lemain), 24, 34, 42, 49, 53, 64, 65, 68, 70, 76, 78, 90, 91
Mali Empire, 6, 19
Malta Plan, 207
Manchester Chamber of Commerce, 87
Mandingos, 12-13, 54, 114, 159, 199, 201
Mande, 15
Mansa Konko, 174, 175
Mansa Koto, 120
Marabouts, 39, 40
Medical Research Council, 176
Medina, 59
Mellacourie River, 83, 90, 98, 100
Messina, 15
Missionaries, Catholic, 69
Missionaries, Wesleyan, 43, 68
Monson, Sir Edward, 106
Moore, Francis, 13, 14, 30, 74
Musa Mollah, 41, 53, 54, 115, 120
Muslim Congress, 194-195, 200

Napoleonic Wars, 35
National Party, 195
Niambantang, 105
Niamina, 54
Niani, 56
Nianibingtang, 53
Nisard, M., 102
N'Jie, P. S., 195, 197, 198, 199
Noreco River, 70
North Africa, 7

O'Connor, L. S. (Gov.) 42, 43, 44, 45, 70

Oil exploration, 159
Omar of Sabaji, 40, 43, 44
Ord, H. St. George (Col.), 51, 69, 76, 77
Othman dan Fodio, 40
Oualicounda, 109
Owen, Lieutenant, 70
Oyster Creek, 44
Ox-plowing, 149
Ozanne, Travelling Commissioner, 67, 113-114

Pakali Ba, 174
Palmer, Sir H. R. (Gov.), 130-131
Panchang, 105
Park, Mungo, 34-35
Patey, C. G. (Adm.), 84, 85
Pauncefote, Sir Julian, 100
Phillips, Millard, 152 ff.
Political Memoranda for the Guidance of Commissioners, 130
Political Parties, general organization, 194-195
Portendic, 27, 33, 73, 81
Porto Novo, 104
Portuguese in Gambia, 18-20
Progressive Peoples Party, 195ff.
Prince Rupert, 21

Quinn & Co., 72
Quinella, 49

Ramaswami, Mr., 148 ff.
Religion:
    traditional, 6
    Christianity, 19-20, 68-69
    Islam, 9, 13, 15, 39-40, 47 ff., 194-195, 200-201
Rendall, George (Lt. Gov.), 67
Rice and rice culture, 143-144, 146-151
Road system improvements, 173, 175
Roseberry, Lord, 107
Rouen Merchants, 27
Roume, M., 107, 109
Rowe, Sir Samuel (Gov. in Chief), 57, 58
Royal Adventurers of England, 22-23
Royal African Company, 23, 25, 26, 27-29, 30, 31
Rubber, 71, 145

Saba, 46
Sabaji, 40, 43, 44
Said Matti, 56, 57, 101
St. Louis, 24, 32, 33, 61, 81
St. Marys Island (Banjol), 2, 22, 36
Saloum, 56, 114
Sankandi, 120

Index

Sapu, 148
Satiyo Tiyo, 126, 127
Seagram, H. F. (Gov.), 70
Segu, 99
Select Committee of Parliament (1842), 70
Select Committee of Parliament (1865), 77, 78, 79
Senegal, 1, 12, 21, 22, 24, 33, 58, 81, 84, 86, 203, 207
Senegal Company, 24, 26, 27
Senegal *rapprochement*, 202-203, 207
Senegambia, Province of, 32
Serahuli, 16, 41, 202
Sereres, 41, 202
Seven Years War, 31-32
Sierra Leone, 44, 64, 70, 78, 79, 89, 94, 98, 99, 102, 104, 207
Sine-Saloum, 48, 49, 57, 101
Sitololo (Carrols Wharf), 109
Sitwell, Commissioner, 113, 120
Slaves liberated, 66-67
Slave trade, 19, 22, 29-30, 36, 37, 54, 61, 66, 67, 114, 119
Slavery, 112, 114-115, 119
Small, Edward, 192
Society of Friends, 68
Songhai Empire, 6, 10
Soninki chiefs, 40, 41
Soninki-Marabout Wars, 16, 39-60, 67, 71, 73, 93, 104, 111, 127
Sosso Empire, 15
Southorn, Sir, W. T. (Gov.), 169
Stibbs, Captain, 29
Strange farmers, 16-17, 132
Sudanic State, 6
Sukuta, 55, 59, 170-171
Suleman Santa, 59
Suwarrakunda, 46

Tekrur, 6

Tenda, 70
Tendeba, 59
Timber resources, 145-146, 152, 155
Togoland, 98
Tomani Bojang, 55, 87
Tomani, Kingdom of, 54
Tractor plowing, 150
Tribalism, 201
Trefgarne, Lord, 152ff.
Tubab Kolon, 50
Tubakuta, 53
Tucolors, 15, 99

United Party, 195ff.
Usi di Mare, Antoniotto, 18

Victoria Hospital, 176,

Waddington, M., 100
Wallikunda, 147-148, 173
War of American Revolution, 32-33
War of Austrian Succession, 30
War of Spanish Succession, 26-27
West African Currency Board, 167
West Indian Regiments, 43, 46, 84
West Indies Company (Fr.), 24
Whydah, 81
Windley, Sir Edward (Gov.), 191
Wolof, 10-11, 48, 114, 159, 201
Wood, Sir Ernest, 155ff.
Wuli, 16, 65, 66
Wyn-Harris, Sir Percy, 148, 188

Yarbutenda, 67, 105, 107, 109
Yundum, 49
Yundum Airport, 172
Yundum Egg Scheme, 146, 152-158, 180
Yundum Teachers College, 180

Ziganchour, 110

244